THE LONG HANGOVER

PUTIN'S NEW RUSSIA AND
THE GHOSTS OF THE PAST

SHAUN WALKER

OXFORD
UNIVERSITY PRESS

OXFORD

UNIVERSITY PRESS

Oxford University Press is a department of the University of Oxford. It furthers
the University's objective of excellence in research, scholarship, and education
by publishing worldwide. Oxford is a registered trade mark of Oxford University
Press in the UK and certain other countries.

Published in the United States of America by Oxford University Press
198 Madison Avenue, New York, NY 10016, United States of America.

Library of Congress Cataloging-in-Publication Data
Names: Walker, Shaun (Journalist), author.
Title: The long hangover : Putin's new Russia and the ghosts of the past / Shaun Walker, author.
Description: New York, NY : Oxford University Press, 2018.
Identifiers: LCCN 2017015739 (hardcover) |
ISBN 9780190659240 (hardcover ; alkaline paper) | ISBN 9780190058845 (paperback ; alk. paper) |
ISBN 9780190659257 (updf) | ISBN 9780190659264 (epub)
Subjects: LCSH: Putin, Vladimir Vladimirovich, 1952-. | Russia (Federation)—Politics and
government—1991-. | Russia (Federation)—History.
Classification: LCC DK510.763 .W34 2018 (hardcover) | DDC 947.086
LC record available at https://lccn.loc.gov/2017015739

1 3 5 7 9 8 6 4 2
Printed by Marquis in Canada
on acid-free paper

CONTENTS

———◆———

LIST OF MAPS

———◆———

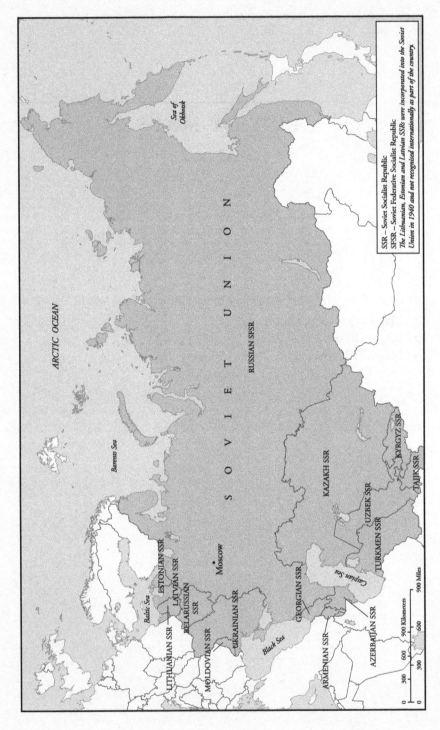

ARCTIC OCEAN

Barents Sea

Sea of
Okhotsk

SOVIET UNION

RUSSIAN SFSR

Baltic Sea

ESTONIAN SSR

LATVIAN SSR

LITHUANIAN SSR

BELARUSSIAN
SSR

•Moscow

MOLDOVIAN SSR

UKRAINIAN SSR

Black Sea

GEORGIAN SSR

ARMENIAN SSR

AZERBAIJAN SSR

Caspian Sea

KAZAKH SSR

UZBEK SSR

TURKMEN SSR

KYRGYZ SSR

TAJIK SSR

SSR – Soviet Socialist Republic

SFSR – Soviet Federative Socialist Republic

The Lithuanian, Estonian and Latvian SSRs were incorporated into the Soviet
Union in 1940 and not recognised internationally as part of the country

0   300   600   900 Miles
0 300 600   900 Kilometers

Map of the Soviet Union

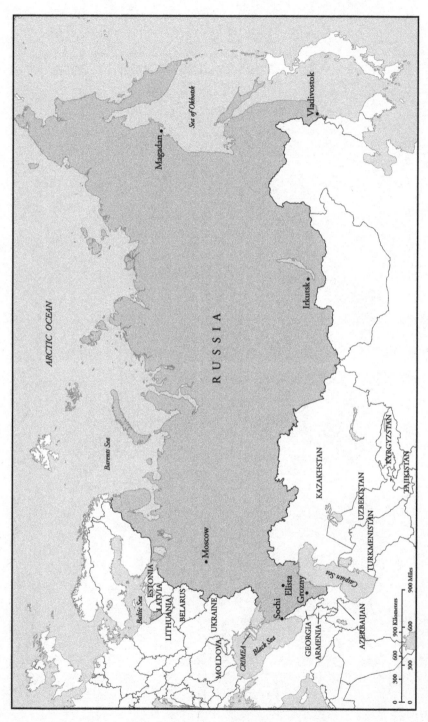

Map of Russia

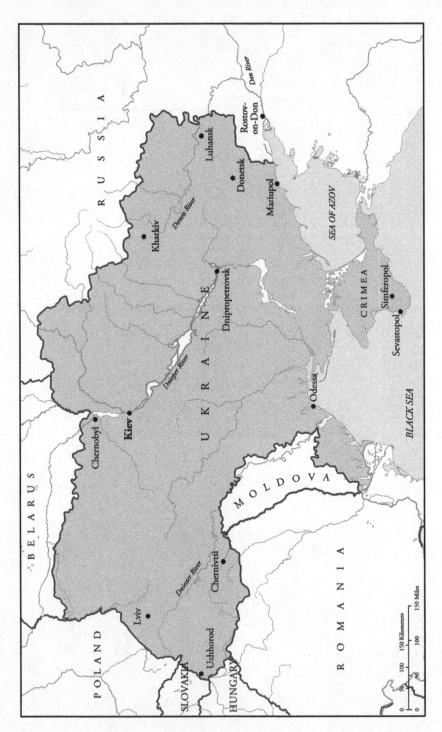

Map of Ukraine

PROLOGUE

October 2014, Torez, rebel-controlled eastern Ukraine

There had been an autumn chill in the air for a few days, and even inside the seized secret police headquarters, it was cold. The Romanian did not seem to notice the temperature, apparently comfortable in his light military jacket and a single, fingerless leather glove. But he clocked me shivering, and declared it unacceptable that the town's heating system had not yet come on. He had been to the power plant the previous day, he said, and laid down an ultimatum. They had a week to get things sorted or he would have the management shot for sabotage.

This might have been taken for bravado, were it not for the fact that the Romanian had organized two public executions in the preceding weeks. Most recently, a young man in his twenties had been caught looting by some of the Romanian's men, and sentenced to the ultimate punishment. 'He thought it was a joke until the last minute,' the Romanian said, puffing his way through the latest in a steady stream of cigarettes held in his ungloved hand.

The young man was executed by a bullet to the back of the head, outside the shop from which he had stolen. A crowd of locals gathered on the street to watch.

Public executions seemed a little out of place in twenty-first-century Europe, I ventured. The Romanian shrugged. 'Nobody blames a surgeon for the fact they remove tumours from the body with a scalpel. That is what we are doing here, with this society.'

Despite the name, he was very much Russian; 'the Romanian' was merely his *pozyvnoi*, a *nom de guerre* chosen because one branch of his family had roots in Romania. All the fighters I met during the war in eastern Ukraine had a *pozyvnoi*. There was the Amp (a former electrician), the Ramone (they were his favourite band), and the Monk (he'd never cheated on his wife).

With their silly names, they often seemed like boys playing at war, but the Romanian was one of the serious ones. He radiated intensity, and had a clipped, military brusqueness when he spoke that bordered on disdain. Nevertheless, it was clear he enjoyed having an audience. He had griped repeatedly when our interview was set up that he did not have time to waste chattering with journalists. But when I arrived, he proceeded to talk about his fiefdom for three hours with little interruption, spraying literary and biblical references, ranging from the novels of Stendhal to obscure conspiracy websites about the Bilderberg Group. Tall and lean, with closely cropped greying hair and a neat, clipped moustache, he sat at the head of a long table, drinking over-brewed tea and ashing his cigarettes into a rusting old tuna tin. The walls were bare save for peeling light-blue paint.

The building had previously been the headquarters of the SBU, the Ukrainian security services, in the grimy mining town of Torez. Now, it was a heavily fortified base, controlled by the Russia-backed militias of the Donetsk People's Republic, a lawless quasi-state that had come into existence a few months previously.

A retired Russian military officer, the Romanian now held the official title of Head of Counterintelligence for the Ministry of State Security of the Donetsk People's Republic. In practice, this gave him license to act as a kind of vigilante ombudsman. A blonde woman, with gold hoop earrings, an elaborate manicure, and a combat jacket lined with faux fur, periodically entered the room to hand him sheets of paper, appeals from locals about looted property, or other grievances linked to rebel forces behaving badly.

He was trying to get to the bottom of one case of a local farmer, whose only cow had been pilfered by rebel soldiers. He had jailed several rebels for theft. The two public executions for looting were justified, he said, because only the lowest form of humanity would steal the few provisions remaining in the town. 'In order to live by the laws of the New Testament, first we must live by the laws of the Old Testament; an eye for eye. If the people behave like animals, we will treat them like animals.'

This was the Romanian's sixth war. The first had been the Soviet invasion of Afghanistan, soon after he signed up. He became an officer in the Soviet and Russian armies, and later in an interior ministry special forces unit. There was no way of verifying his claims; he never even told me his real name. But I doubted he was lying.

Having been through the blood, mud, and brutality of both Chechen wars during the 1990s, he left the army. Afterwards, he tried his hand at civilian life, setting up a small construction company in Moscow. It was not a success, and he ended up working on the building sites himself to make a living.

The Romanian did not like corruption; his eyes sparkled with fury whenever he brought the subject up, which was often. If he had his way, he would have all the corrupt officials shot. Joseph Stalin had been right, he said; there may have been repression back then, but the country developed, and progressed, and that was the main thing.

'Giving a bribe makes you feel like a gay. It's like being raped. This repulsive man standing in front of you with a leering smile and his hand open. It's disgusting. I never gave a single bribe when I was working in construction.' He continued, pensively, after a pause: 'That's probably why nothing ever worked out for me.'

The Romanian had come to eastern Ukraine of his own accord, he insisted. Nobody had sent him. He made regular, informal reports to old friends in the Russian security services back in Moscow, but was spending his own small savings pot to subsist here. He had seen footage on the news a few months previously, of pro-Russian protesters burning to death in Odessa's trade union building, a horrific event in any terms, but one that Russian television had upgraded to a Nazi-inspired pogrom. He decided there was nothing for it but to travel to Donetsk himself. Just as patriotic Russians had come together to defeat the Nazis in the Second World War, he said animatedly, it was again time to join in unity against the modern-day 'Ukrainian fascists' and their backers in Western capitals. On his lapel, he wore the orange-and-black St George's ribbon. It marked the Soviet victory in the Second World War, and had become the symbol of the Donetsk rebels in this new war.

Although he despised the corruption of Vladimir Putin's Russia, he was pleased that over the past year the president had done 'at least something' to restore Russian prestige, annexing Crimea and providing support to the rebels. The army was being revamped again; money was being spent on defence. Maybe soon, Russia would once again become a country of which he could be proud.

The Romanian's trajectory over the past two decades was an extreme variation on a recurrent theme of post-Soviet malaise that I encountered during my years reporting from Russia and other former Soviet countries, first as correspondent for *The Independent* and then for *The Guardian*. He had lost his way in the aftermath of the Soviet Union; now, as he meted out summary justice on the battlefields of a messy war, he felt that he was finding his bearings again.

By any measure, his presence in Ukraine, commanding a ragtag bunch of armed separatists and ordering public executions, was illegal. But the Romanian did not consider himself to be outside his homeland. His home was the Soviet Union. That was the country in which he was born, the country to which he first swore a military oath, and the country that still lived on in his heart. He admired the coal miners and steelworkers of eastern Ukraine, 'simple, hardworking and morally outstanding people' who made him feel he was back in the Soviet Union.

The Romanian mourned the Soviet Union's passing, but it was not quite right to say that he longed for its resurrection. His nostalgia was not about a devotion to Leninist philosophy. It was not necessarily even a striving for the same kind of lives people had lived before Mikhail Gorbachev's *perestroika* and the subsequent Soviet collapse. What the Romanian really missed was something more fundamental.

'We need to rebuild the country. The Soviet Union, the Russian Empire, it doesn't matter what you call it. I want a Russian idea for the Russian people; I don't want the Americans to teach us how to live. I want a strong country, one you can be proud of. I want life to have some meaning again.'

PART ONE

Curating the Past

I

A first-tier nation

I

To assert that the collapse of the Soviet Union cast a long shadow over subsequent events in Russia and the other former Soviet republics is to state the obvious. It is hardly surprising that the death of a whole system would irrevocably shape the future for years, if not generations, to come. But I feel that the particular way in which the Soviet Union disintegrated, and the vacuum of ideas and purpose it left in its wake, is undervalued when it comes to our understanding of Russia and the whole post-Soviet world.

In 1991, Russians experienced a triple loss. The political system imploded, the imperial periphery broke away to form new states, and the home country itself ceased to exist. There were few committed Communists left by 1991, but that did not make the collapse any less traumatic. Russians felt they had lost not an empire or an ideology, but the very essence of their identity. If they were no longer Soviet citizens, then who were they?

Images of toppling Communist monuments and the tearing down of the Berlin Wall were the easy metaphoric expressions of the Soviet collapse; the multitude of Lenins that remained, standing proudly amid the capitalist cityscapes of modern Russia, were a sign that attitudes to the Soviet past in Russia were not so clear-cut after all. But the visual, surface issue of how to deal with Communist symbols was just one small part of the picture. Almost every story I have written during many years of reporting from Russia and the broader post-Soviet region

7

has been, at least in some way, about the effects of the Soviet downfall, and with it the requirements of reformatting national ideologies, the international geopolitical balance, and the emotional and psychological makeup of 250 million people.

For a great many Soviet citizens, the collapse came as a long-awaited blessing: the end of a stifling political system and the arrival of a multitude of exciting opportunities. But even for those who despised Communism, the collapse of the country along with the system was a jarring moment. They had spent their lives walking along a particular path: it had been hard going, the progress was minimal, and it was unclear if they would ever make it to their destination. But they at least understood the terrain. Suddenly, the ground beneath their feet gave way. All that had constituted the fabric of everyday life—accolades and punishments, status and rank, linguistic and behavioural codes—was suddenly rendered meaningless. The established order had dissolved, and in its place was a new world that was difficult to navigate and full of pitfalls.

It was a sensation I would hear about again and again from people who had failed to find their way in the post-Soviet years. The vague sense of unease and nostalgic longing created fertile ground for manipulation. It often seemed to be most acute in those aged between forty and fifty: people who had come of age just as the system collapsed. Men often seemed to struggle more than women to find the emotional resources to deal with the transition: there are many confused and angry men to be found in these pages.

What people remembered about the Soviet period did not, perhaps, bear much resemblance to what they had actually felt at the time. But memory, both individual and collective, is fickle, more dependent on the vantage point of the present than on the reality of the past. Viewed through the prism of the miserable 1990s, the previous decades took on a rosier hue.

Appeals to a visceral and intangible sense of the past, what the Russian émigré thinker Svetlana Boym labelled 'restorative nostalgia', can gain traction in any society: witness the 'taking back control' of Brexit, or Donald Trump's promise to 'Make America Great Again', with little explanation of when the exact period of previous greatness started and ended. In Russia, there were more specific historical hooks on which to hang these appeals, most of all the Soviet collapse, which could be recast in people's minds not as the juddering death of an untenable system, but as the nefarious dismantling of a great state by malevolent external forces and their helpers within.

This book charts Vladimir Putin's mission to fill the void left by the 1991 collapse and forge a new sense of nation and purpose in Russia, though it is by no means a chronological history of the Putin era. The first section explores the curation of the past in the service of the present: the attempt to meld collective memory of the painful and complicated Soviet decades into something Russians could be proud of, particularly the elevation of victory in the Second World War to a national founding myth. Putin had no interest in resurrecting the Soviet system, but the sense of injustice over the way it collapsed would prove a powerful rallying point.

The later sections explain how this historical discourse, along with a parallel process in Ukraine, helped lead to the events of 2014, which left ten thousand people dead and changed the geopolitical map of Europe. By 2017, with record-high approval ratings at home, and much of the Western world looking towards Moscow with trepidation, Putin appeared to have succeeded in his quest to consolidate Russia, and turn a weak and traumatized country into a major world player once again. But with what collateral damage?

This book is not an apology for Putin's policies during his years in the Kremlin. Putin's mission to unite Russia involved the manipulation of history and an aggressive stifling of dissent; the system he constructed also allowed his old friends and inner circle to become fantastically rich. But neither is the book an anti-Putin polemic. Putin, after all, is only one of a large cast of Russians featured in these pages. He too had his moment of personal trauma as the Soviet Union collapsed, which strongly influenced his later worldview and actions. Putin was, to some extent, the director of the post-Soviet story for modern Russia, but he was also very much a character in it.

II

There is a rather well known story about a lieutenant colonel of the KGB, who in 1989 was stationed in the East German city of Dresden.

His was just one of millions of individual experiences that would remain seared into the memories of those who had lived them for years or decades to come. But for the future direction of Russia, this particular one would have great resonance.

The thirty-seven-year-old lieutenant colonel, Vladimir Putin, watched nervously as angry crowds stormed Dresden's huge Stasi compound in December 1989. Overrunning the offices of the East German secret police, the crowds moved on to the KGB headquarters, the inner sanctum. Putin called for armed backup to protect the employees and sensitive files hidden inside, but was told there was no help on the way. 'Moscow is silent,' said the voice on the line. He had no choice but to go outside and lie to the crowds that he had heavily armed men waiting inside who would shoot anyone who tried to enter. The bluff worked, the mob dissipated, and the KGB's files on informers and agents remained safe. But the psychological scars ran deep, at least in Putin's own telling a decade later.

As delighted crowds in Berlin tore down the wall separating the two Germanies and drank in the new atmosphere of freedom, a shocked Putin set to work destroying the compromising documents of the KGB, an organization that had until recently seemed omnipotent. It would be another two years before the Soviet Union collapsed for good, but the way Putin recalled it later, his personal moment of realization that the game was up for the Communist superpower came that day in Dresden. He felt he was watching one of the largest and most powerful empires the world had ever seen unravel in the most pathetic and humiliating way. 'I had the feeling that the country was no more,' Putin remembered. 'It had disappeared.'[1]

It might seem strange that Putin would mourn the passing of the Soviet Union, given his life trajectory in its wake. Like millions of Soviet citizens, Putin grew up in spartan, even squalid conditions, his whole family crammed into one room of a communal apartment that had no hot water. Having worked his way up to what was only a middling position in the KGB by the late 1980s, he did remarkably well out of the decade following the Soviet collapse, inserting himself into the St Petersburg mayoral office at a time when being part of the government meant proximity to contracts and financial flows. In 1996 he was called to the presidential administration in Moscow, and by 1998 he was made head of the FSB, the successor organization to the KGB.

In a few short years, Putin had made a spectacular rise from mid-ranking cog in the periphery to overlord of the whole sprawling organization. A year later, the ailing Boris Yeltsin made Putin his prime minister and, ultimately, successor. The 1990s were good to Putin, and he proved far more adept at rising through the post-Soviet system than he had the Soviet one.

But he never forgot that moment of helplessness in Dresden, and however well he did personally from the Soviet collapse, he was deeply angered by the manner in which the country had disintegrated. He seemed to mourn not the human cost or material tribulations, but the national humiliation of a powerful state simply imploding. He later claimed to have had a sense for some time that the collapse of Soviet power in Europe was inevitable. 'But I wanted something different to rise in its place. And nothing different was proposed. That's what hurt. They just dropped everything and went away.'[2]

Even those who had been far less committed to the Soviet cause than Putin felt these pangs of regret at how the end of the seventy-four-year political experiment brought the country itself tumbling down with it. 'I was delighted that the end of Communism had come about,' Alexander Voloshin, chief of staff to Yeltsin and then to Putin, once told me. 'But the Soviet Union was my homeland. That was different. How can you be happy about your homeland collapsing?'

During Putin's early years in Moscow serving Yeltsin, he saw up close how weak the country had become. The Russian Army fought a miserable and bloody war to stop the southern republic of Chechnya from seceding, costing tens of thousands of lives and ending in *de facto* defeat for Moscow. Russian society was in turmoil, goods scarce, and the majority of the populace impoverished.

On the international stage, things were little better. In 1998, when President Bill Clinton called Yeltsin to tell him the United States was considering air strikes on Serbia, Yeltsin was furious. He screamed '*Nel'zya!*'—something like 'it is impermissible!'—several times down the phone at the US president and then hung up. The bombing raids went ahead anyway. A country that had only recently been one of the world's two major lodes of power was now utterly powerless to stop bombs falling on the capital city of an ally. American diplomats and politicians were constantly warned during the Yeltsin era that such a state of affairs would not last forever.

'Russia isn't Haiti and we won't be treated as though we were,' Yeltsin fumed to Clinton's point man on Russia, Strobe Talbott. 'I don't like it when the US flaunts its superiority. Russia's difficulties are only temporary, and not only because we have nuclear weapons, but also because of our economy, our culture, our spiritual strength. All that amounts to a legitimate, undeniable basis for equal treatment. Russia will rise again! I repeat: Russia will rise again!'[3]

On the eve of the millennium, Yeltsin announced he was stepping down. He left the country mired in poverty, the wealth in the hands of a few greedy oligarchs and the army fighting a grim and demoralizing war in Chechnya.

Perhaps most troubling of all, Yeltsin's years in charge did not provide a clear idea of what kind of country modern Russia should be. Gleb Pavlovsky, a spin doctor and 'political technologist' who worked for both Yeltsin's and Putin's Kremlin, later told me about the panic during the handover period: 'There was a real sense that Yeltsin could leave and there would be utter chaos. Most of the population didn't recognize the Russian Federation as a real thing. They felt like they lived in some kind of strange offshoot of the Soviet Union. We had to ensure the handover, but we also had to create some sense of nation.'

Yeltsin, a man who had once embodied hopes of future prosperity, cut a sorry figure, of unfulfilled expectations and missed opportunities, as he gave his slurred farewell address on the eve of the millennium: 'I am asking your forgiveness for failing to justify the hopes of those who believed me when I said we would leap from the grey, stagnating totalitarian past into a bright, prosperous, and civilized future. I believed in that dream. I believed we would cover that distance in one leap. We didn't.'

III

I first travelled to Russia in January 2000, a few weeks after Yeltsin stepped down. I was eighteen, and before starting at university spent four months teaching English at a secondary school in Moscow. The Russian capital then was a dark, chaotic city. The cautious optimism that some people had felt about the future a decade earlier had all but evaporated. Life in the 1990s had progressed along the lines of a particularly implausible episode of a job-swap reality TV show: biochemists were now taxi drivers; market stallholders were CEOs. The criminals became the authorities and those who tried to stand up against them became the criminals. A few people had pilfered all the ladders, leaving the rest to be devoured by snakes.

The poverty among the majority of the population made for widespread squalor and rampant exploitation. At Komsomolskaya metro station, in the centre of Moscow, there was a Dostoyevskian tableau of despair on emerging at ground level: dazed homeless drunks, penniless grannies hawking a few sorry wares spread out forlornly before them on the concrete, and a shabby market selling cheap Chinese electronics and knock-off DVDs of hardcore porn.

Sex, which had been a taboo topic in Soviet times, was everywhere. At several points on the Garden Ring, the multi-lane highway that encircles the very centre of Moscow, prostitutes stood by the roadside in skimpy outfits, offering their services. Their leather-jacketed pimps paid off the police to turn a blind eye. Any sensible citizen knew to avoid the police, who were far more likely to shake you down for a bribe than help you out. Heroin abuse was rampant; the country was on its way to having the world's fastest-growing HIV epidemic. If Moscow was bad, outside the capital life was much, much harder.

The shortages of the late-Soviet period had created a nation of resourceful barterers, and now, absolutely everything was for sale: sex, marriage, a doctor's note to avoid being called up to fight in Chechnya, your acquittal or someone else's conviction in a court case, or a ready-made PhD thesis to boost your qualifications. The appeals to 'traditional Russian values', that would become official Kremlin rhetoric much later, resonated because of their aspirational quality: people wanted to believe in a country of supposed purity and chastity exactly because what they saw before their eyes was so at odds with it.

After my months in Moscow, I spent several weeks traversing Russia in the third-class *platskart* carriages of Trans-Siberian trains. The dormitories on wheels puttered across the endless Eurasian landmass, the air inside thick with a blend of sweaty feet, fish lunches, and a sooty tang emanating from the coal-fired samovars that dispensed boiling water for tea. I remember snippets of conversations with my fellow passengers in the open-plan carriages: a skinny young conscript who had nervously bade farewell to his parents and was en route to his army base; two gossipy matriarchs travelling on a four-day journey home to Irkutsk, after visiting children who had fled the nest to Moscow; a pair of go-go dancers from the Siberian city of Ulan Ude who dreamed of moving to South Korea and making a fortune working the restaurants and nightclubs there; and a duo of young wheeler-dealer businessmen from Vladivostok who force-fed me vodka amid much bravado and then vomited all over the carriage at night, much to the despair, if not the surprise, of the beleaguered attendant who had to mop up the mess.

My unexpected presence in the cheapest class was met with ever-changing combinations of warmth, aggression, inquisitiveness, drunkenness, and flirting, depending on the interlocutors, the time of day or night, and the general mood of the carriage. Back then, my Russian-language skills weren't good enough to launch complex conversations about nostalgia, or probe people's memories of the Soviet Union, which had collapsed less than a decade previously. But I remember a palpable sense of confusion with the state of affairs in the new country. A few young business-oriented types saw it as a time of great excitement and opportunity, but most people seemed lost on some kind of existential level—plaintive, overwhelmed, and alarmed by the chaos that a decade of 'democracy' had brought. Two years earlier, a financial meltdown had meant millions of Russians lost whatever paltry savings they had managed to put aside. More recently, explosions had torn through several apartment blocks in the capital, supposedly the work of Chechen terrorists.[4] People longed for normalcy and stability. This much-craved *stabil'nost'* became an altar at which many freedoms would later be sacrificed.

Public opinion surveys from the time show that the majority of people were unimpressed with the new Russia. In March 1993, 63 per cent of Russians said they regretted that the Soviet Union had collapsed. By the end of 2000, the figure had risen to 75 per cent.[5]

After six months in Russia, I returned to Britain to go to university, but I already knew I would be back before long. The coexistence of beauty and horror, hope and despair, glory and absurdity was frustrating and alluring in equal measure. Russia got under my skin, as it had done to foreigners for centuries.

I studied Russian and Soviet history at Oxford, and moved back to Moscow at the end of 2003, working for an NGO for a year before taking up journalism. The city was slowly becoming more prosperous and humane. Over the next decade, oil prices rose so high that, even allowing for the rampant corruption in Putin's inner circle, money did trickle down and provide real benefits to people in the cities.

In Moscow and other major settlements, abject squalor disappeared from the central streets, and a middle class began to develop. With it came coffee shops, wine bars, and frequent flights to Europe. But trips to the regions were a reminder that for the majority of the country, life was still hard. The heroin and HIV epidemics worsened; when authorities did crack down on heroin supply, people switched to *krokodil*, a synthetic opioid made from cooking codeine pills, lighter fluid, and industrial cleaning products until they formed a brownish gunk. In Tver, just a couple of hours from Moscow, I met *krokodil* addicts whose flesh was quite literally rotting away from injecting the drug.

Across Russia's multiple time zones, there were endless towns and villages where similar scenes played out. In Alexandrovsk, a small town on Sakhalin island in the far east of Russia, an eight-hour flight from Moscow followed by an overnight train, the roads were made of mud and stray dogs howled relentlessly. Alexandrovsk's only point of interest was a museum that marked Anton Chekhov's visit there a century previously, after which he had written at length about what a miserable hellhole it was. Half the town seemed to be drinking *spirt*, chemical ethanol, because they could not afford vodka. A friendly drunk explained the drill: you had to exhale fully before drinking; if you didn't, it would burn a hole in your oesophagus. Millions of Russians drank ethanol, window cleaner, perfume, or other industrial spirits that were marketed more cheaply than vodka. There was both an economic and an existential sense of hopelessness, interconnected and mutually reinforcing.

IV

Putin's task, as he took over from Yeltsin, was to imbue this vast, creaking country with a new vitality. Shortly before he became acting president on the eve of the millennium, Putin wrote a lengthy, pro-grammatic text about the challenges facing Russia. It touched on pov-erty, social upheaval, and other human issues, but its main thrust was a worry about the health of the Russian state rather than that of its people. Russia, Putin wrote, was undergoing one of the most difficult periods in its long history.

'For the first time in the past 200–300 years, Russia faces the real danger that it could be relegated to the second, or even the third tier of global powers,' the article's conclusion warned. 'In order for this not to happen, we will need a huge mobilization of all the intellectual, physi-cal and moral strengths of our nation. We need unified, constructive work. Nobody else will do it for us. Everything now depends on our ability to understand the level of danger, to unite, and to set about car-rying out the long and difficult task.'[6]

The poverty and divisions of the 1990s were a symptom of this broader malaise, Putin believed. The health of the state was the most important thing: if Russia could regain the global importance the Soviet Union once possessed, then people's well-being would auto-matically improve. Putin's article tapped into a long line of Russian political philosophy that fetishized the strength of the state and sovereignty.

To facilitate this renaissance, Putin faced the enormous task of creat-ing a sense of nation and national pride among Russians. At his inau-guration, on 7 May 2000, Putin explicitly laid out the mission ahead of him as he saw it: 'I consider it my sacred duty to unite the people of Russia and to gather citizens around clearly defined tasks and aims, and to remember, every minute of every day, that we are one nation and we are one people. We have one common destiny.'

But what was this common destiny, and what was this new 'first-tier' Russia meant to look like? Should it be a neo-Soviet superpower, and strive to resurrect as much as possible of the Soviet past? Or was the Soviet period, in fact, a horrible error and thus the new Russia should be a continuation of the tsarist empire, with its triple ideology of Orthodoxy, Autocracy, and Nationality? Was Russia a bastion of 'tra-ditional values' in opposition to a decadent West? A 'Eurasian' power that could bridge the gap between East and West? Or simply a 'normal' European nation, albeit one of dramatically bigger size than the others and with a more traumatic past, that could in time integrate with the democracies of the continent's western half?

Putin, and those around him, at various times appealed to elements of all these visions of Russia. Foreign leaders who met Putin in the early years say he floated the possibility that Russia could join the EU at some stage. In one of his first interviews in 2000, he suggested Russia might even become part of NATO one day.[7]

The Russian president was a political chameleon in both domestic and foreign policy, but whatever the changes in backdrop and mood music, his various political incarnations were all designed with the broader goal in mind of restoring what he believed to be Russia's rightful place on the global stage, lost when the Soviet Union collapsed. If the West would play by Putin's rules, the quest to regain status as a first-tier nation could be achieved through cooperation. If it would not, confrontation would be required.

V

Leaders of all stripes, faced with the task of rejuvenating wounded nations, have looked to history to do so. Back in 1882, the French thinker Ernest Renan recognized that for a sense of nation to take hold, shared glories and common suffering were far more important than customs posts or heavily guarded borders.

The fifteen nations to emerge from the Soviet collapse all took different approaches to dealing with their pasts as they built new national identities. In the three Baltic states, where Soviet rule had been imposed only in 1940, and large swathes of the populations had always been strongly antipathetic to rule from Moscow, new governments worked feverishly to undo the Soviet legacy. Museums opened that equated the Soviet period with the Nazi occupation. The old KGB archives were opened, and monuments erected to the victims of the occupying regime. The national narratives saw 1991 as an unequivocally celebratory date: the end of oppression, the restoration of a past, interrupted independence, and a return to the European family.

In Belarus, by contrast, President Alexander Lukashenko offered his people the limited but comfortable 1970s version of Soviet power: high on tractor production and agricultural targets, low on political freedoms. It was as if nothing had changed; 1991 was an irrelevance. In the new ethnic republics of Central Asia, where there was little in the way of pre-Soviet ethnic-based statehood to hark back to, new national identities were manufactured that traced the nations back centuries on semi-historical or pseudo-historical grounds. Lenins were replaced by portraits of the smiling, geriatric local autocrats, just as ubiquitous and just as hagiographic. The Soviet past was quietly excised from the official narrative, neither demonized nor nostalgized, a historical elephant in the room that was simply ignored, despite the fact that the dictatorial leaders were all former party bosses in a new nationalist guise.

The only two of the fifteen countries not to come up with a coherent, unifying national-historical narrative in the first two decades after the collapse were Russia and Ukraine. The events of 2014—the revolution in Kiev, Russia's annexation of Crimea, and the war in eastern Ukraine—were, at least in part, a clash between competing Russian and Ukrainian attempts to transcend the conundrum of 1991 and mint new national identities.

By the time Putin took over, Russian attitudes to the Soviet past were ambivalent and confused. Back in 1991, crowds in Moscow had toppled the monument to Felix Dzerzhinsky, founder of the Cheka (the Bolshevik secret police that would later be called the NKVD and then the KGB), which stood outside the Lubyanka, the KGB headquarters in central Moscow. Leningrad reverted to its imperial name, St Petersburg. But after this initial flurry of activity, the disposal of the iconography of the Soviet past came to a halt. Most cities still had a Lenin striking a stirring pose in their main squares; many streets retained their Soviet names. There were Lenin, Marx, Komsomol, Red Partisan, and Dictatorship of the Proletariat streets across the country. Russia was like a party host who awoke the morning after, started making a cursory effort to clean up the mess all around, but after a while simply gave up and slunk back to bed to nurse its hangover.

The visual representation of history was dizzying and disorientating. Lenin's mummified corpse remained on display in a glass case inside his marble mausoleum; stern soldiers watched over visitors to ensure they treated the embalmed Soviet leader with respect (no talking, no hands in pockets). Meanwhile, on the other side of Red Square, the new rich dropped obscene amounts of money in the upmarket boutiques of a flashy department store. The last tsar and his family were made saints by the Russian Orthodox Church, and yet a Moscow metro station still bore the name of Pyotr Voikov, the man who was directly responsible for organizing their execution.

Hammer and sickle motifs adorned dozens of government buildings; sumptuous mosaics of happy collectivized peasants and stoical workers lit up metro stations. Looked at through contemporary eyes, it was hard to say if they should be taken merely as culturally valuable artefacts of a bygone age, or if they still celebrated the achievements for which they had initially been designed. Most disturbingly, the Lubyanka, the imposing mustard-coloured KGB headquarters, famous for basement interrogations and executions during the purges of the 1930s, remained the headquarters of the FSB, the KGB's successor agency. Inside, there was no 'lustration' of those cadres who had taken part in the worst excesses of the Soviet regime, no purge of Soviet functionaries in the way that many Central and Eastern European countries implemented in the aftermath of 1991. In most of those countries, there was a consensus that the Communist period had been an occupation, or an unwanted external imposition. In Russia, the issue was far more slippery and confusing. After all, both Gorbachev and Yeltsin had themselves been Soviet officials.

The Moscow of the early 2000s was a palimpsest; the monumental buildings and heroic archetypes of the Soviet past were still visible beneath the tacky veneer of modern construction and the gaudy capitalist hoardings advertising casinos, loans, and burgers.[8]

The new president's nation-building task was unusually thorny, as he inherited a multi-ethnic, post-imperial state with a recent history that was as bewildering as it was painful. Putin took a selective approach to the Soviet past, picking out individual elements that could help provide a sense of continuity, starting with the old Soviet national anthem, which was restored in 2001, albeit with new lyrics. But simply creating a Soviet Union 2.0 was not going to work. While there was much nostalgia for the Soviet period, calling for its return would alienate the business community and younger Russians, who enjoyed the opportunities that capitalism and Putin's oil wealth had brought them. Putin tapped into the sense of injustice among many Russians, famously calling the Soviet collapse the 'greatest geopolitical tragedy of the twentieth century'. But he also equivocated, saying that while only a person without a heart could fail to miss the Soviet Union, only someone with no head would want to restore it.

In the new Russia, the old Soviet pantheon of revolutionary heroes and dates was no longer applicable, and it was not clear from where new ones might emerge. The Orthodox Church could help provide some kind of moral code and a new sense of purpose for a portion of Russians freed from the confines of official Soviet atheism. Moscow's Cathedral of Christ the Saviour, blown up under Stalin in 1931 and later replaced with a swimming pool, was rebuilt during the 1990s and reopened during the first year of Putin's rule. The Church became an important part of Putin's identity project for modern Russia, but it could not alone unify the nation, especially in a country with large Muslim and smaller Buddhist regions.

Putin enjoyed reading history books and came across many figures in the tsarist past whom he admired, mainly those who had strengthened the state and ensured political continuity. At different times he would reference various statesmen and thinkers as inspirations, and draw from both the tsarist and Soviet periods. But in all of Russia's long and complicated history, there was only one event that had the narrative potential to unite the country and serve as a foundation stone for the new nation, something that could help to foster a sense of national pride, just as the oil revenues led to improved economic indicators. That was the victory in the Second World War, or in the Soviet parlance that was still used in modern Russia, the Great Patriotic War. Pride in the defeat of Nazism transcended political allegiance, generation, or economic status, and had been used by the later Soviet leaders to cement the regime's legitimacy. Putin would once again draw on the war victory as the key to creating a consolidated, patriotic country. Only as this kind of country could Russia regain its rightful place as a first-tier nation, Putin felt, and as the years of his rule over Russia continued, the role of the war victory in official rhetoric grew steadily. The answer to the implosion of 1991, it turned out, was the triumph of 1945. The ideology of victory would become the touchstone of Putin's regime: an anchor of national legitimacy in an ocean of historical uncertainty.

2

The sacred war

The four years between 1941 and 1945 had a logical place as the defining cataclysmic event for generations of Russians in a century that had been full of them. Putin's own parents lived through the siege of Leningrad, which lasted more than two years, and his older brother died in it. There was barely a family in Russia that was not linked to the war effort in some way, and in most there were missing grandparents or great-grandparents, among the millions who died in those years.

The modern-day victory legend that Putin would create built on the late Soviet narrative. It was under Leonid Brezhnev, who led the Soviet Union between 1964 and 1982, that the legend in its current form began to take shape. In the immediate aftermath of the war, the subject had been too raw, and Stalin was jealous of the acclaim given to the top military leadership. Georgy Zhukov, the man who led Soviet forces during the war, was demoted and consigned to relative oblivion. Victory Day was made a normal working day;[4] Labour Day and Revolution Day were the main celebratory dates. After the legendary 1945 victory celebration, Red Square held no victory parades at all in the first two post-war decades.

As the economy stalled under Brezhnev, and the path towards a utopian future of Communist plenty seemed less easily navigable, the regime sought validation in the past rather than the future. The heroism of the war, in which the Soviet people came together to defeat the ultimate enemy, became a foundational pillar of the state, and 9 May became the biggest holiday in the calendar.

Despite the official pomp, for ordinary Soviet citizens the holiday remained primarily about spending time with real veterans, many of whom were still alive. Unlike other Soviet holidays, Victory Day had a visceral, personal element for millions of families who retained indelible memories of the war years. During the 1970s, veterans wore their uniforms on Victory Day and gathered in parks across the country, bringing their children and grandchildren, and happily receiving flowers from well-wishers. But the tone was one of solemn commemoration rather than joyous celebration. One report of the day from the Siberian city of Nizhny Tagil recalled the following scene: 'There was an endless stream of people moving along the road to the cemetery. More than an hour before the designated start time, the cemetery was filled with people of various ages. . . . During the solemn meeting there was a tense silence; many of those present were sobbing. The participants placed wreaths and bouquets of flowers on the graves of the fighters. Not one grave was left forgotten.'[5]

The official narrative, of a unified Soviet people marching forward to a glorious victory, a black-and-white tale of the triumph of good over evil, was always vulnerable to historical enquiry. In 1965, the Soviet historian Alexander Nekrich published a book called *June 22, 1941*, which dealt with the events around the launch of Operation Barbarossa, the Nazi invasion of the Soviet Union. Nekrich, himself a veteran who had spent much of the war on the front line, wrote about the purges of the army leadership in the years leading up to war, and the intransigence of Stalin in the face of evidence that the Nazis were preparing for an attack. Conceived during the brief 'thaw' under Nikita Khrushchev, by the time the book came out, Brezhnev had taken over and the critical viewpoint was not welcome. Nekrich was denounced and expelled from the party. He eventually emigrated.

With the advent of *perestroika* in the mid-1980s, there were still many people alive who remembered the war vividly. As the archives opened and the fear of taking the 'wrong' line dissipated, it was no longer possible to silence alternative voices. Difficult questions about Stalin's unpreparedness and the huge casualty count resurfaced, together with some new ones. Why were returning Soviet soldiers who had been

captured by the Germans sent to labour camps? Why were whole eth-
nic groups deported from their homelands to other parts of the Soviet
Union during the war? And what exactly was it that motivated the
Soviet people?

Secret NKVD reports into the private moods of writers and intellectuals during the war came to light that showed just how much resistance there was to Soviet power during the first months of the conflict.
A Moscow journalist claimed he was ready for another three years of
war and a million deaths, if by the end of it the 'despotic, awful order
in our country' was defeated along with the Nazis.[6] Other intellectuals,
including those considered loyal to the regime, apparently had similar
thoughts.[7]

There remained no doubt that millions of Soviet citizens did fight,
heroically and to the death, but it was clear that the picture was not
as simple and clear-cut as the previous historiography had made out.
The Soviet order, after all, had existed for less than a quarter of a century and had embarked on a series of bloody attacks on huge swathes
of its own population. Some people fought for the Soviet Union or
for Stalin, while others fought in spite of them, for a deeper sense of
Russianness and homeland.[8]

It turned out that prior to the Nazi invasion, Stalin had received more
than a hundred warnings of the impending attack, coming from sources
as diverse as moles inside the German air force, Winston Churchill, and
an intelligence agent in Japan who had seduced the German ambassador's wife. He ignored them all, convinced that Hitler was not planning
an attack, and failed to make elementary preparations to repulse the
initial advance,[9] a blow to the idea of Stalin as the wise and brilliant
military tactician who had steered the Soviets to victory. When it came
to the fighting itself, the sanitized, glorious portrayal of the war also
began to crumble. Soviet tactics paid scant concern to human lives; it
was often a case of victory by sheer numbers. In one Crimean operation, Red Army soldiers were ordered not to dig trenches because they
spoiled the 'spirit of aggression'. In under a fortnight, 176,000 soldiers
died.[10] Historians dug up many such examples.

There were also many examples of tactical brilliance, and the Western
image of terrified Soviet soldiers who lived in fear of execution and
fought only through coercion is equally problematic.[11] But the reality

of war is never pretty, and the Eastern Front was perhaps the most sav-
age theatre of the most awful war in human history. There were indeed
many cases of extreme bravery and extraordinary feats, but this did not
lessen the horror. Many who fought heroically were persecuted after
the war, especially those who had succumbed to the 'shame' of being
captured rather than fighting to the death.

In 1985, the director Elem Klimov's *Come and See*, one of the most
disturbing war films ever made, hit Soviet cinemas. Released as the
first hints of *perestroika* were in the air, the film had been planned
since the mid 1970s but was deemed inappropriate by the censor.
Nobody who has seen it can forget the expression of horror on the
face of the main protagonist, Flyora, a young boy from a village in
Belarus who leaves his mother to fight with the pro-Soviet partisans
against the Nazi occupants. With the exception of very brief moments
of graphic violence, the film's power is channeled through the reflection of events on Flyora's face, a masterly and disturbing piece of
acting. It certainly does not besmirch the memory of the Soviet war
dead or show the Nazis as anything other than monstrous killers. But
it does not glorify the war either; it shows events in all their appalling
misery. When it was released, there were reports of people fainting
inside the cinema. Nevertheless, nearly thirty million Soviet citizens
went to see the film and were subjected to this shockingly realistic
portrayal of the conflict.

The official, Brezhnev-era historiography was coming apart at the
seams. In 1989, Moscow admitted the existence of the secret protocols
of the Molotov-Ribbentrop pact, by which it had carved up Eastern
Europe together with Nazi Germany, moved into the Baltic States and
eastern Poland, and deported tens of thousands of people in 1940 and
1941.[12] There was finally an admittance that the mass execution of 21,857
Poles at Katyn and two other sites, which the Soviet government had
for decades blamed on the Nazis, was indeed Moscow's doing. In the
countries of Central and Eastern Europe, historians and activists who
had always balked at the Soviet insistence that 1945 should be seen as a
liberation, rather than a new occupation, began writing their own, new
histories.

In this atmosphere of soul-searching, the Soviet ministry of defence
commissioned a new history of the war from the director of the

army's main history institute, General Dmitry Volkogonov. By 1990, Volkogonov had prepared a draft in which he criticized the terror and slaughter in the years leading up to 1941, suggested that the Red Army had won the war in spite of Stalin's tactics rather than because of them, and intimated that the death count was far higher than it had needed to be. With access to more archives than anyone previously (and more than any historian would have today), Volkogonov was able to piece together a disturbing portrait of the war, which even in the atmosphere of *perestroika* was extremely controversial. When attacked by other generals over the tone of his work, he said, 'We don't need blind patriotism. We need the truth!'[13]

Gradually, attitudes were changing, and during the first years of Yeltsin's rule there was a flourishing of interest in a new historiography of the war, one that would take in the more problematic sides of the victory as well as the glory. In parts of the periphery, there was also a flourishing of interest in one of the least publicized crimes of the Soviet war effort: the deportations.

II

Kalmykia, a chunk of arid steppe on the Caspian Sea, is only a two-hour internal flight from Moscow, but when my plane landed in the region's capital, Elista, I felt as though I had made a civilizational shift. The ethnic Kalmyk population is of Mongol origin, and the city's skyline is dominated by a splendid Buddhist temple.

Kalmykia's story during the war was one of many reminders that the black-and-white version of the Soviet war narrative was deeply problematic. In 1943, the Kalmyks, along with many other Soviet nationalities, were accused of supporting the Nazis. Every man, woman, and child of Kalmyk ethnicity was rounded up, expelled from the ancestral homeland, and resettled in scattered settlements deep in the heart of Siberia, thousands of miles away. It was extraordinary, when one stopped to think about it: like deporting the whole of Wales to Australia.

Vladimir Ubushayev, the head of the history faculty at Kalmykia's main university, had written the only proper book on the subject, published locally in pamphlet form in 1991, amid the new atmosphere of intellectual permissiveness. By the time I visited him in his Elista home in 2007, he was a pensioner with a swept-back shock of grey hair and chunky glasses of the type favoured by Soviet-era intellectuals.

For Ubushayev, the subject was more than simply historical grazing ground. He had been a toddler in 1943 when the Kalmyks were deported, and spent his early years in Siberia. His father fought and died at the front, for the same country that would soon deport his entire family. Ubushayev recalled days as a young child spent with his grandfather scouring the frozen Siberian earth for potatoes, while his mother worked until late at night on the collective farm, each day returning home to find her daughter more and more ill, until one day she died. He was certainly a historian with a connection to his subject. 'It's the question that's bothered me my whole life,' he said, as we sat on spongy sofas in his living room, the television flickering silently in the corner. 'Why did it happen? Why us?'

Despite the fact that even mentioning the deportation publicly was not allowed until *perestroika*, it was a question that Ubushayev had a chance to put privately to Vyacheslav Molotov, the Soviet foreign minister during the war, when he visited the ageing Molotov at his dacha outside Moscow in the late 1970s. Molotov recalled a 1943 meeting of the State Defence Committee, the Soviet war planning body that consisted of just a few top Soviet leaders. Stalin had a list with different nationalities on it. The military top brass criticized the 110th Kalmyk Cavalry Division, which had fought the Germans on the River Don near Stalingrad and had eventually surrendered. 'Molotov told me that Beria was in favour of deporting the Kalmyks. I asked him why he didn't speak out against it, and he said that nobody at the time had any real information, and if Beria said it, who were they to disagree?' If Molotov's story is to be believed, the fate of the Kalmyks was sealed on the basis of a few words from Lavrenty Beria, one of the most odious of Stalin's henchmen, and a flick of the Soviet leader's pencil.

I headed to a bungalow on the outskirts of town to meet Boris Ochirov, a stocky pensioner, dressed for the summer heat of the steppe in only a pair of shorts. His torso was hairless and wrinkle-free, and he had a full head of closely cropped grey hair. He greeted me cheerily, and we took seats in his kitchen, where he decanted me a cup of traditional Kalmyk tea, a lukewarm buttery brew liable to induce retching in the uninitiated.

He started to tell me about 28 December 1943. He was only seven years old at the time, but the events remained seared into his mind. It was a viciously icy morning on the steppe, and almost all the young and healthy men were away at the front, so the villages were filled with women, children, and the elderly. It was just a few days before New Year's Eve, and while few people were in a festive spirit, families were nonetheless planning small celebrations and events to humour the children and forget the difficult times in which they were living. As dawn broke, the roar of engines could be heard approaching every village in Kalmykia, and out of the mist came shiny new Studebaker trucks. Given to the Soviet war effort by the Americans through the lend-lease programme, the trucks were part of convoys shipped to Murmansk, and had been brought all the way down from the Arctic Circle to the Caspian Sea.

Out of the Studebakers hopped soldiers from the NKVD, recalled Ochirov. They read the bemused villagers a decree informing them that the entire Kalmyk people were to be deported for treason. Elista had been occupied by the Nazis in August 1942, and was under German control for around five months, until the Soviets retook it at the end of the year. The Kalmyks were accused, en masse, of collaboration. They were given about half an hour to gather their possessions and prepare for permanent exile.

Some Kalmyks were cruelly beaten and robbed by the soldiers; others, such as Ochirov's family, were treated relatively well. They were allowed to slaughter a cow and pack the meat for the journey ahead; his mother took her sewing machine. 'They put us in the trucks with our things. The dogs were barking, and the cows and sheep were stamping their feet. People think only dogs can sense this kind of thing, but the livestock also knew something bad was happening. It was such chaos, such a terrible, terrible scene. The dogs ran after the trucks as we drove away, howling like mad. I'll never forget that scene.'

They were driven to a railway station, where a long train made up of cattle cars was already waiting. The Kalmyks were told to get in, fifteen or twenty families to each wagon. 'It was absolutely freezing—the height of winter, and we were journeying into Siberia. It must have been minus thirty or minus thirty-five most of the time. The journey lasted about twelve days, and by the end we were disgusting, lice-ridden wrecks. I remember there was a hole cut into the floor of the middle of the carriage for pissing and shitting. If we stopped at a station, sometimes they would let one or two people out to get some hot water. But I didn't get out once for the whole journey.'

At each station, guards walked along the platform and called up to enquire if there were any dead bodies. 'There would often be one or two people who had succumbed to the cold. We'd throw out their bodies, and they'd be taken away.' Parents bade farewell to children this way, husbands to wives.

By 4 January 1944, Beria was able to report personally to Stalin that '26,359 families, consisting 93,139 persons, were loaded onto 46 special trains'.[14]

The Kalmyks were one of many nationalities to be deported. The Chechens, Crimean Tatars, and ethnic Germans living inside the Soviet Union were deported to either Central Asia or Siberia, as well as several other smaller nationalities. In total, the Soviet Union deported around two million of its own citizens during the war.[15] The Kalmyk operation alone, one of the smallest in scale, required 2,975 officers of the NKVD as well as thousands of soldiers. It also entailed the logistical challenge of freeing up the trucks required, and took dozens of trains, which could have been helping the war effort, out of action for several weeks. The deportation of the much larger Chechen and Ingush populations in early 1944 saw 83,003 regular Soviet troops and 17,698 from the NKVD move into the region in the weeks prior to the roundup, ostensibly to reinforce the rear of the Soviet war effort, but actually to prepare for the deportation.[16] When it occurred, it involved 190 trains and an entire tank division.[17] For a country that was stretched to breaking point fighting the Nazis, it was an extraordinary use of energy and resources.

There is no doubt that some Kalmyks had indeed welcomed the Nazis when they occupied the region, and it is not hard to see why. The Soviet regime had closed down most of Kalmykia's Buddhist temples, and the territory had suffered as much as anywhere else in the country from the previous two decades of civil war, collectivization, and terror. When the Nazis took Elista on 17 August 1942, after rounding up around eight hundred locals, mostly Jews, and shooting them on the outskirts of town, they immediately set about a 'hearts and minds' operation. Buddhist temples were reopened in many settlements, and a Kalmyk-language newspaper called *New Life* was set up. Some Kalmyks voluntarily went over to fight for the Germans.

But even if there was sympathy for the Nazis among certain sections of the Kalmyk population, there were also many Soviet patriots who fought to the death for their country. More than twenty-three thousand went to the front, and 22 were given the 'Hero of the Soviet Union' medal, the highest military award. Kalmyk soldiers in the Red Army, who knew nothing of what was going on back home, were removed from the front as the deportation got under way—the officers were told they were being sent to form a special regiment in the east of the country. Instead, they were sent to labour camps.

Roughly two weeks after embarking on their forced journey through the coldest part of the world at the coldest time of year, those Kalmyks who had been hardy enough to survive arrived at Siberian rail hubs. There, they were divided up and scattered across remote towns and villages. A decree published in 1948 stated that the Kalmyk people had been deported 'forever, and with no right of return to the previous place of habitation.' Ubushayev estimated that about 40 per cent of those deported died either on the journey or during the first months of adaptation to their harsh new living conditions. Escape attempts were punishable by twenty years in the Gulag, and anyone caught abetting an escapee could count on five years of the same. To leave their 'special settlements' even for a few days required written permission.

Ochirov told me that when his family arrived at their new Siberian home, the villagers looked at the Kalmyks with disgust, scared by their Asian faces. For the first few months the newcomers were referred to as 'cannibals'. His schoolteachers did not use his name but referred to him as 'Enemy of the People' when calling the register. In the first five years of exile, over 90 percent of Kalmyk newborn babies were still-born or died in infancy, as whole families went starving and succumbed to illness.[18] It was only in 1957, during Khrushchev's 'thaw', that the Kalmyks were allowed to return. Many of them found the houses they had once lived in had new occupants, ethnic Russians who had moved in during their absence.

Perhaps, given the primary purpose was not physical extermination, the deportations were not technically genocides. But the Kalmyks, like all the deported nations, were scattered across a huge territory, with the goal of destroying any sense of national cohesion. Mentions of them were excised from official Soviet encyclopaedias and textbooks, and discussion of the deportations was taboo. It was as if these peoples had never existed, had never had homelands. By the time Stalin died in 1953, thousands of Kalmyks had perished in Siberia. If it was not genocide, it certainly came close to it.

III

Most Russian settlements of more than a few hundred people have a monument to those who perished in the Great Patriotic War, and often it carries the inscription: 'No one is forgotten; nothing is forgotten.' But in reality, in order to provide the required narrative, first for the Soviet war legend and then again for Putin's updated version, millions of people had been quite deliberately forgotten. If the war was to become the event that bound the nation together, dark chapters like the deportation of millions of Soviet citizens by their own government were best left unexplored. The spirit of enquiry that characterized *perestroika* and the early 1990s dissipated, as the war narrative gradually became more and more central to the nation-building project.

Yeltsin resumed the Soviet tradition of victory parades every 9 May in 1995, but they were modest affairs. With the economy imploding and the army mired in a horrendous war in Chechnya, there was little appetite for victory celebrations, especially for a victory linked to a country that had recently ceased to exist.

In 2000, Victory Day came just two days after Putin's inauguration, and this time, the ceremony of the day was much more pronounced. The celebration was the biggest since the Soviet collapse. On Red Square, thousands of soldiers lined up alongside veterans, who proudly wore their vintage uniforms, the lapels dripping with medals. They marched across the square in columns arranged by their wartime battlefronts.

In a speech given from outside Lenin's mausoleum, Putin described the war as a 'severe test of our statehood and people's spirit'. That Putin saw the devastation of the Second World War first and foremost as a challenge to statehood is telling, illustrating again that he saw sovereignty and the strong state as sacrosanct, and more fundamental than the well-being of individual citizens.

'Today you stand together with the new generation of defenders of the motherland,' Putin told the assembled veterans. 'Through you, we got used to being winners. This entered our blood. It was not just responsible for military victories, but will also help our generation in peaceful times, help us to build a strong and flourishing country.'[1]

In fact, the current generation did not feel much like winners, and there had been little by way of victories to celebrate in living memory. A few months later, the disconnect between the glorious military rhetoric and the modern Russian reality was underlined when the Kursk submarine sank in the Barents Sea. The country watched in horror as 118 sailors died, while the generals appeared indifferent and Putin did not return to Moscow from holiday for five whole days. Putin learned a number of lessons from the public relations disaster, including the potential bite of a free and critical media, and the urgent need to modernize the vast but creaking military resources inherited from the Soviet Union.

Amid the disintegration of the present, the memories of the war were a rare and powerful symbol of what it meant to triumph through adversity, of how it felt to be a winner in life. Putin wanted to imbue young Russians with this philosophy of winning. As the economy began to stabilize during Putin's first years, and people were paid pensions and salaries on time for the first time in more than a decade, there was more appetite for talk of a victorious nation. On occasions, the idea of 'handing down' the victory from one generation to the next was explicitly ritualized. Shortly after Victory Day in 2005, sixty thousand members of the Kremlin-sponsored youth group *Nashi* marched through central Moscow in matching T-shirts. When they reached the end of their route, they were handed bullet casings by war veterans, which bore the inscription: 'Remember the war, defend the Fatherland'. Then, the youth swore an oath: 'I take the homeland from the hands of the older generation. Yesterday, you fought at the front for freedom, independence, and a happy life. Today I continue this fight—wherever my country needs me.'[2]

The strength of feeling that the victory narrative evoked in people of all ages did not go unnoticed in the Kremlin. The post-Soviet years had bred a generation of cynics, and it was common among the country's 'political technologists' to see ideology as merely a useful tool with which to manipulate popular opinion. People had watched the once-rigid ideological constraints of the Soviet Union crumble, and had then seen the lofty democratic slogans of the 1990s disintegrate in an orgy of cynical stealing. It led to a situation where nobody really believed in anything at all. It was a society where, as the author Peter Pomerantsev put it, 'nothing is true and everything is possible'. I once visited a political technologist who was working on an electoral campaign for a regional mayor. He welcomed me to an office covered from floor to ceiling with Orthodox religious icons; behind his desk was an extra-large image of a dusky Byzantine Christ. I mentioned to him that the devout backdrop seemed slightly at odds with his outfit, a black jumpsuit and a fluorescent orange bandana. 'Oh, I'm not at all religious,' he told me with a laugh. 'I just like to change my ideological surroundings every few weeks for inspiration.' Ideas were a means to an end, not something genuine. With the Second World War, though, it was different.

Over the years, Putin's chief strategist Vladislav Surkov concocted all manner of fake movements, political parties, and ideologies that were run from the Kremlin, with the aim of keeping Russians occupied in a giant political 'matrix'. Pro-business liberals, hardcore Russian nationalist movements, and pro-Putin youth groups were all conjured into existence by Surkov's magic wand, to give the impression of a vibrant political culture and to allow safety valves for protest. But most of these ventures soon reached their sell-by date and had to be replaced.

Amid this cynicism, the war victory was a rare case of something genuine. It was a unique event that evoked real emotions and uncontested agreement from the vast majority of the population. As well as the personal sacrifices in almost every Russian family, the victory narrative also deeply resonated among a population that was hungry for things to be proud of, for good news. Its rise to prominence came about symbiotically. 'You can't say that Putin forced the war cult on the people, but you also can't say that the people independently demanded it,' the far-right Russian philosopher Alexander Dugin opined to me. 'It was a natural process that flowed in both directions. It was organic.'

In 2005, a state news agency for the first time distributed the orange-black St George's ribbons, as a symbol of victory, ahead of 9 May. The practice took off, and with each subsequent year, the orange-and-black colour palette became ever more widespread in the weeks before Victory Day. The holiday took on more and more importance, as the iconography of victory dominated the city for weeks and months before the date itself.

In 2008, the parade featured heavy weaponry, for the first time since the Soviet collapse. 'This is not sabre rattling,' Putin told a cabinet meeting on the eve of the holiday. 'We threaten no one and do not intend to do so. We have everything we need. This is a simple display of our growing defence capability, the fact that we are now able to protect our citizens, our country, and our riches, which we have in great quantity.'[3] Exactly three months later, Russian tanks rolled into neighbouring Georgia.

As time passed, the victory rhetoric became more and more explicitly linked to contemporary Russia. Every year on Victory Day, surviving veterans still donned their uniforms and strolled proudly through the streets, to be showered with affection and flowers. But with each passing year, the tone of the day continued to change. Under Putin, gradually but inexorably, the day became less about remembering the war dead and honouring the survivors, and more about projecting the military might of contemporary Russia. The message was one of unity, around the idea of a resurgent, victorious nation.

IV

As the focus on the glory of victory intensified, the sense that it was 'unpatriotic' to dwell on the darker pages of the war history became more pronounced. The war was meant to be a unifying memory, not a controversial and divisive one. Modern Russian school textbooks contained just a single line about the deportation of two million of the country's own citizens during the war.

According to Putin's logic, the war victory underpinned the strength of modern Russia, and it thus stood to reason that anyone trying to undermine or complicate the narrative was also attempting to undermine Russia itself. This applied both to 'unpatriotic' Russians at home, and other nations abroad who had ambiguous feelings towards the Soviet war effort because of the Molotov-Ribbentrop pact and Soviet actions in the eastern half of Europe after the war. 'Today we see not only attempts at distorting the events of the war, but also cynical lies and impudent defamation of an entire generation of people who gave up everything for this victory, who defended peace on earth,' Putin complained at one point. The goal of such distortions was obvious, he said: 'to undermine Russia's power and moral authority, to deprive it of its status of a victorious nation, with all the ensuing international legal consequences, to divide peoples and set them against each other, and to use historical speculations in their geopolitical games.'

The Russians did have legitimate questions about the veneration of Nazi-allied wartime formations in the Baltic States or Ukraine, but 'cynical lies' in Putin's terminology was code for anything that questioned a black-and-white narrative of the triumph of good over evil. There was something epic, almost religious, about the victory narrative: of suffering, triumph, redemption. The Soviet Union had been a Christ-like martyr, undergoing immense torment for the sins of all mankind. And along with pride, there was anger when others refused to see the Soviet victory in these terms too, and show gratitude for the sacrifice.

The horrific price the Soviet nation paid for the war victory became something to be brandished aggressively, rather than sombrely reflected upon. People often played the numbers game, pointing out that the numbers of British or Americans killed were a fraction of the millions of Soviet citizens who perished fighting the Nazis. Russia, having lost so many, had earned a moral right to be respected, went the narrative.

It became a mantra of Putin and other top Russian officials that 'it is unacceptable to rewrite history'. But history is always being rewritten, as new sources and new interpretations come to the fore. In a country that for decades had lived with a politicized and proscribed study of history, rewriting the history books should have been not only acceptable, but a matter of the first importance. In fact, history in Russia *was* rewritten, but rewritten so as to excise the difficult questions and grey areas that had been raised by the historiography of *perestroika* and the 1990s. The central archive of the defence ministry held ten million documents about the war, but only two million of them were available to researchers; the rest remained classified, including almost everything about wartime repressions.[19]

In 2009, the Kremlin set up a 'Commission to Prevent the Falsification of History to the Detriment of Russia's Interests', focussed mainly on countering Baltic and Central European narratives about Soviet occupation and wartime collaboration. The implication in the commission's name was as disturbing as it was obvious: falsifying history to the *benefit* of Russian interests would be quite acceptable. The same year, the Kremlin-connected historian Natalia Narochnitskaya said Russia should demand respect for its view of the Second World War by 'putting the issue side by side with the issue our Western partners are really interested in—the energy sector'.[20] The idea, destined to remain unimplemented, was to calibrate oil and gas prices in line with the level of respect accorded to the Russian war narrative.

Inside the country too, subjecting the sanitized version of the war to proper scrutiny became a moral outrage, something akin to Holocaust denial in the West. When the independent television station TV Rain asked its viewers for their thoughts on whether Leningrad should have been surrendered in order to avoid the horrific starvation and attrition during the 872-day siege, which cost over a million lives, it faced a political and legal backlash so strong that the channel was almost closed down.[21] There were, perhaps, strong and convincing arguments that Stalin was right to decide it was not worth surrendering the city at any price, but it at least seemed a question worthy of discussion and debate.

Sometimes, there was a curious doublethink at play, a tacit admission that maybe the war myth was not as clear-cut as the official narrative made it out to be, but that the topic was too sensitive to be subjected to questioning. Back in 2002, the British historian Antony Beevor wrote an account of the Red Army's march on Berlin, which concluded that Soviet soldiers conducted the worst episode of mass rape in human history as they moved through Germany in the final months of the war, with around two million German women raped,[22] many of them multiple times.

On the publication of Beevor's book, the Russian ambassador to the UK, Grigory Karasin, penned a furious letter to the *Daily Telegraph* decrying the allegations as 'lies and insinuations', despite a wide body of evidence from Russian and German archives provided by Beevor. 'It is a disgrace to have anything to do with this clear case of slander against the people who saved the world from Nazism,' wrote the ambassador. But separately, and privately, Karasin invited Beevor to lunch. The ambassador told Beevor that given the horrors of the past century of Russian history—the revolution, civil war, famines, purges, and then the brutality of the Nazi invasion, the victory had to be seen as 'sacred'. He said Russia would only be able to face up to these pages of its history when all the veterans had passed away, by implication admitting that what Beevor had written may indeed have been true.[23] Dredging it up now was inappropriate and unseemly; it was better to leave the Victory as a sacred myth.

Russia is far from the only country that has simplified its war narrative and excised the darker moments. In 1992, a monument was erected in London to Sir Arthur Harris, otherwise known as 'Bomber' Harris and responsible for the saturation bombing of German cities, most notoriously Dresden, at the end of the war. In perhaps the closest parallel to the Soviet deportations among the Allied nations, the US rounded up and interned over 100,000 Japanese Americans, more than half of them US citizens, during the Second World War, deeming them untrustworthy. It was the 1980s before the government issued an apology and paid reparations.[24]

But in Russia, the obsession with 'remembering history' in fact masked a desire to wilfully forget, or at least distort it. Popular pseudo-history books on sale at the biggest Moscow bookshops spun tales about a Western plot against Russia that had gone on not for years but for centuries, with Adolf Hitler in fact part of a Western project to attack Russia. On occasions, people even angrily claimed to me that Britain had joined with the Nazis and both had been fought off by the Soviets. This all made it much easier to transpose the historical events onto the present-day situation. As the Soviet people had once won the ultimate struggle against fascists, so today's Russians could be called upon to fight in echoes of the same battles, against those who currently opposed Russia. The 2014 conflict in Ukraine, which is dealt with later in this book, borrowed much of the rhetoric and symbolism from the Second World War narrative. It was in many ways the logical culmination of the steady increase of the importance of Victory in Putin's narrative: the flames of a new conflict were fanned by the memories of an old one.

v

As the seventieth anniversary of victory approached in 2015, Moscow oozed victory from every pore. At the airports and train stations, screens flashed up congratulatory messages. Muscovites, with orange-black victory ribbons pinned to their lapels, scurried about their business along boulevards lined with 'Our Victory' billboards. Hammer-and-sickle flags fluttered from the streetlights throughout the city centre; far below ground, trains repainted with orange and black sashes pulled into the elegant marbled stations of the Moscow metro.

Murals of heroic wartime images, five stories high and bearing the legend WE ARE PROUD, appeared on the facades of apartment blocks, while government agencies got a makeover for the occasion: the hulking ministry of defence headquarters was wrapped up like an over-sized orange-and-black gift. On Aeroflot planes, repainted in victory livery, the stewardesses intoned 'velkam to hero city of Moscow,' on every descent into the Russian capital.

On television, there were war films and military documentaries all day long. Shops promised victory discounts and advertisements offered special VICTORY IS OURS bank accounts. Some people daubed slogans onto their cars: 'Thanks Grandad for victory!' or 'To Berlin!' One popular graphic showed a man whose head had been replaced with a Soviet hammer and sickle pushing down a man with a Swastika head, and penetrating him from behind. The caption read: '1941–1945. We can do it again if necessary.'

In the month preceding the date, traffic was frequently diverted to allow tanks and other heavy equipment to roll down Tverskaya, Moscow's central thoroughfare, and rehearse their display on Red Square ahead of the big day. The military hardware growling through everyday urban scenes made for an unnerving sight.

On New Arbat, a multi-lane avenue of Brutalist high-rises, huge neon hoardings the length of several tennis courts flashed up statistics about the Soviet war effort. As I walked home from a bar late one Friday night, the screens glowed with information about the Battle of

Stalingrad, relayed in block letters so large that the street below was bathed in light each time new text appeared.

201 DAYS!
3,280 DEAD EVERY DAY!
284,000 GERMANS SURROUNDED!
86,000 GERMANS TAKEN PRISONER!
ONWARDS TO VICTORY!

When 9 May finally came around, it was a warm morning in Moscow, and crowds lined the streets hours before the parade was due. People jostled for position and held Soviet and Russian flags in eager expectation, as I weaved my way through the metal barriers and police cordons in the direction of Red Square, the asphalt of the traffic-free streets glowing in the early morning sunlight. I had secured an invite to the VIP viewing stand, and passed through multiple security perimeters, a passport check each time, before I finally reached the square itself. The elite of Vladimir Putin's Russia was assembled in the tribune—ministers and parliamentarians, Orthodox priests and military officers, patriotic bikers and Kremlin-friendly journalists. I sat next to an FSB general, who was chatty until he found out I was a Western journalist. A few rows in front of me, a four-year-old wore a child-sized vintage Red Army outfit; when the national anthem played, his father repeatedly elbowed him, making sure he held a military salute the whole way through. As the day went on, I saw dozens of these army children. One couple had transformed their child's pushchair into a tank; the uniformed baby peered out curiously over the papier-mâché gun turret extending in front of him.

'In spring 1945, the Red Army brought freedom to Europe,' boomed a baritone voice straight from the wartime Soviet newsreels, the words reverberating around the vast square. A military march struck up, and eight soldiers goose-stepped the length of the square, holding aloft the Russian flag and the Victory banner, melding the two concepts into one. The rest of the troops, sixteen thousand of them, looked on saluting. The defence minister, Sergei Shoigu, stood in an open-top limousine, and held a long salute as he was driven the length of the square past the rows of troops assembled before him.

"Greetings Comrades!"
"Greetings Comrade Minister of Defence!"
"Congratulations on seventy years of Victory!"
"URAAAAAAAAAA!"

The loudspeakers crackled with the best known of the Russian war marches, Sacred War, piping it across the square at top volume. Just hearing the strains of the rousing minor-key tune conjured grainy black-and-white images of brave Red Army soldiers charging in slow-motion at the enemy. The tone of the ceremony was overbearing, but it was impossible not to be moved, in the same way a splendorous religious service elicits an emotional response even in an atheist. I found myself inadvertently humming the march on a daily basis for months afterwards.

Arise, vast country,
Arise for the deadly battle
With the dark fascist forces,
With the cursed horde.

Let our noble rage
Rise up like a wave.
This is the people's war,
The sacred war.

When the music finished, Putin took to the podium and addressed the assembled soldiers and veterans: 'As we mark this sacred date, we again take stock of the full importance of the victory over Nazism. We are proud that it was our fathers and grandfathers who were able to overcome and crush that dark force.'

Putin paid lip service to the other Allied nations, but also made a thinly veiled comparison between the Nazi threat of yore and American hegemony in the modern world. 'Back then, in the 1930s, enlightened Europe failed immediately to see the deathly threat of Nazi ideology. Seventy years later, history calls on us to be aware and alert once again,' said Putin. 'We have seen an effort to create a unipolar world, and we are seeing force-oriented thinking gain traction.' Putin said Russia should not repeat the 'mistakes of the 1930s': it was necessary to fight attempts to gain world domination before it was too late. He never once named the United States explicitly, but he did not have to.

After Putin's speech, the parade began. Thousands of soldiers marched with exquisite precision; some of them wore Second World War uniforms, while others were dressed in their modern army gear. A terrific growling of engines announced the arrival of military hardware: first, columns of vintage wartime vehicles, and then the best and most sinister hardware the modern Russian Army had to offer. Armoured cars, tanks, and multiple-launch rocket systems all rolled across the square; bringing up the rear were the enormous, phallic intercontinental ballistic missiles, mounted atop elongated, slow-moving trucks. A spectacular flyover completed the ceremony, dozens of planes roaring overhead in formation, the final group leaving a smoky trail in the colours of the Russian flag. The crowd went wild.

VI

A few days before that year's Victory Day, I paid a visit to Evgeny Kuropatkov, a sprightly ninety-one-year-old with a moustache that was as impressively well-tended as his bushy eyebrows were unkempt. He was in the midst of packing up his apartment into boxes, with help from his daughter. His second wife had died the month before, and her son from a previous marriage wanted to take possession of the flat. 'He'll be coming to live with me now; it'll be nice to live together,' the daughter said, stoically. Most of his clothes, papers, and trinkets had already been boxed up, but his medal-laden military jacket was set to one side; he wanted to wear it with pride on Victory Day.

Evgeny had been eighteen when Nazi Germany invaded, and he was called up to the army immediately. He fought around Stalingrad, and in the defence of Leningrad, with the 196th rifle division. He was in charge of weaponry supplies for the division; his task was to ensure the men had sufficient ammunition at all times. Of the thirteen thousand men in the division at Stalingrad, just 1,658 survived, he said.

The day Evgeny went to war also marked the last time he saw his closest relations. All three men in the Kuropatkov family were sent to the front: Evgeny's twin brother Vladimir fought in an anti-tank battalion and died in Belarus in 1944. His father was also called up, though

Evgeny did not know which part of the front he ended up in. He was never heard from again. During *perestroika*, a television crew making a documentary helped Evgeny track down information, and he discovered his father's entire regiment had been wiped out in the battle for Novgorod. No remains were ever found. All Evgeny had to remember his twin and father by were two passport-sized photographs, yellowed and dog-eared.

'The grass of the steppe smells of grief, Robert Rozhdestvensky wrote,' said Evgeny, quoting a Soviet poet. 'He was right. I had my face in that grass while we were retreating; I smelled that grief myself. The things I saw in Stalingrad, and in Leningrad, to see those things not in a book or a film but in real life, it's impossible to put into words what it was like.'

When Evgeny looked at twenty-year-olds today, skipping around Moscow carefree and innocent, he could not quite believe they were the same age he had been when he witnessed the horror of Stalingrad. 'Of course, a person becomes different after this, of course it changes you. I still see those things in my dreams.'

Evgeny's lines were well rehearsed. He rattled off figures and dates with the precision of someone who had told his story a thousand times before. If I had returned a month later, I suspect he would have repeated the same sentences almost verbatim, in the way that distant memories coagulate into set monologues. And yet, despite that, there was still something raw about the recollections. Every now and then, the old man's voice became rasping and he would gulp for air, as if he had surprised himself by the emotions the stories still raised, seventy years and hundreds of tellings later.

Evgeny had been invited to Red Square for the parade and planned to attend; he liked the fact that 9 May was still celebrated. But although he enjoyed wearing his army jacket, festooned with medals, and he took understandable pride in being part of the victory, his bearing and tone were very different to the official propaganda. He spoke of the war as a terrible, not a glorious, experience; of loss and violence and unspeakable imagery. I doubt he would have wanted to dress his great-grandchildren up in Red Army uniforms, as if for a party.

3

Chechnya: the deal

I

When Putin took over as acting president on the eve of the millennium, the most pressing issue he faced was that of Chechnya, where the violence of the 1990s embodied the helplessness of the Russian state. For Putin, bringing order to Chechnya was the first part of his plan to reunite Russia. Just a few hours into his acting presidency, on 1 January 2000, Putin flew to Chechnya and awarded medals and hunting knives to Russian troops fighting there. 'This is not just about restoring the honour and dignity of Russia,' Putin said, in televised remarks beamed into homes across the country. 'It is about putting an end to the break-up of the Russian Federation. That is the main task. Russia is grateful to you.'[1]

The Chechens, a mountain warrior people who speak a guttural language with no Slavic roots, had a long history of resistance to Russian rule. In the nineteenth century, they waged guerrilla war against the tsar's army, alongside other Muslim nations from the North Caucasus, led by their spiritual and political leader, Imam Shamil.

Chechen society was based on fierce loyalties to family and clan rather than to class, and many Chechens were never fully on board with the Bolshevik project either, with its collectivization of agriculture and focus on an industrialized, proletarian future. In 1931, more than thirty-five thousand Chechens were arrested and most of them were shot, in a crackdown on religious leaders, nationalists, and kulaks.[2] Nonetheless, when the Second World War came, thousands of Chechens fought and died at the front. As with the Kalmyks, this did not spare them deportation. In Operation Lentil, launched on 23 February 1944, 450,000 Chechens and Ingush (a closely related ethnic group) were rounded up just as the Kalmyks had been, by NKVD men in Studebaker trucks. Most of the Chechens were sent to the punishing, barren lands of the Kazakh steppe.

Their crime was alleged collaboration with the Nazis, though unlike Kalmykia, the vast majority of Chechen lands were never occupied by the Nazis; most Chechens had never even laid eyes on a German soldier. The punishment was more likely due to broader suspicions about whether the Chechens would ever fully acquiesce to the Soviet system. Tens of thousands of Chechens died in the early stages of the deportation, both from the icy, inhumane conditions on the train and from the difficulty of adapting to life on the Kazakh steppe. Even by the NKVD's own accounting, up to a quarter of the deported Chechens died in the first four years of exile, with child mortality rates particularly high.[3] The real figure was almost certainly higher.

Khrushchev allowed the Chechens back home in 1956, but the memories were not easily erased. During the years of deportation, many villages had been destroyed and graveyards desecrated. Soviet attempts to curate historical memory had mixed success, as national legends and sometimes embellished tales of the glorious past of the Chechens remained alive, through oral storytelling traditions. They trumped the official propaganda that 1945 was a glorious date for all the Soviet people to celebrate. For the Chechens, the war had meant tragedy. Although many Chechens did become Sovietized, taking up positions as teachers, doctors, or even party officials, a spirit of resistance remained. Alexander Solzhenitsyn wrote that the Chechens were the only nationality in the camps who never brown-nosed the guards, and refused to resign themselves passively to their fate.

When *perestroika* came, this sense of rebellion only intensified. Dzhokar Dudayev, a Chechen general in the Soviet air force, with dashing looks and a pencil moustache, was posted in Estonia as the Soviet Union collapsed and saw the small nation push for freedom from Moscow. He may have been a Soviet officer, but he too remembered the injustices of the past. He had been an infant during the deportation, when his entire family were branded traitors despite the fact that two older brothers had fought in the Red Army. In November 1991, under Dudayev's leadership, Chechens declared independence.

But Chechnya was not Estonia, and this was a red line for Yeltsin. The Baltic States, like Ukraine and the Central Asian republics, had all been full-fledged 'SSRs' (Soviet Socialist Republics), with at least theoretical rights of secession from the USSR. Chechnya, by contrast, had been a region of the Russian SSR. Moscow had voluntarily given up control of the other Soviet republics, but there were plenty of other regions with similar status to Chechnya inside the Russian SSR boundaries. Allowing Chechnya to slip away could set a precedent that would see more and more territory ebb from the new, post-Soviet rulers in Moscow, as inexorably as their tsarist predecessors had once acquired it.

In late 1994, Yeltsin ordered what was meant to be a speedy operation to take back control of Chechnya, but the rump of the old Soviet Army was in no shape to fight a war against a motivated, nimble opponent on its own mountainous terrain. After an attempt to seize Grozny by land ended in defeat, Yeltsin resorted to crude, criminal tactics, pounding the city from the air. Thousands of civilians died in the attacks on the capital. The mess in Chechnya came to symbolize the hopelessness of the Yeltsin era. Two years of gruesome fighting killed tens of thousands of civilians and probably fifteen thousand Russian soldiers. It ended in a humiliating defeat for Moscow, and a brief period of *de facto* Chechen independence in the late 1990s, during which the territory became a Hobbesian nightmare of violence, kidnapping, and extortion.

Putin, as prime minister and then acting president, cemented his rise to power by launching a new campaign that would be equally bloody, but would eventually bring the territory back under Moscow's control. He filled the airwaves with tough talk, promising to hunt down the Chechen bandits and 'waste them in the outhouse' if necessary. The Chechen battle was portrayed as a terrorist struggle against the legitimate Russian state. This was partly true—the Chechens did begin to use terror as a weapon. But the context of extreme violence against them, both during the two wars but also further back in history, was ignored.

II

In early 2000, Putin used one of his first interviews as president to tell the Chechens they were not under attack from Russia, but being brought under its protection. 'We don't want them to develop the syndrome of a defeated nation. The people should understand that they are not a defeated people. They are a liberated people.'[4]

Putin said this as his fighter jets were bombing Grozny, raining more misery down on a city that already seemed as though it had reached total devastation. The damage was on a scale not seen in Europe since the Second World War. There was not a building that had remained intact from the two wars—Yeltsin's, then Putin's.

A survey by Médecins Sans Frontières in the aftermath of the second Chechen war found that nine out of ten Chechens had lost someone close to them during the two wars, while one in six had witnessed the death of a close relative with their own eyes, and 80 per cent of people had seen someone wounded. Two-thirds said they never felt safe, and almost every single respondent said they had come under shelling or aerial bombardment, or been caught in crossfire.[5]

After the ruthless military action came attempts at peace. Moscow knew it could not win over Chechnya without at least some portion of local support. Akhmad Kadyrov, the rebel mufti during the first war, changed sides and agreed to do Moscow's bidding. Kadyrov and his clan benefited personally from collaborating with the old enemy, but after years of misery he also believed that further resistance was a path to extinction. Many Chechens agreed, and were willing to give peace a chance at any price, even if that meant collaborating with the Russians. Kadyrov, with Russian backing, granted amnesty to thousands of Chechen men who had fought against the Russians. Fighters emerged from the mountains and forests, and joined new battalions loyal to Kadyrov. Although they were theoretically integrated into the Russian state, the battalions essentially became Kadyrov's private army, and were known as the Kadyrovtsy. Those who refused to lay down their arms were hunted down, first by the Russians in ruthless 'cleansing' operations and filtration camps, then by the Kadyrovtsy, who terrorized anyone suspected of having links to the insurgency, which took on an ever-more Islamist bent.

Akhmad Kadyrov was killed in a bomb blast in Grozny in 2004, and his son Ramzan, then a stocky twenty-seven-year-old with a cropped ginger beard, effectively took over. Ramzan travelled to Moscow and was received personally by Putin, who voiced condolences on the death of his father. In a pale-blue tracksuit, Ramzan looked absurdly out of place in the Kremlin's ornate interiors, but he and Putin formed a personal bond. Over the next years, Moscow showered Chechnya with cash. Ramzan used it to rebuild the region, but also to cement his personal rule.

By the time I made my first trip to Grozny, in 2009, the city was unrecognizable from the eerie photographs of Stalingrad-level destruction from less than a decade previously. Neat tree-lined avenues, of new apartment blocks and pleasant cafes, were intersected by pedestrian crossings where digital counters flicked the seconds down until the green man appeared. If you didn't look too closely, it could have been Belgium.

Each time I returned to Grozny, there were newer and shinier additions paid for with Moscow's roubles: a whole street in which the charred husks of apartment blocks had been replaced with brand-new versions; empty squares newly filled with white marble-effect ministerial buildings; and to top it all off, Grozny City, a thirty-two-story skyscraper housing a five-star hotel with a rooftop restaurant, a gym, and plush bedrooms with luxury toiletries. Next door, an enormous Ottoman-style mosque appeared, its minarets stretching far into the sky. The cognitive dissonance with the state of the city a decade previously was loud enough to cause tinnitus.

The money from Moscow came as part of a deal, offered by Putin via the medium of Kadyrov. In exchange for a free hand inside Chechnya, Kadyrov paid obsequious lip service to Putin, an almost mediaeval pledge of feudal loyalty. Portraits of Putin found their way onto flags, posters, and billboards across Grozny. Together with Ramzan and his slain father, they made up a Holy Trinity for modern Chechnya.

In 2008, less than a decade after Putin had ordered the bombing of the city, Grozny's central avenue was renamed from Victory Avenue to Putin Avenue. Kadyrov spoke at a ceremony to mark the switch: 'Terrorists from sixty countries came to Chechnya, not to make it an independent country, but to transform it into a springboard for destroying Russia.

They didn't succeed, thanks to Putin's will and resolve,' said Kadyrov. 'This avenue is being renamed after Vladimir Putin because he is the saviour of the Chechen people. He saved us from genocide.'

For Putin, the deal with Kadyrov was primarily about Russia's sovereignty, not about his own ego. It was not important that Chechens should see him as a personal saviour, but vital that they recognize the Russian state and its power as legitimate, despite the two terrible wars. A peaceful, loyal Chechnya was a key part of his mission to create a unified, great Russia.

In return for providing this supposed stability, Ramzan was given leeway to settle his personal scores with enemies and rivals: Chechens who might have represented alternative power bases, or those who had spoken out against the abuses of his rule, met violent deaths not only in Grozny and Moscow but also in Dubai and Vienna, an extraordinary series of extrajudicial assassinations to which the Kremlin turned a blind eye. Inside Chechnya, Kadyrov's forces were accused of carrying out all manner of crimes against those Chechens who refused to lay down their arms.

Kadyrov did have a real insurgency to fight against, the continuation of the 1990s movement he had once been part of, which with time had lost its focus on local independence and grown closer to the international jihadi cause. Kadyrov's people insisted that the harsh methods were the only way to keep order. A decade earlier, the whole of Chechnya had been engaged in partisan warfare against the Russians; bringing people back to peaceful life meant dealing ruthlessly with those who did not play by the rules. Anyone who broke the stifling codes of silence and questioned the tactics used to fight the insurgency—the ritualized torture to gain information and the punitive house-burning of relatives—was also at risk.

Natalia Estemirova was one of the last of the people trying to exercise some kind of oversight over the human rights situation in the region. In July 2009, she was kidnapped and murdered, with government-linked militias implicated. A month later, I went to Chechnya to write about the atmosphere in the aftermath of her killing. During my visit, Zarema Sadulayeva and Umar Dzhabrailov, recently married charity workers, were kidnapped from the offices of the Save the Generations charity in central Grozny, where Sadulayeva worked. Six men burst into her office in the broad daylight of a Monday afternoon, four of them in combat fatigues and the other two in civilian clothing, and dragged the pair off. With characteristic impunity, they returned later to seize the couple's mobile phones and Dzhabrailov's car. I spent the evening with the region's few remaining human rights activists, brave but terrified, traipsing from one police station to the next in the eerie darkness of the Grozny night, trying to find news. But nobody was talking. The next afternoon, a call came: Dzhabrailov's car had been found, with the bullet-ridden bodies of the newlyweds in its boot.

At the funeral in a nearby village, plain-clothed officials combed the streets keeping an eye on the mourners. Inside the house, female relatives performed the grim task of preparing Sadulayeva's mutilated body for burial, sponging down the naked corpse with wet cloths. Sadulayeva's work could not possibly be considered political. Some suggested her husband might have links to the Islamist insurgency. But the line between those who were legitimate law-enforcement targets for terrorist activities, and those who were targeted simply because they were critics of Kadyrov, grew more and more blurry as the years passed.

The leadership cult, the social contract of prosperity in return for unquestioning loyalty, and the ruthless handling of critics deemed unhelpful to the overarching project of renaissance: what Kadyrov offered Chechnya was a souped-up, more violent version of what Putin offered Russia, without the window dressing of democracy and niceties that the broader Russian project demanded. It was Russia as reflected in a circus mirror.

So it was with memory too. The people had been liberated. Not defeated. That was the official mantra, and that was the deal.

III

In locations far from Chechnya, I met with Chechens who had escaped Kadyrov's torture chambers and fled the region. One claimed to have seen a man doused in petrol and set alight. A dignified elderly gentleman, whose sons had been in the insurgency, told tales of awful beatings, of being handcuffed to the radiator in a damp cell for days and nights on end, and of electric shock machines that looked like they came from 1950s black-and-white horror movies, a spaghetti of leads that attached to fingers and toes and delivered a shock that sent your muscles into wild spasms of pain when the torturer pumped the hand-wound lever. Another told me how his captors tied his ankles to his wrists and trussed him up from the ceiling with a belt. They carefully positioned him at an angle that meant when he urinated or defecated, it would run down over his torso and onto his face.

Russian and Chechen officials denied such practices in public; in private, they justified them by the need to prevent terror attacks. The more the insurgency resorted to attacks on civilians, the more Kadyrov and the Russians felt vindicated about their own heavy-handed tactics; the more aggressive the tactics, the more entrenched and depraved the terrorist aims became.

Throughout the 1990s and early 2000s, the Chechen independence movement had called for the establishment of an independent Chechen republic, to be known as Ichkeria. The movement used Islamist rheto-ric, but even the appalling hostage takings at a Moscow theatre in 2002 and Beslan's School Number One in 2004 were aimed at putting pres-sure on Russia to withdraw its troops. The militants showed themselves more than willing to cause civilian casualties, but unlike al-Qaida or ISIS attacks, massacre was a side effect when things went wrong, not the end goal.

Doku Umarov, a ginger-bearded militant who was the self-styled president of Ichkeria, in 2007 announced the establishment of the Caucasus Emirate. Henceforth, the goal was not an independent Ichkeria, but an Islamic emirate that would spread across the Caucasus, with Umarov as its so-called Emir. The militants, on the run in the high mountains and thick forests of the Chechen interior, promised to rain down terror on Kadyrov and his Russian backers. A series of attacks in the Moscow metro in 2010 left dozens dead; the next year a sui-cide bomber struck at the capital's Domodedovo Airport killing at least thirty-six people in the international arrivals hall. Umarov approved both of the operations, he said, in videos claiming responsibility. Now, the insurgency 'negotiated' using random slaughter.

Determined to keep attacks inside Chechnya to a minimum, Kadyrov endorsed collective punishment for the relatives of those in the militant underground. Quietly, Russian security services allowed suspected insurgents to leave the country, figuring they would do less harm outside Russia than inside. Doku Umarov died in 2013 after the FSB managed to poison food that was brought to his hideout by a messenger. In the years that followed, many of the group's members went to fight in Syria for the cause of global jihad, lending belated credence to the Russian claims that they were fighting the evil of international terror rather than a local conflict brewed over many years of grievances under tsarist, Soviet, and post-Soviet rule. Most Russians knew nothing of the brutal deportation of the Chechens and the role the memories of it had in the demands for post-Soviet independence.

It was clear that with time, many in the Caucasus Emirate had become fully converted to radical Islamism and were willing to use terrorist methods to push their agenda. But on the numerous occasions I met people linked with the insurgency, they always cited very specific grievances about the way they had been treated by Russia throughout history, rather than speaking in the Islamist rhetoric of global jihad.

In 2011, two years before Doku Umarov was killed, I met his brother Akhmed in Istanbul. He was one of many Chechens I interviewed in the offices of an NGO near the city's Fatih Mosque, and the first time we spoke he did not reveal his true identity. When I later put the pieces of his story together, it dawned on me with whom I had been speaking, and I arranged to see him again. He admitted that he was indeed the brother of Russia's most wanted man. He was still in touch with his brother, via secure communication methods, he told me.

Akhmed, who spoke eloquently and thoughtfully, had spent eight years in his youth as the secretary of his local branch of the Komsomol (the Communist youth movement) prior to the Soviet collapse. In the 1990s, he set up a small business, but then war broke out and he joined the fight against the Russians. He claimed that during the second war, he did not fight, but helped the insurgency with supplies. He was arrested in 2005.

Capturing the brother of Russia's number one terrorist was a huge prize for Kadyrov. Akhmed recalled a year of torture and beatings: a cellophane bag was placed on his head and he was dangled in handcuffs from a hook on the ceiling. His captors approached from behind and prodded him with electric shock sticks. Sometimes, there were just simple old-fashioned beatings.

One day, he told me, instead of his Chechen torturers, a soft-spoken Russian man came into the room, who Akhmed suspected was a high-ranking intelligence officer. By this point, Akhmed was black with bruises, but the Russian told him he was not there to beat him. 'He was a philosophical kind of guy, he wanted to talk about life and the world. He asked me whom I would support if America started fighting Russia. I thought for a while, and then I said America. If Russia had behaved with a human face towards the Chechens for the past three hundred years, then without a doubt I would fight for Russia; it's our neighbour after all. But that hasn't been the case.'

Akhmed was eventually brought to Kadyrov, who told him his father had also been arrested. Kadyrov promised Akhmed his father would be set free, on one condition: he had to go on television to denounce his terrorist brother, and pledge allegiance to Kadyrov as the true leader of Chechnya. For the sake of his father, he agreed. Kadyrov ordered his handcuffs immediately removed, and rushed to embrace him warmly. Akhmed was taken to a luxurious room where he was told to shower and given a change of clothes. A team of six psychologists was made available for the next weeks, to ensure he was ready for his coming out, and he was given a security detail.

He did give the interview to Russian television, but only part of it ever aired. The correspondent wanted him to say, on camera, how grateful he was to the Russians for having rebuilt Grozny so beautifully. Akhmed, whose father had still not been freed as promised, lost patience. He refused to take part in the wilful amnesia. 'I told him it was beautiful before, and it was destroyed by the Russians. Why should I be grateful if you've now rebuilt it, to fool people? Putin became president on the blood of the Chechens; if you want to create peace here, then just withdraw all the special units that are kidnapping and torturing people.'

After the scandalous interview, he was put back in a cell, and was held for a further two years. He was no longer beaten but he would often hear the screams of men being tortured and women being raped, he claimed. One night, he executed a long-planned escape (he wouldn't give away the details) and made it out of Chechnya, through other parts of Russia, to Ukraine, and across the Black Sea to Istanbul.

Akhmed expressed sympathy for his brother's goals, and glossed over the appalling terrorist methods used by the Caucasus Emirate, but even he spoke in the language of an oppressed ethnic group, not that of jihad. Islamism was merely the best way for the peoples of the Caucasus to unite against Russia, Akhmed said. In these times, it was the only possible vehicle through which to realize the long-standing desire for independence.

'Ever since the Russians started their conquest of the Caucasus, there has never been a generation when fathers could pass on the fruits of their labour to their sons: either they were killed, or deported, or humiliated. Every new generation had to start life again, from nothing. They can't understand that we are free people, a free nation. They want to make us like them. But I don't want to be like them. They tell us you should live in our system, and the system will give you bread, flour, and sugar. But if I don't like the system I don't want to live inside it. What am I supposed to do, then?'

IV

In the new Chechnya, however, it was no longer Russians telling Chechens how to live. Almost every key government post in the republic was occupied by a Chechen, who answered to Ramzan rather than to Moscow. Chechens were free to speak their native tongue and practice Islam, and were effectively ruled from Grozny, not Moscow. It was everything that the early proponents of Chechen independence had wanted. That was the compromise Moscow had made to keep control of the territory. But in return, the Chechens were required to recalibrate their memories of the past, and tolerate the Kadyrov personality cult. When Ramzan wanted to make a political point, hundreds of thousands of Chechens were rounded up and sent to the streets for 'spontaneous' marches. The crowds surged through the streets of Grozny waving flags, clutching balloons, and holding aloft giant portraits of Ramzan, who in time was branded *Padishah*, the emperor.

Most Chechens were genuinely relieved that Ramzan had brought peace; they knew the horrors of war all too well. Some of those appearing on television or at parades shrieking about their love for Ramzan were perhaps doing so genuinely. But the Chechens were a proud nation with a history of fierce adherence to the individual and the family; it was humiliating for them to prostrate themselves before an absolute leader.

Many people whispered privately that they were horrified by the pomp and personality cult. Watching the Grozny parades, I was reminded of the words attributed to Dmitry Shostakovich about the bombastic end of his Fifth Symphony, premiered at the height of Stalin's purges in 1937: 'It's as if someone were beating you with a stick and saying, "Your business is rejoicing, your business is rejoicing," and you rise, shaky, and go marching off, muttering, "Our business is rejoicing, our business is rejoicing."'[6]

Kadyrov's methods made him an international pariah, but Putin's backing meant he enjoyed immunity from retribution, and the West served as a useful rhetorical punchbag. He nevertheless sought to confer legitimacy on his rule over Chechnya using the approval of mercenary Western celebrities. Like nineteenth-century traders seeking favour at the courts of the Central Asian emirs, they happily came to Grozny, flown in on private jets to genuflect to Kadyrov and laud his pet projects, all in return for a fat cheque. Over the years, Brazilian footballers arrived to take part in a rigged kickabout at the central stadium (Kadyrov missed two penalties but managed to score twice nonetheless) and Mike Tyson came to watch a boxing match. The French actor Gérard Depardieu, who would later be given Russian citizenship, came to shoot a mediocre film and hang out with his 'good friend' Kadyrov. He grew upset when I asked about human rights in the press conference. Wafting through the lobby of Grozny City later the same day, his elephantine frame clad in a tent of a white linen shirt, he wagged a finger at me in mock sternness: 'So, they haven't killed you yet, English?' He looked immensely pleased with his joke, the basis of which was apparently that this ignorant Western journalist thought Chechnya a dark and violent place, when actually his friend Ramzan had built a charming new capital with beautiful five-star hotels.

Ramzan's thirty-fifth birthday in 2011 coincided with City Day, a newly anointed public holiday. Lavish celebrations culminated in a gala concert in the evening. Ostensibly the event was to honour the resurrection of Grozny, but everyone knew the real celebration was of its patron. After all, the fates of Kadyrov and his city were inextricably intertwined.

I crouched with my back to the stage at the newly constructed outdoor arena, which seated around two hundred VIP guests. I watched

Ramzan reclining in a front-row armchair, grinning with pleasure as a litany of second-tier Western stars performed for him, voicing eulogies from the stage. Jean-Claude Van Damme, the violinist Vanessa-Mae, and the singer Seal all took their turns to perform for Kadyrov.

'I could feel the spirit of the people, and I could see that everyone was so happy,' gushed the actress Hilary Swank, before offering a sultry 'Happy Birthday Mr President' to Kadyrov, who beamed like a Cheshire cat. The patronage and praise of these ignorant Western stars helped sustain the official narrative of Ramzan, and ultimately Putin, as the benefactor of the Chechen people, liberated and not defeated. The locals at least had understandable reasons for going along with Kadyrov's charade; the foreigners had little excuse.[7]

The deal became ever more distorted as Kadyrov grew increasingly drunk on absolute power, hauling subjects in for a televised dressing-down if his security services caught them sending critical text messages about the government. He kept exotic pets at his numerous residences and sped across Chechnya in a high-speed motorcade made up of dozens of luxury cars. Critics continued to be beaten up or worse. Kadyrovtsy were jailed for the murder of Boris Nemtsov, the Russian opposition politician, in Moscow in 2015, apparently an ill-judged attempt by Kadyrov to please his feudal overlord. In 2017, his security forces began a gruesome round-up of Chechen men suspected of being gay. I met with gay men who had fled the republic, some of whom had been subjected to the same electric-shock torture in Kadyrov's secret prisons as suspected Islamist militants.

But even as the personality cult and dictatorial rule became ever more grotesque, the essence of the deal between Chechnya and Moscow remained the same: we will lay our historical grievances to one side, we will name our main street after the man who bombed our capital, and we will pledge him allegiance in the most obsequious terms, in order that we may enjoy the fruits of his coffers.

Putin and Kadyrov always had different reasons for the deal: for Kadyrov it was about his personal role as the leader of the nation, while for Putin it was about a pledge of loyalty to Russia. It was proof that 'stability' had come to Chechnya, and that Moscow had been right to fight for the territory, given how happy it was now under what was, at least theoretically, Russian rule. A peaceful Chechnya of Russian flags and portraits of Putin was the ultimate sign to the Russian president that he had succeeded in his mission of healing the pain and disaster left behind by 1991. But Kadyrov was now the only person who could provide the stability so vaunted by the Kremlin, and he became ever more demanding of resources and special dispensation from the centre. As the journalist Anna Politkovskaya put it before she was killed, probably in retaliation for her writings on Chechnya under Kadyrov, 'the Kremlin has fostered a baby dragon, which it now has to keep feeding to stop him from setting everything on fire'.

Ordinary Chechens were left with a difficult choice. They could face up to the ghosts of the past, which meant either leaving their homeland as refugees or continuing to fight against the Russians and the Kadyrov regime in ways that were becoming ever more perverse and nihilistic. Or they could push the past to one side, engage in the false rejoicing, and be thankful that however difficult the political situation might be, there was no war. There was no point wallowing in the past; after all, they were a liberated nation, not a defeated one, and their only tears should be tears of joy. The Chechens had been good at remembering their history, and it had brought them only misery. Perhaps it was time to try the alternative.

v

One hot summer's evening in 2015, I found myself at a kitschy, upmarket Grozny restaurant having dinner with a group of Kadyrovtsy. We sat in a faux-wooden cabin, one of many laid out amid manicured grass verges in the outdoor restaurant. Ornate wooden walkways bridged the artificial streams that meandered between the huts. The Chechens ordered a platter of grilled meat from a supplicant waiter. Among their number were man-mountains built like cartoon superheroes with ripped, contoured muscles and thick necks, and lithe wiry men who nevertheless looked ferociously strong. Apti, the man I had come to meet, was short and stocky, and with his sandy close-cropped beard bore an uncanny resemblance to Kadyrov himself.

Apti had progressed through Kadyrov's battalions until he retired in 2012, but it was clear he still held rank. The summer before, he had surfaced in eastern Ukraine commanding the Death Battalion, a grouping of two hundred Chechens who fought on the side of the pro-Russian separatists, one of the more confusing cameo appearances of the war. In eastern Ukraine, the Chechens inspired fear among all they encountered, both opponents and allies.

Apti had a certain charm to his manner and a warmth to his voice, which was heavily accented in Russian, but some of the others enjoyed playing up to the fearsome reputation of the Kadyrovtsy. One in particular scared me, a broad-shouldered giant with a cropped black beard, who wore a two-piece suit in emerald velvet and a prayer cap to match. He spoke slowly and deliberately, his eyes staring at me but somehow vacant, sounding me out and turning his manner on a sixpence between friendly joshing and deadly serious threats.

'Dangerous job you have,' he said, stroking his beard, before grasping and squeezing my upper arm far too tightly. 'Any time you write the wrong thing, you'll be killed straight away.' I wriggled from his grasp and tried to steer him towards something resembling a normal conversation, asking what he thought of Kadyrov. He softened.

'My generation has grown up on war; we don't know anything else. Even if people are scared of Ramzan, that's a good thing. Chechens need to be scared of someone. If we are left to ourselves, chaos breaks out. Ramzan is putting so much money into education, into sport. Maybe finally the next generation will have things better. Maybe finally people will be able to live normally here.'

It was an understandable desire. There were no adults in Chechnya who could say they had lived their lives 'normally'. Apti was thirty-six; he had just turned a teenager when the first war broke out, and did not receive any more education. He and friends fought despite their young age; they were underage partisans making explosive mixtures to lob at tanks. They hid in the forests, luring Russian soldiers into traps.

I wanted to get Apti away from his friends, to have a proper conversation about the past. He was initially evasive, but on my last night in Grozny he called me at two in the morning, and summoned me to the carpark outside my hotel. We perched on a bench, while a friend of his remained in the car listening to Chechen ballads on the stereo. Apti spoke in non-linear fragments of memories, not always related to the questions I had asked. 'I remember 31 January 2000, I was in Grozny, and it was utter chaos. I remember trying to cross the bridge, right there.' He pointed over at the spot, where several high-rise buildings clad in neon lights now stood, and pulled out his mobile phone to show me a photograph of the scene of devastation fifteen years previously. It seemed impossible that the picture could show the place we were now sitting, but Apti remembered. There were almost no physical reminders of the war in modern Grozny, but it was still there inside people's heads.

We discussed *yakh'*, a Chechen word for which there is no real translation in either English or Russian. The concept of *yakh'* encompasses codes of honour and masculinity, bundled together with a healthy dose of courage. It seemed it was at least in part the spirit of *yakh'* that had kept the Chechens going for so long in the face of oppression, though perhaps it had also contributed to their problems.

'Do you know how, in the year 2000, the fighters escaped from encirclement? Through a minefield. Seven thousand people. Four hundred of them were blown up on the mines. They walked and they walked and they kept exploding. For twenty-four days they went across the minefields, through the mountains. There was snow, and they exploded in the snow. You know, it wasn't my fault that war started here. I never wanted to fight anyone, but I had to. They called us bandits, but in the first war, nobody felt like a bandit.'[8]

In 2001, two of Apti's cousins disappeared, presumably seized by Russian forces. The bodies turned up horribly mutilated, with the ears chopped off. Especially for a Chechen, raised in a culture where honour and revenge play important roles, the desecration of the bodies was unforgivable. But nevertheless, Apti gave up the independence fight in 2002. Under Akhmad Kadyrov's guidance, the Russians allowed men like Apti to lay down their weapons and come out of the forest, to reintegrate slowly back into society and join the new pro-Moscow battalions. Apti was not just saving himself, but also his parents, who had been harassed by Russian security services demanding to know where their son was.

Almost all the men in the new battalions had lost relatives in the wars, many in horrific circumstances. In the rigid behavioural codes of the Chechens, there was little place for a man to display sorrow, but that did not mean it wasn't there. 'We feel a heavy burden and a void, an overwhelming void,' Apti said.

Apti found solace in the new life. In 2008, he was promoted to major, and became commander of a whole battalion. Apti had not travelled widely, just a couple of trips to Moscow and to fight in Ukraine. But he had also journeyed to Mecca to perform the hajj six times over the past years. 'Six times! Just think, if I had stayed in the mountains with the rebels, or if the war had continued, I would not have had the opportunity to do it even once.'

Still, it was extraordinary that after all the Russians had done in Chechnya, Apti could countenance fighting alongside them in Ukraine. Talking to Apti about his youth, it was clear that the painful memories were still there. After a childhood wrecked by war, after growing up with Russian bombs exploding around him, after losing relatives and loved ones in Russian air strikes and artillery barrages and filtration camps and extra-judicial executions, after years of partisan warfare against the Russian Army, how could a man then fight on the side of the Russians? Many of the rebel commanders in Ukraine were the very same Russian officers Apti had once fought against. Now they were fighting a clandestine war in a neighbouring country side by side. Apti had decided to take Putin and Kadyrov's deal, and it was an extraordinary turnaround.

He sighed. 'I can't be angry with Russia for my whole life. There were Russians who helped us also. People are sick of war, they want to live normally. They want to live here, speak Chechen, practice their religion and live without terror and fear. Kadyrov has made all of that possible.'

I had written many stories about the crimes carried out by Kadyrov's special battalions. The fact they were allowed to exist, and act with impunity, was a terrible indictment of Kadyrov's Chechnya and Putin's Russia. It was probable that Apti's service had involved performing all kinds of appalling tasks, but I found it hard to dislike him. Unlike some of his friends, he had something genuine left in his eyes; the sparks of empathy had not quite died. He might have many terrible deeds on his conscience as a consequence of his decision to take the deal on offer. But after being surrounded by blood, loss, and sorrow since his early teenage years, who was I to judge him for his choice?

VI

Ramzan mourned his late father with the zeal of a Caucasian Hamlet. Grozny's main museum was a vast shrine of marble and gold columns in memory of Kadyrov Sr. Inside, the life story of the elder Kadyrov was told in a number of photographs and life-sized oil paintings. There was a display about the heroism of the Second World War effort; about the deportation of the entire Chechen people during the very same war, there was not even a mention. The recent Chechen wars were also conspicuous by their absence, especially given the role that Kadyrov Sr had played in the first war on the side of the rebels. It was not that people in Chechnya did not know about these things. They were simply moved to one side; unspoken events pushed out of the consciousness. That, after all, was the deal.

Sometimes, even Kadyrov himself veered off script. Operation Lentil, the NKVD manoeuvre to deport the Chechens in 1944, was launched on Red Army Day, and in modern Russia, 23 February was still a public holiday, renamed as Defenders of the Fatherland Day. It was meant to be the day in which the army's heroic deeds were celebrated, not a day to moan about the injustices of the past. But in 2010, Kadyrov made a surprise announcement. Henceforth, 23 February would officially be known in Chechnya as the Day of Memory and Sorrow. 'We will not forget the terrible suffering that befell our people, and we will do everything to make sure such tragedies do not happen again,' he said. It seemed as if a new chapter had been opened, one in which it was acceptable to talk about the awful events of the past.

But commemorating the deportation was a double affront to Putin's memory politics, both sullying a day that was meant to be about military glory, and injecting an unwanted element of negativity into the war narrative. The impulse to remember did not last long. The very next year, the Day of Memory and Sorrow was moved from 23 February to 10 May, the anniversary of the burial of Kadyrov's father. In his address marking the day, Ramzan did speak about the deportation, and about the wars of the 1990s, but this time he suggested the events were the fault of the Chechens' own weaknesses. 'Our people's downfall has been that we never had leaders who were able to unite everyone, to take responsibility for the fate of the nation,' Kadyrov said. Today, when the Chechen nation was 'united like never before,' such tragedy would be unthinkable. It turned out that all the years of Russian oppression could have been avoided, if only Ramzan or his father had been on the scene previously.

In 2008, a memorial to the deportation in Grozny that had been erected in the 1990s was closed off to the public. In 2014, it was partially dismantled, and the real gravestones that had been used in its construction were removed and reused for a monument to the police who died in the bomb blast that killed Akhmad Kadyrov.[9] It was an extraordinary physical manifestation of the metaphysical memory process: shifting emphasis from the tragedy of an entire nation to the death of one man.

A few days ahead of the seventy-year anniversary of the deportation in 2014, with official commemoration absent, a small group of historians and activists organized an unofficial conference on the topic in Grozny. When Kadyrov found out, he was furious, and ordered them summoned to him for a personal dressing-down. The conference's main organizer, Ruslan Kutayev, declined to show up, saying he had nothing to answer for. He was arrested a couple of days later, beaten up by members of Kadyrov's close circle, tortured with electric shocks, and forced to sign incriminating documents. He was then accused of heroin possession and sentenced to four years in prison.[10] It had literally become a criminal offence to talk about the deportation in an unsanctioned way: the wrong kind of memories were now illegal.

VII

Interviewing Chechens, I would often find one of two scenarios. Sometimes, the walls they had built around certain events in their minds were so strong they would only speak in half-memories and platitudes about the past, no matter how carefully the questions were phrased. Other times, the opposite happened. Everything tumbled out, as at a long-overdue therapy session. Even then, it was not clear whether I was getting to the bottom of the reservoir of pain or merely skimming the surface. Sometimes, after I had been speaking to a person for a while, they would confide other, more terrible memories, with a plea not to print them. Memories of the Russian filtration camps at the end of the war, hints of sexual abuse, or of female family members taunted or humiliated. Often, I suspected another layer of things they would not confide even with a guarantee they would not appear in print, and perhaps a further layer still, of things they had successfully blocked from their own consciousness. It was a *matryoshka* nesting doll of painful memories.

At funerals and other big gatherings, Chechen men lose themselves in the *zikr*, an otherworldly Sufi ritual in which they dance, stamp, and chant. Dozens of them whirl in a circle several men thick, this way and that, like a wheel spinning back and forth. Amidst the stamping, again and again comes the rhythmic pealing of *la ilaha illa'llah*; there is no God but Allah. This goes on for ten minutes, thirty minutes, an hour, everyone in a hypnotic trance, a mass of undulating bodies soaked with perspiration. The *zikr* is an ancient ritual; maybe it always induced such peaks of religious ecstasy. But in contemporary Chechnya, where suffering has been plentiful but there is little opportunity to speak openly of grief, it feels remarkably therapeutic. The catharsis of the *zikr* is as palpable as the stench of sweat.

There was no excuse for the excesses of Kadyrov's forces or for the disgusting acts of terrorism perpetrated by the insurgency, but to deny that both the horrific past and the current denial of it played a role in the genesis of such extremism would be perverse. I was reminded of Arthur Koestler's remark on the consequences of victimhood: 'If power corrupts, the reverse is also true: persecution corrupts the victim, though perhaps in subtler and more tragic ways.'

In Russia proper, there was little recognition of the whirlwind of violence that had been unleashed in Chechnya both during the recent wars and over the past century. Chechens were seen as wild, uncivilized bandits. There was rarely an acknowledgement that Russia might have a debt to the Chechens, albeit one that could have been paid back in more nuanced ways than buying off a local warlord to pledge feudal allegiance to the Kremlin. There was no understanding that memories of the deportation had played a large part in the determination to fight for independence after the Soviet collapse, and that the brutality of those wars and the policy of forced amnesia all helped inform the current violence in the region.

For Chechens, the horror was all too recent to be forgotten properly. Of course nobody could forget the wars, nobody could forget their dead relatives, or what the Russians had done with the territory. But people knew not to talk about it, either publicly or privately, through a mixture of state coercion and their own desire to forget.

VIII

On Victory Day 2015, at the very same time as Putin was surveying the parade on Red Square, Ramzan Kadyrov rode down Grozny's central street on horseback, dressed in full military uniform with the orange-black St George's ribbon pinned to his chest. Kadyrov thanked the Chechen veterans of the Second World War, and praised the victory in similar terms to Putin in Moscow.

'The Soviet army cleansed our country and Europe from Hitler's invaders, and saved the world from fascism,' said Kadyrov, in his accented, growling Russian.

Speaking in front of a stage crafted in the shape of a swirling orange-black ribbon, Kadyrov said the younger generation had learned something from the Red Army soldiers. The patriotic spirit handed down from the veterans had allowed this new generation of Chechens to prevent Western secret services sowing discord in Chechnya more recently. It had helped preserve the territorial integrity of Russia, he said. In Kadyrov's rewritten version of history, the wars of the 1990s had not been Chechens against Russians, but the nefarious West on one side, and the Russians and Chechens on the other, infused with the spirit of the Second World War. The fact that he and his father had fought against the Russians in the first war was an inconvenient and ignored detail.

After the speeches came the spectacle. In the centre of Grozny, a mock-up of the Reichstag had been constructed. Soldiers in period Soviet uniforms rushed towards it, shooting Nazis dead as they went. Fake explosions sent plumes of smoke into the air, and the reconstruction culminated with Soviet soldiers scrambling onto the roof of the Reichstag and raising the red flag. Afterwards, a group of 'Soviet soldiers' paraded a group of 'Nazi prisoners', dressed in grey uniforms with Nazi regalia, in a procession through the streets. The soldiers tossed Swastika flags and Nazi banners at the feet of the grinning Kadyrov.

As in Moscow, there was then a parade of heavy weaponry, and a fly-over. A tennis-court-sized Soviet flag was paraded down the main street, while two helicopters flew above flying the Chechen and Russian flags. Nowhere in Kadyrov's speech, nor in his interior minister's speech, nor in a twelve-minute, pomp-filled news item on the day's celebrations broadcast on local television,[11] was there a single mention of the fact that the victory being celebrated came a year after the entire Chechen people had been rounded up and deported from their homeland. At the moment when Soviet soldiers had lifted the red flag above the Reichstag, the Chechen people were dying in their thousands of hunger and hypothermia as they adapted to their new lives in deportation.

The forced forgetting had the goal of pacifying Chechens and making them part of a new, united Russia. Perhaps, in a generation, the memories of the deportation, along with the hideous trauma of the more recent Chechen wars, would be airbrushed and forgotten. Perhaps, the next generation of Chechens would grow up strolling along Putin Avenue and Kadyrov Street and push the memories of their dead parents, dead siblings, their sorrow and humiliation, so far into their subconscious that eventually they would disappear. Perhaps, Putin and Kadyrov's deal would work.

With each passing year, however, it seemed that demanding a people excise the memories of such recent tragedies would eventually prove counterproductive, especially when a man as despotic as Kadyrov was in charge of the show. One night in Grozny, I was given a lift back to my hotel by a fighter in one of Kadyrov's battalions. We slowly got chatting, and his initial patriotism for Russia gradually peeled away. I asked if he thought the current peace in Chechnya would last, or whether one day the Chechens would again end up fighting the Russians.

'We need peace, we need time to breathe. We know what war is, and we are grateful for peace. But of course this is temporary. If you know anything about the history of the Chechens, if you read a single book about the history of Russia and the Caucasus, you will realize that this is not the end. This is far from the end.'

The deal, in other words, was temporary.

4

Kolyma: the end of the earth

I

The deal offered to the Chechens was in some ways simply a more extreme version of the one offered to Russia as a whole. Putin wanted Russians not so much to forget the past, but to view it in a particular way, and the government's attempts to curate historical memory found favour in a population tired of bad news and economic hardships. The impulse to take pride in the Second World War victory as a black-and-white triumph of good over evil was understandable. But it meant not only skipping over the darker pages of the war effort, but also whitewashing the nature of the Soviet regime at the time. To celebrate the war victory was to celebrate the continuation of this system. This was often not explicit: Putin calibrated his rare words about Stalin very carefully, and the more liberal Dmitry Medvedev, during his four years as figurehead president, condemned Stalin directly on occasion. But even if Stalin was not officially revered, for the war narrative to make sense he could not be reviled either. The goal was to neutralize the Stalin era, not to lionize it, but it often had the latter effect by default. The artificial famines, the ruthless terror of the late 1930s, and the sprawling system of Gulag labour camps, which continued until Stalin's death, had destroyed the lives of millions, touching almost every family in the Soviet Union. But across Russia, I met many people who either denied Stalin's crimes entirely or declared them to be a necessary evil, justified by the extenuating circumstances of the era and the great victory over the Nazis.

I made the long journey to Kolyma, to try to understand how this wilful amnesia was possible. There had been camps all across the Soviet Union, but Kolyma was the most notorious outpost of the Gulag system. For the first two decades of its existence, the whole region was simply one big prison colony. A thousand miles north of Japan, tucked into the armpit between the far east of Russia's mainland and the Kamchatka peninsula, Kolyma is famously isolated. Peering from the window as my plane approached the capital, Magadan, it was hard not to feel a sense of helplessness against the desolate landscape visible below. Even when travelling on the Trans-Siberian railway, the never-ending ticker tape of Motherland passing by the window revealed factories, villages, and small stations at regular intervals. Here, far north of any railway, there was nothing at all; the brownish land was uninhabited, uncultivated, and untamed for hundreds of miles. Low, brooding clouds hung ominously in the sky, and hills stretched to the horizon, undulating like leathery wrinkles on an elderly face. Tickets for the nine-hour flight from Moscow cost more than flying to New York, and plane was the only way in, save for several days' perilous driving along the Kolyma Highway, nicknamed the Road of Bones due to the deaths of so many of the Gulag prisoners who built it. In Magadan, they call the rest of Russia 'the mainland'. Kolyma is not an island, but it may as well be.

In 1926, there were just fifteen thousand people living in Kolyma, almost entirely indigenous nomads and Cossacks. But geological surveys in the late 1920s showed that the desolate region was uniquely rich in gold and other precious metals, and Stalin set up the Far North Construction Trust, Dalstroi, to organize Kolyma's cultivation. In reality, Dalstroi was a slave enterprise, bringing prisoners to the region to extract natural resources for the Soviet state in miserable conditions. By 1941, the population had risen to 270,000, and the arrivals were almost entirely prisoners and their guards, brought in on ships plying the rough, ten-day voyage from Vladivostok.

After Stalin's death, the camp system slowly wound down. The region was repopulated with workers from across the country, in search of well-paid work at the empire's extremities. Then when the Soviet Union collapsed, so too did the system of subsidies that had kept the isolated region alive. Most of those who had somewhere to go fled; those who stayed lived in extreme poverty. During the Putin years, Magadan had a minor renaissance, with promising oil finds offshore. But overall, it remained a depressing place.

At Magadan's hangar-like airport, the walls were livened up by fantastical mosaics depicting happy workers toiling, native peoples herding reindeer, and butch pilots taking charge of their aircraft. In the arrivals hall, a huge map of the Soviet Union, cast in metal, was attached to the wall. The map, like most things in the airport, was clearly of a vintage that predated the empire's collapse, and showed the major airports of the Soviet Union, with an embossed pictorial accompaniment for each: from the spires of Tallinn and Lviv in the west to the minarets of Samarkand in the south and the volcanoes of Kamchatka in the very far east. It was hard not to feel awed by the size and diversity of the long-vanished country.

I took a stroll around the city with Sergei Raizman, a mild-mannered local historian who ran Magadan's branch of Memorial, a small, beleaguered organization devoted to keeping memory of the Stalin-era repressions alive. It was early September, and a damp, icy wind coming off the sea zipped through Magadan's avenues, heralding the approaching long winter. Raizman was unfazed by the weather, but downbeat about the political climate. 'The increasing patriotic atmosphere has made it even harder to talk about these things,' he said with a sigh. 'People ask you why you need to keep bringing up such things; people are ashamed if they have a family history with the Gulag. It's normal if your grandfather fought at the front, or if your grandfather was a hero of labour. It's not normal if he was in the camps.'

We walked past what was formerly the local headquarters of the NKVD, an imposing building with neo-classical columns, built in the grand post-war Stalinist style. This had been the secret police administration for the most notorious Gulag region in the whole Soviet Union. And yet not only was there no plaque outside nor any kind of information as to its former function, but the building was adorned with official flags. It was now the headquarters of the regional governor, Putin's representative in the region. Like the Lubyanka in Moscow, the ongoing use of the building suggested continuity of power rather than a break. A block away, Raizman showed me the former NKVD prison, now the local parliament. Again, there was nothing to mark the past function.

In front of another administrative building, there was a bust in honour of Edvard Berzin, the first boss of Dalstroi. Like so many of those in charge of implementing the early stages of Stalin's repressions, Berzin himself was arrested in 1937. He was called back from Magadan to Moscow for consultations, pulled off the train just before reaching the capital, and charged with 'counterrevolutionary sabotage-wrecking activities'. He was shot in August 1938. Mainly due to the extreme bloodiness of those who followed him, Berzin has been reinvented as a kind of benevolent figure who had the best interests of the prisoners at heart. While it is true that the monstrous cruelty that would mark the next decade was absent, Berzin nevertheless presided over the cultivation of an entire region by the slave labour of people who for the most part had been falsely convicted. Of the sixteen thousand prisoners sent to Kolyma in Berzin's first year in charge, fewer than ten thousand arrived alive.[1] He may not have been a monstrous sadist, but building a monument to him seemed like celebrating the executioner while ignoring the victims.

The only monument in Magadan to deal with the overwhelming trauma of the Gulag was outside the city, a large Easter Island head called the Mask of Sorrow, designed by the émigré sculptor Ernst Neizvestny and opened in 1996, in the Yeltsin-era atmosphere of historical enquiry. Since then, nothing else had been built.

II

There were few Gulag survivors still alive in Magadan, and even fewer who were willing to talk about their time in the camps. But I tracked down Olga Gureyeva, who reluctantly agreed to tell me her story. I met Olga at her small apartment, two neatly arranged rooms inside a Khrushchev-era block that had been badly battered by the climate. A tiny, stooped figure wearing a floral blouse and with a bob of thick black hair, her dark eyes were glazed with a milky film. She peered closely at me as she let me in, and I realized she was almost blind. She shuffled slowly but with purpose, ushering me into the living room, and pulled two chairs close to each other so she could just about see me while recounting her story.

Olga was born in 1928 in Roshniv, an ethnic Ukrainian village in an area under Polish control, near the regional capital of Stanislawow.[2]

The urban population was largely made up of Poles and Jews, while the villages were predominantly Ukrainian. As a child, Olga learned Polish at school, and spoke Ukrainian at home. She remembered the Greek Catholic religion of the western Ukrainians playing an important role in her upbringing. Western Ukraine had been part of the Austro-Hungarian Empire, but in the convulsions after the First World War it became part of Poland. The region was occupied by the Soviets in 1939, taken by the Nazis in 1941, and recovered by the Soviets again in 1944, after which it was incorporated into the Ukrainian SSR. Most of the region's Jews were massacred by the Nazis, and those Poles remaining who had not been killed by Ukrainian nationalists or Nazis were deported to Poland after the war by the new Soviet authorities. To complete the task, the new authorities swept the area for Ukrainian nationalist fighters and potential anti-Soviet elements. Had the Ukrainians not been such an enormous nation, Stalin might have deported the lot of them, like the Kalmyks or the Chechens.

In December 1945, the Red Army entered Olga's village, looking for Ukrainian nationalist fighters. She remembered a 'real terror', with soldiers looting the village for clothes, money, and livestock, and going from house to house demanding to know where Ukrainian insurgents were hiding. She had just turned seventeen, but was suspected of collaboration with the Nazis and membership in the Ukrainian nationalist organization, the OUN. After a day of questioning, she and her even younger brother were taken away to the regional capital, suspected of aiding the partisans. She was not allowed to take so much as a hairbrush or a toothbrush with her, and it would be decades before she returned to her home village. She would never see her brother again, and does not know what happened to him.

In the holding prison, the inmates had to sleep on hard stone floors; the cell was so crowded that if one person needed to turn over, the whole row had to turn, 'like a tin of herrings'. Each night, there were interrogations, accompanied by ruthless beatings. She denied everything, and the beatings intensified. 'I was half-dead and black with bruises, like a piece of meat, by the end of it. After four months I didn't have any strength left so I signed everything they put in front of me.'

She was convicted of collaboration, betraying the motherland and being part of the OUN, by a troika of judges in a trial that lasted a matter of minutes. The sentence: twenty years of *katorga*, exile to the labour camps. The Soviets mopped up hundreds of thousands of people in newly conquered territories during and after the war, dispatching them to the camps. Often, they were blanket arrests of those social groups thought likely to pose a threat to the Sovietization of territories: people were arrested for potential crimes rather than actual ones. But *katorga*, a tsarist-era term meaning penal servitude, was reintroduced at the end of the war for genuine war criminals, rather than just people who might turn out to be hostile to the Soviet regime. Those sentenced to *katorga* were meant to be 'especially dangerous enemies' who had no chance of being reformed. They had a particularly hard time in the camps, with an extra-strict regimen and separation from 'normal' prisoners. About sixty thousand people, many of them from central European liberation movements, had been sentenced to *katorga* by 1947.[3] Some of them had certainly been involved in war crimes, or collaborated with the Nazis. Among the Ukrainians there were undoubtedly those who had taken part in the massacre of Poles and Jews, or those who had enthusiastically joined the Nazis. Equally undoubtedly, many thousands were arrested who had committed no crimes at all.

Olga said the charges in her case were nonsense: her father, a farmer, had tried to keep a low profile during the war years, and she herself recalled the Nazi occupation as a gruesome time. 'I remember the terror the Germans caused in our village; they were animals. They hanged several people from lamp posts and put signs next to them saying, "If you touch them, you'll share their fate". What kind of collaboration could there have been with people like that?'

As for betraying the Soviet Union, it was a country her village had only been part of for two years, between 1939 and 1941. The territory had been Austrian, then Polish, then Soviet, then Nazi, then Soviet again. She had been born to Ukrainian parents in a Ukrainian-speaking village, and it was unsurprising that this would be her first allegiance. It was hard to fathom how you could betray a homeland that had only just been forced upon you. In any case, when the Nazis occupied the region, she had been twelve years old. Even if she had sympathized with the goals of the Ukrainian nationalists, it seemed highly unlikely she could have been a dangerous criminal.

Freshly sentenced to twenty years of *katorga*, she was loaded onto a filthy cattle wagon with dozens of other prisoners and dispatched on the journey to Siberia. The long, snaking railway routes of the Soviet Union were again put to use to transport cargos of prisoners. At the station in Lviv, she spotted a bedraggled woman from her village trying to pass a parcel to her arrested husband, who yelled out to inform Olga that her parents had also been sentenced and had already been sent to Siberia. It was the last thing she would hear about them for more than a decade.

The train of prisoners travelled at night, and sat in sidings by day. Each day they were given stale bread, some dried fish, and a cup of dirty water for drinking and washing. Most of the women got ill during the long journey: more than a month of sleeping, eating, and washing in the train. Only once, in Novosibirsk, were they let out for a proper wash in a banya, the Russian sauna. Olga passed out, and was scooped from the floor by the guards and put back on the train. It took them forty days to get to Irkutsk, about two-thirds of the way across Russia. There, they were unloaded and were marched, on foot, around ninety miles to a labour camp. The journey took nearly a week. The women slept overnight in barns or barracks by the side of the road, where bugs and insects feasted on their tired flesh. At one of the stops, a convoy of male prisoners arrived as night fell and made to settle in the same building as Olga's convoy. The women began to protest, but the men told them not to worry; they were hardly in any state to make advances.

'They were half-corpses, grey people, shadows of human beings. Without seeing it you wouldn't believe humans could look like this. It was a devastating sight. Of course, we didn't look much better either.'

The convoy trekked on, accompanied at its edges by guards and dogs.

'We supported each other, people would fall at times, and we would pull them back up. Sometimes people died in front of our eyes. A medic was with us, and would feel the pulses. If they had died, there were carts at the back for corpses.'

Olga was moved between various Siberian camps several times. Her recollection of those months was a litany of appalling stories: scrubbing the blood from the barrack floors after an execution, scrabbling to pick potatoes in the hard frozen earth, applying tar to any square of exposed flesh in a vain attempt to keep the horrendous clouds of hungry midges from feasting on them.

'I was so ill, I looked more haggard than I look now. They weighed me at one of the camps, I was thirty-eight kilograms [six stone; eighty-four pounds]. I remember my ribs sticking out. People got typhus, dysentery, TB. We were completely isolated from the world. In the evenings we prayed and sang. Some people cried.'

In autumn 1948, Olga was again put on a freight train and sent to Vanino, a Pacific port close to Vladivostok. On 25 October, she was loaded with thousands of other prisoners onto the *Nogin*, one of the boats that plied the long route to Magadan. The autumn seas were already rough, and the prisoners were stashed in the hold where it was cold, dark, and dirty. Water flooded the hold, sloshing their knees with icy seawater, which before long became infused with vomit as almost everyone grew seasick. Many people got seriously ill, and a number died. The boat arrived in Magadan's Nagayev Bay on 7 November, but because it was the anniversary of the revolution, they were kept waiting for two more days so as not to spoil the celebrations with the arrival of prisoners.

'Everyone was half alive, it was freezing, there was wind and snow. There were so many people that it took several days to remove and process everyone. It was one of the most humiliating moments; they stripped us naked, and men in uniforms walked up and down and decided whether we were fit for work.'

Olga was dispatched to work at a tin mine at Vakkhanka, in the Kolyma interior. The work was loud, dusty, and painful. She was given a number that was sewn onto the back of her prison overalls, and by which she was referred to at all times. She was no longer Olga Gureyeva; she was now M-323. On one occasion, she complained about the food and was given three days of solitary confinement, standing upright in a damp and cold cell, which made her so ill she ended up spending months in the camp hospital. There were no newspapers, and the women were forbidden from writing letters. They had no pens or paper, anyway. The days were monotonous and endless.

'They woke you up at six. You would march in a line to the canteen. Then to work, then at sunset back. The barracks were searched frequently, which would mean you'd have to stand outside in the cold while they did it. I only had one pair of trousers; I wore them to work and to sleep. In the winter you could never get properly warm, never.'

The cold, unsurprisingly, is a recurring feature of Gulag memory. It was the kind of cold that 'crushed the muscles and squeezed a man's temples', wrote Varlam Shalamov, the best-known literary chronicler of life in Kolyma. At Olga's camp, the working day was cancelled if the temperature went below minus fifty-three degrees Celsius. This was rare, but there were a good four months when the temperature was below minus thirty most days. Outdoor work was miserable in these conditions, and often deadly. 'I remember my best friend collapsing and dying while chopping wood. She lifted up the axe, it stayed in the air for a minute and then she fell, dead.'

After Stalin died in 1953, the camps slowly became more humane, and by 1956, when Khrushchev gave his 'secret speech' denouncing the crimes of Stalinism, the mass incarceration gradually ended. The camp system would go on functioning in some form until the end of the Soviet Union, but it shrank to a tiny fraction of the size at its Stalinist peak. Olga remembered the sudden appearance of unimaginable luxuries in the months after Stalin died: the bread was fresh rather than rock-hard, the prisoners were paid small salaries, and a shop appeared at the camp where jam and sugar could be purchased. They were allowed to write letters, and she wrote home to western Ukraine to enquire about her parents. She waited months for the letter to cross all of Russia and Ukraine, and the reply to return. Her parents were in a camp in the Urals, came the reply from distant relatives. It was bad news but hardly the worst news possible. For a decade, she had feared they must be dead.

In 1955, she was transferred to a brick factory in the city of Magadan itself, which after years in the wilds of Kolyma seemed like a luxury assignment. Then, in March 1956, she was officially freed, though she was forbidden from leaving the confines of Magadan region. The official who processed her release gave her a word of advice: never speak about what happened to you. Not to anyone.

During her decade in the camps, through all the hardship and humiliation, the bone-crunching journeys, the never-ending work, and the debilitating illness, she had never once cried. Now, she walked out into the Magadan street holding her release documents in her hands and burst into tears. She was twenty-seven years old; it was the first time she had been a free woman since her arrest as a teenager.

A passing man with a kindly face asked her why she was crying. 'I was just freed, and I don't know what to do,' she said. 'If you were freed, why are you crying? Let's go for a walk, I'll cheer you up.'

Vladimir had been a cinema engineer in Kolomna, a small town near Moscow. He told her he too had just been released from the camps. He had been accused of being part of a counterrevolutionary group that secretly organized screenings of forbidden films. The charges were nonsense, but enough to get him sentenced to fifteen years in Kolyma. The pair bonded over their experiences and before long they married. They moved into a tiny room in a communal apartment, and Olga trained to be a nurse in the evenings while doing nannying work in the day. She got a job as an ambulance nurse, and for the next thirty years worked shifts picking up the injured, the ill, and the deceased from across Magadan. The couple did not particularly want to stay in the city, but had nowhere else to go. All the while, Olga remembered the words of the man who had signed her release papers: never speak about what happened to you. After she and Vladimir had shared some of their camp stories with each other, the pair decided to keep their memories private, and when Olga gave birth to a son a few years later, whom they also named Vladimir, they did not tell him that both of them were former prisoners. Throughout his youth, neither parent said a word to their son about their secret. They even stopped mentioning it to each other, pushing the years of pain deep into the back of their minds. Sometimes it seemed like they had truly forgotten. But then, in the late 1970s, the younger Vladimir was doing his military service in the Soviet armed forces and was due to be sent to serve at a base in East Germany. On the eve of the departure, his commanding officer told him he would not be travelling with the other soldiers: due to his parents' background as enemies of the people, he was not considered suitable to be sent abroad.

'He came home, and he was in tears, it was awful, there was such drama,' Olga recalled. 'We told him some of the stories then. He was so upset. I tried to explain to him that it was such a traumatic experience that neither of us wanted to talk about it. It was really hard to explain to him, and to convince him that neither of us had actually been guilty of anything.'

Olga's case was hardly unusual. Many camp survivors never spoke about their experiences, even to family members. The poet and singer Bulat Okudzhava wrote an immensely moving short story, many decades later, of how he met his mother in Tbilisi in 1947 on her return from a decade in a camp on the Kazakh steppe. He cleaned the house and planned a surprise trip to the cinema; he trembled with excitement at the catching up they would have to do after a decade apart. But when she arrived she was distant, and strange. She did not respond to questions, and seemed to be inhabiting a different world.

'I looked into her eyes. They were dry and absent. She was looking at me but did not see me. Her face was lifeless and stony, her lips slightly open, her strong, suntanned arms lying feebly on her knees.'

There are numerous cases of camp returnees never uttering a single word about their time in the camps in the years after their return. People whose parents had been shot in the purges, or expired in the camps, often told future generations that their parents had died in the war, to hide the shame. Even after telling her son about the ordeal, Olga did not speak to neighbours, friends, or colleagues about her time in the camps.

Therein lies at least part of the reason why Russians have so successfully buried the knowledge about the Gulag; how people can be so blasé about a tragedy that devastated their own ancestors, and hit if not every family in the Soviet Union, then certainly a large percentage of them. Public acknowledgement of the camps was forbidden in the Soviet period, save for the occasional flurry of discussion or literature that was quickly quieted down. Most former prisoners adhered to the omertà, and by the time *perestroika* came, the majority of those who had been incarcerated were either dead or psychologically unable to begin remembering their buried trauma after so many years of silence.

Nevertheless, there was a moment when it seemed some kind of reckoning might be possible. From the start of *perestroika* there was an interest in the theme of the repressions. Gorbachev declared open season on historical enquiry; there would be no more obligatory 'rose-tinted spectacles' when looking at the past, he promised. On the seventieth anniversary of the revolution, in 1987, he spoke of the 'immense and unforgivable' guilt of Stalin and those close to him for the repressions.

'Even now, we still encounter attempts to ignore sensitive questions of our history, to hush them up, to pretend that nothing special happened. We cannot agree with this. It would be a neglect of historical truth, disrespect for the memory of those who found themselves innocent victims of lawlessness and arbitrariness.'[4]

The wave of interest in the repressions came in conjuction with the new inquisitiveness about the darker sides of the war, as people demanded answers about what had happened to their parents or grandparents back in the 1930s and 1940s. A group of activists and historians formed Memorial, and appealed to people for stories and information about family members who had suffered. Between 1989 and 1991, a number of newspapers carried daily items about victims, often accompanied by photographs or documents related to the case.[5] Television documentaries about the purges and other dark aspects of the past abounded.

In the 1990s, Olga began attending a church group, where a visiting American priest persuaded her and other survivors that through remembrance could come catharsis, and she began to share her experiences at weekly meetings of survivors. It was the first time she had spoken about her ordeal since the showdown with her son. In 1993, she was officially rehabilitated, a process tens of thousands of those who were unfairly convicted in the 1930s and 1940s went through in the immediate years after the collapse of the Soviet Union. In 1996, the Mask of Sorrow opened on the outskirts of Magadan. But already the tide was turning. Magadan residents grumbled about the monument: life was already hard enough; was there really a need to air the dirty laundry of the past?

Olga saw the 1990s as a chance to give her life an unexpected and happy coda. Her husband Vladimir had died of lung cancer; his health had never been right since he left the camps. She made contact with distant Ukrainian relatives who had emigrated to the United States after the war, and they invited her to come and live with them in Chicago. She made the long journey, but found life in America hard. Her Ukrainian was rusty after so many decades in Russia, and she spoke no English. Her relatives seemed to her to be materialistic and showy. Probably, horrified by the tales of her life over the past decades, they wanted her to rest and relax, but she found it suffocating and patronizing. The whole experience of living in America was disorienting, and she missed her son, so a year later she moved back to Magadan.

In 1998, she made another attempt, travelling all the way back to Roshniv in western Ukraine, where she had grown up. The family house was still there, and she decided there was a pleasing harmony to the idea of finishing her life in the same place it had started, the same house where her childhood abruptly came to an end when the Red Army seized her. Again, the dream turned sour. Ukraine in 1998 was in financial turmoil, like most of the former Soviet lands. The region was rural and poor, and nobody had time to help a lonely old woman with a deeply traumatic past. She decided that being close to her son was her main priority, and resolved she would move back to Magadan and see out her days in the city that had caused her so much misery. And so she returned yet again to the small apartment at the end of the world.

But her final ordeal was still to come. Shortly after she returned, her son died. Of all the horrors she had recounted, it was clear that talking about this one was the hardest for her. 'That is my one real tragedy,' she said, almost farcically given the appalling nature of the tales that had preceded it. Her tiny, fragile frame shook with gentle tremors at the mention of her son, and I decided I could not torture her further by asking how he had died. His portraits were everywhere in the apartment, a face of handsome innocence topped with a dark, bushy mop of hair. He had, at least, left her a grandson, who by this point was a healthy nineteen-year-old young man, she said, brightening up. The grandson was currently serving his time in the Russian Army. It was a supremely dark twist of fate, I thought, that there was a possibility her grandson would be dispatched to fight in the Kremlin's secret war in Ukraine, the country his grandmother had been deported from seventy years previously.

I got up to leave many hours after arriving, reeling with emotion from our conversation. She padded slowly towards the door to let me out. 'It probably sounds to you like I'm calmly telling these things to you, like it's easy for me to talk about this. But inside it destroys me to remember, these are things that should be forgotten. Every time I talk about it, I have pains, headaches, trauma for days and weeks. I wake up in the night, upset, again and again. I don't know why God chose such a life for me.'

III

I felt guilty for making Olga relive her experiences once again, but also angry on her behalf. It was clear that the majority of Gulag survivors had spoken little about their ordeal, but there were some like her who had found the strength to do so. And yet the official narrative, which seemed to be willingly accepted by most Russians, glossed over the period and played down its horrors.

I wandered down to Nagayev Bay, the natural harbour where Olga's ship had arrived in 1948. This was where every prisoner ship to arrive in Kolyma had docked for years on end. Hundreds of thousands of convicts had arrived at the bay, and tens of thousands had died on the journey. But all I found there was a cafe, some benches, a monument to a popular Soviet singer, and a plaque that read: 'This is where the construction of Magadan began in 1929'—the merest hint at the bay's past.

At the city's main museum, there had been an overhaul of the dreary Soviet exhibits and I found all the displays shiny, new, and well presented. The Gulag was not ignored, but it was consigned to just one room, while the war victory got four rooms. Oil paintings in the Gulag exhibit depicted happy workers toiling in bucolic rural scenes. The display also included a wooden watchtower and barbed wire, but the overall tone was not one of horror; there was none of the bleak despair that could be sensed from the briefest of conversations with survivors like Olga. One exhibit listed the number of 'passengers' who had arrived in Magadan on ships during each year of the 1930s, an odd way to refer to prisoners locked into the dark fetid hold of a slave ship, ridden with lice and disease.

The war exhibit was as bombastic as usual, with all the glory and none of the horror. A chronology of the war mentioned only that 'the Second World War started on 1 September 1939 when Germany invaded Poland,' mentioning nothing about the Molotov-Ribbentrop pact, nor the Soviet move into the rest of Poland and western Ukraine. Everywhere, there were photographs of happy, smiling men in uniform. The war, in this telling, was all about heroic feats, with no sign of any suffering. The final display announced that 'as a result of victory, the Soviet Union became a world superpower and the Soviet Army was recognized as the strongest in the world'.

This view of history was reinforced when I met with a local history teacher to find out how Magadan's horrific past is taught in its schools. Larisa, a stern forty-year-old who was deeply suspicious of me and my questions, told me there was just one lesson on the school curriculum about the purges and the Gulag. She taught it by dividing the blackboard into two halves. On one side, she would write the 'military and industrial achievements' of the Stalin era; on the other, the 'unfortunate side effects'. Pupils could then make up their own minds. Surely, I protested, anyone who had done the smallest amount of research into the history of the camps could not fail to apprehend their horror, and would be unable to dismiss them as mere 'side effects'?

Larisa shrugged, and gave me a withering look.

'Was there a military threat from Germany? There was. Were there spies in the country? There were. There was no time to decide who was guilty and who wasn't. We should remember the innocent victims but I think it was all necessary.'

Little matter that the purges and the Gulag swallowed the lives of some of the country's brightest talent, holding it back rather than advancing it as the war approached, and that the numbers of those incarcerated in the camps actually peaked after the war was over. The whole system was justified by the war effort, she believed. You can't make an omelette without breaking eggs, was Larisa's basic take on Stalinism.[6] No matter that making this particular omelette had involved not only breaking a few eggs, but also requisitioning the chickens, destroying the kitchen, then executing the chef and half the diners.

IV

Olga's arrest and transfer to Kolyma had been tied to the aftermath of the war, and people like Larisa would perhaps claim that the Soviet authorities, sweeping into hostile territory in the wake of the Nazi defeat, had no choice but to act harshly. But the terror that preceded the war had affected hundreds of thousands of loyal Soviet citizens. While labour camps and political trials characterized most of the Soviet period, the peak of the violence came in 1937–1938, a period known as the Great Terror. The self-inflicted tragedy of the terror, perpetrated by a regime drawn into a vortex of paranoid bloodletting, came just four years before the start of the tragedy imposed from outside by the Nazis.

The terror affected most of the top strata of the political and social elite: old Bolsheviks, party commissars, factory managers, and army generals were all subjected to ruthless purges, as were musicians, artists, and sports stars. In one shooting range on the outskirts of Moscow, Butovo, more than twenty thousand people were executed between August 1937 and October 1938.[7] While there is no reliable figure for executions across the Soviet Union during the brief period, a conservative estimate is around 680,000.[8] The total number of violent or 'manmade' deaths during the whole of the 1930s numbers many millions: those who were shot, who died in the camps, who died on the journey, or who were killed in the unnecessary, manmade famines.

The system's bureaucratic machine went to great lengths to extract confessions from those who were shot in the purges; the appearance of due process remained important. Because of this, the crimes were meticulously documented, but in Putin's Russia, case files on those who had been shot in the terror were difficult to access. Usually, only relatives could see them, and then only with difficulty. Even though most of them should long have been declassified, the intelligence services used various excuses to ban access, including the argument that declassifying the files could give away the operational secrets of intelligence work. It was a sinister line of argument, with the unfortunate implication that the modern-day FSB did not just work out of the same building as the NKVD, but also used the same methods.

In Ukraine, the archives were open, providing an opportunity to get inside the world of the Soviet terror. One summer's afternoon in Kiev, I went to the old KGB archive and requested to see some files from 1937. I told the archivists to pick anything from the year that took their fancy, and was presented with a stack of thick cardboard folders. I chose one of the fatter files at random, and began reading about the case of Petr Nechiporenko, who had been a professor at Kiev State University and the Deputy Director of the Kiev Astronomical Observatory. There were 330 pages in the file, arranged in chronological order, and I soon found myself absorbed in Nechiporenko's world.

Born in 1892, Nechiporenko was by all accounts a zealous Bolshevik. He had volunteered for a pro-Soviet Ukrainian battalion in 1918 and fought in the Civil War, then studied at Dnipropetrovsk Mining Institute and became a decorated academic, winning posts at the university and the observatory.

They came to arrest him on 9 May 1937—a certain Comrade Miller searched his house and seized multiple items, all of which were carefully accounted for in the file, right down to the sets of cufflinks taken. According to the document ordering his arrest, Nechiporenko was accused of being 'an active participant in a fascist terrorist organization that pursued the goal of overthrowing Soviet rule and implementing a fascist dictatorship in the USSR.' He had been implicated by fellow academics who were already under arrest. The file contained the full transcripts of several interrogations, all meticulously typed up.

It was true that many in the Soviet Union were uncertain in private about the new order, just two decades since the revolution. But Stalin's regime saw plots, saboteurs, and foreign spies everywhere, an obsessiveness that nevertheless left Stalin blindsided when there was an actual fascist attack in 1941. Nechiporenko explained the operations of the almost certainly fictional grouping during an interrogation on 15 May: 'Since 1933 a counterrevolutionary fascist organisation has existed and functioned on the territory of Ukraine as an arm of the analogous organization that exists in a number of cities in the Russian SSR with its headquarters in the city of Leningrad.'

Each time he sat down with his captors, Nechiporenko admitted to ever more outlandish things. The language was stilted, presumably because the text had been written for him to sign. I imagined him being beaten and tortured as it was demanded that he sign more confessions. 'The organization of which I was part had the task of actively fighting the Soviet authorities, with the goal of the overthrow of the current system and the implementation in the USSR and in Ukraine in particular of a fascist dictatorship,' he said a few days later. 'In order to achieve the organization's goal, we hoped for the support of fascist Germany and expected its armed intervention to help us.'

Nechiporenko subsequently 'admitted' that while waiting for this Nazi intervention, the group's members had carried out various acts of sabotage, with the goal of ruining Soviet industrial production and trying to bring the economy to its knees.

Suddenly, I came across something that shook me: a page in which Nechiporenko implicated fourteen others in the leadership of the organization, presumably under intense pressure and probably physical violence. Did the fact he was naming co-conspirators, even under torture, undermine his status as a victim? Then, another document revealed that at least three of the fourteen had implicated Nechiporenko first. The events threw up agonizing questions. Did he know that these people had already informed on him? Were the people he implicated friends, or enemies? What would I have done? How much torture would I have been able to take before I falsely implicated others in the hope it would stop?

I leafed my way further through the thick file, and the tale wound its way towards an inevitable conclusion. Nechiporenko was given the indictment against him to review on 1 September, the day before his trial. His signature, in wobbly pencil, was there in the file to say he had received it.

The next day, a troika heard his case, in secret, and with no defence permitted. According to the file, Nechiporenko confirmed his testimony, but in his brief statement insisted that although he had been a member of the fascist conspiracy he had not known about any terror acts. He begged the court to spare his life.

The hearing began at 4.15pm, and by 4.30pm the troika had already given its verdict. Nechiporenko was sentenced to death. A small slip of paper recorded that the very next day, the sentence was carried out. The document contained formulaic printed sentences with spaces to fill in the specific details of the execution. A certain Lieutenant Shevelev had scrawled Nechiporenko's name, the date, and the city in which the execution took place on the slip in purple pen. Hundreds of thousands of similar slips of paper were filled out across the Soviet Union in 1937 and 1938.

The file did not end with his death, however. The final document was a handwritten letter from Nechiporenko's wife, dated 1957, two decades after he was shot. Presumably, she had been emboldened by the atmosphere of Khrushchev's thaw, when it became just about acceptable to talk about the excesses of Stalinism, though the focus was still on crimes against the Party rather than crimes against the country and its citizens.

Her husband had been taken from their home in Kiev in May 1937, she wrote, and she had no inkling of his fate ever since. She begged to be informed about what had happened to him. She presumably feared the worst, but it must have been hard not to know for sure, harbouring a faint hope that perhaps her husband was not dead but languishing in a prison somewhere.

She herself had been arrested in October 1937, she wrote, and deported to Siberia without so much as a trial, merely on the basis of her marriage. She spent eight years in the Gulag and was then released, but forbidden to return to Ukraine. The couple's apartment and personal items in Kiev had all been confiscated. The letter had been mailed from a small town in Siberia, where she now resided.

After all I had read, her ignorance two decades after the events seemed an unbearable dramatic irony. In just two hours sitting with the documents, I had been given a window into the room where Nechiporenko had been interrogated, the charges against him, the brief and awful trial, and his execution, whereas for twenty years his wife had not heard a peep about his fate. Neither was there any sign that she ever received a reply to her letter, which had been carefully filed along with her dead husband's case. It was quite possible she had lived for decades longer and never discovered the fate that befell her husband. I marvelled at the malevolent organizational power of the system, which had been quite able to file a handwritten letter sent by his wife all those years later into the same cardboard folder as the hundreds of pages of interrogations about him, just one of thousands from Kiev in the year of 1937, but had apparently been unable to send a response to a grieving woman to tell her that her husband had been shot years previously.

Having read to the end of the file, I turned back to the beginning and started again. The yellowed sheets in front of me radiated intense emotional power. The squiggly Cyrillic accusations, the legalistic justifications for the insanity—here it all was, staring out at me from the page. There were moments when I found myself physically shaking. I kept going back to look at Nechiporenko's penciled signature, the last mark of a man who knew he was about to be killed for something he had not done. I had studied the terror at university and been fascinated with the period for years. But this was the first time I had come face-to-face with an original document, and it was more shocking than I had expected.

Even when the files were available, many Russians had no interest in delving into their family histories. In Magadan, Sergei Raizman of Memorial told me about a teenage girl who attended his classes for young history buffs, and wanted to find out more about her granddad, who had been in the camps. The girl did not even know on what charge her grandfather had been sent there, and was eager to find out more. But in order to get access to the files, all close family members had to sign a document saying they agreed. The girl's parents refused to sign. Why dig up old family history, open old wounds, they said. Better to forget the past than reawaken long-sleeping demons.

But it was really important, I thought, that people were able to read these documents. Written about second hand, those shot in the purges were much easier to dismiss as human collateral; as the 'unfortunate side effects' of Stalin's industrialization, as Larisa's history lessons put it. What better material for a school history lesson than to sit with copies of this kind of file and go over the moral dilemmas they threw up?

'The fear rises in my throat,' wrote one terrified Muscovite in her diary back in 1937, 'when I hear how calmly people say it: he was shot, someone else was shot, shot, shot. I think that the real meaning of the word does not reach our consciousness.'[9]

If she felt that at the time, eighty years later in Russia it was even more the case. People made glib justifications about how it had been a cruel time in which painful measures were necessary, without thinking through what it really meant. Spending time with the case files was a helpful reminder of the real pain behind the dry facts. Behind every death sentence, there was a story of human misery, of beatings and interrogations and families torn apart.

v

I heard about a man, Ivan Panikarov, who had spent years collecting Gulag paraphernalia and creating a museum of the Gulag in his own flat, in the town of Yagodnoye, deep in the heart of Kolyma. Yagodnoye was an eight-hour drive from Magadan along the infamous Road of Bones, but I was determined to see the museum. Maybe Panikarov would have some answers as to why so few people were interested in preserving memories of the horrors of Stalin's system.

I hired Oleg, a jovial fifty-one-year-old who had lived his whole life in Magadan, to drive me there. His parents had moved to the city in the early 1960s, after the Gulag system had been disbanded and Khrushchev's Soviet Union was looking for risk-taking workers to help 'conquer' its northern and eastern extremities. Oleg had worked for twenty years at the thermoelectric station that provided power to Magadan, and was able to retire at age forty-five due to the toughness of the job. The pension he received was so miserly that he had taken to driving people along the Kolyma Highway for extra income. He didn't mind: he enjoyed the emptiness and the huge distances. He loved getting out into the vast, bleak nothingness of Kolyma and seemed to revel in nature's power and danger; he rattled off story after story culminating in tragic death as we drove deeper into the wilderness. Here a jeep had attempted to ford a river and been swept away by the current, neither the vehicle nor the family inside ever to be found; there a woman went strawberry picking and was savaged to death by a bear; close to this village a friend's car had broken down in winter, and he was found only a day later by a passing truck, on the verge of dying with severe hypothermia. In Kolyma, death never seemed far away.

For our relatively modest journey of just 350 miles down the Kolyma Highway, Oleg had stocked the car with several days' worth of food, two litres of vodka in plastic bottles, and a gun to fend off bears, in case we had to sleep in the car due to collapsed bridges or swollen streams. At one point we drove for three hours with no sign of civilization, before passing a village that lay in ruins, abandoned. A brief autumn was under way before the long winter came on, the trees ochre and the shrubs a tainted crimson, as if buckets of blood had been tossed over the landscape and left to dry out. The hills on all sides blocked out the horizon; some of them already had a dusting of snow on their peaks, although it was only early September.

We arrived in Yagodnoye as night was falling and rented a decaying two-room apartment. The next morning, Panikarov met me outside to walk me to his apartment-museum. A gruff but amiable sixty-one-year-old, with a corpulent frame, oversized 1980s glasses, and a grey moustache, he shook my hand heartily and led the way along muddy pathways. The temperature was closing in on zero, with icy rain drizzling down. Mangy stray dogs dodged the huge puddles. Tyres that fenced in a small children's playground had been freshly painted in bright colours, but the gesture only served to accentuate the depressive nature of everything else around. Someone had daubed FORGIVE US MUM in foot-high red letters on a dilapidated shed. I wondered what their transgression had been.

Panikarov lived on the ground floor of a shabby apartment block near the ugly hulking power station that provided the hot water and heating for the town. It was a vital piece of infrastructure, given that this part of the Road of Bones was the coldest inhabited region in the world. Temperatures frequently fell below minus forty. There had been winters in the early 1990s when the power station broke down and the town froze over, residents huddling in their apartments and burning what they could to stay alive. The expense of keeping these isolated towns warm was one of the reasons so many of them had been 'closed' in the years after the Soviet collapse. Yagodnoye itself had fallen in population from twelve thousand to around three thousand; most of those who had the opportunity to escape had done so. It seemed only a matter of time before the whole region died out. It was hard to imagine any possible upswing in Russia's economic fortune that could provide for urban regeneration here.

Panikarov grew up near Rostov in southern Russia, close to the border with Ukraine, and worked as a plumber and ventilation specialist. In 1981, when he was in his late twenties, he felt his work was going nowhere and he was having frequent arguments with his wife. One evening, over a drunken game of cards, a friend said he had heard from an acquaintance that a gold mining interest in Kolyma was looking for new workers. The pay was meant to be fantastic. There and then, Panikarov and his three other friends made a pact to sign up. On a sober head the next day, his friends came to their senses and decided the plan was ludicrous. But Panikarov decided to go for it. A month later, he was on his way, and ended up working at the Maxim Gorky gold mine, living in former Gulag barracks transformed into hostel accommodation for the workers.

Kolyma in 1981 was a place where it did no good to delve into the past. Half a century before, there had been nothing here. The land had been tamed exclusively by slave labour; the bones of thousands of those who perished there lay in the earth, often without proper burial, and the watchtowers and fortifications of many of the old camps were still visible, half ruined, sometimes in the very same places where free men like Panikarov had now come to seek their fortunes. But nobody ever spoke of the Gulag. It was a forbidden topic, absent from public and even private discourse. Although Khrushchev had criticized Stalin's excesses in his secret speech in 1956, he focussed on crimes against the Communist party, and the huge network of camps was never discussed publicly.

But one night, the older man with whom Panikarov shared a small room in the makeshift barracks at the gold mine got drunk, and confessed that he had been a prisoner in previous years. Panikarov was equal parts horrified and fascinated by his tales, and demanded nightly stories about the camps. The interest lingered, and several years later, when *perestroika* lifted the taboo on speaking about the Gulag, he could fully indulge his curiosity.

In the late 1980s, Panikarov started visiting the abandoned ruins of old Gulag sites and picking up whatever objects he found lying around; he became an archaeologist of events still in living memory. He started prying in the limited archives to which he could gain access, trying to find as much information as possible. But there had been hundreds of camps, and their locations remained a state secret. The makeshift roads had been hacked out of the landscape by prisoners, to reach the site of some gold or mineral deposit, and were often now lying abandoned and forgotten. Panikarov struck up a friendship with the local KGB chief in Magadan, who agreed to smuggle out a map of camp locations for him to copy. In return, the KGB man wanted Panikarov to see if he could dig up information on his own grandfather, who had been a prisoner. Panikarov's interest soon became an obsession, and he started work as a journalist on a local newspaper, writing mainly on the Gulag. He was one of the pioneers of a new openness that allowed the darkest chapters of Soviet history to be explored. By 1994, he had collected enough to open a small museum. The collection grew, and soon he opened up in a separate warehouse. The local authorities did not like the idea much. Yagodnoye was miserable enough already; they did not want to make the town's only attraction a monument to the region's past horrors. Panikarov found obstacles put in his way. If he wanted to hold an exhibition or a public talk, the venue he booked would get a last-minute call from the authorities booking it for their own youth event. Eventually, he even lost his museum space, and decided the only option was to set up the collection in his own home.

As I stepped through the door to his apartment and took off my coat and shoes, I was already face-to-face with the exhibits; the entrance corridor was plastered with placards and displays giving the biographies of various Gulag administrators and well-known prisoners. Off to the right there was a small bedroom with just enough space for a double bed, and a kitchen with yellowing wallpaper. Every other square inch of space in the flat had been made into museum. A cupboard overflowed with boxes filled with the protocols of interrogations and other camp documents, while the living room housed the main exhibit: rusting tools, clothing, and photographs. There was a spoon, cunningly sharpened at its base to make it double as a weapon, teapots crafted from old tuna tins, and bullet casings gathered from execution spots. There was space for only 20 per cent of his collection in his tiny flat, he said; the rest was in storage in a garage.

He seldom received visitors. Russians were not interested, save for the occasional researcher, so the tiny trickle of guests was made up mainly of foreign adventure tourists driving the Road of Bones, and the occasional foreign journalist or historian. I had imagined he would be pleased to have a rare visitor, but he seemed irate from the outset of our interaction. Before long, he blurted out the reason for his annoyance.

'You come here and you're looking for negative things. It used to be fashionable to say bad things about the USSR, now it is the same thing again. People fell in love in the camps, people got pregnant, it wasn't all bad.'

It was not the line I had expected him to take, but he continued in the same vein, lecturing me that the Western view of the Gulag was one-sided. He dug out a box of documents from the immediate post-war years at Elgen, a camp for female prisoners around sixty miles from Yagodnoye. Typewritten sheets announced punishments of solitary confinement for crimes such as the theft of flour or 'undermining socialist morals', while a fat ledger contained the verbatim transcriptions of interrogations over the pettiest transgressions, recorded in neat purple handwriting. This was the mid-1950s, long after the summary executions had ceased, but the absurdity of the questioning and language stood out.

'You see, people claim prisoners were just shot with no ceremony, but you can see here how carefully all the interrogations were recorded, how everything was done with due procedure,' said Panikarov, as I perused the interrogation files.

The presence of interrogation protocols hardly went any way to justifying the punishments, I thought. Even in Nechiporenko's interrogations in 1937, the Soviet system had insisted on a pretence of legality, meticulously extracting confessions for the most outlandish betrayals from its loyal servants.

I was beginning to realize that Panikarov's views on the Gulag were not what I had been expecting. I had imagined he would be one of the few people in Kolyma who would be unequivocal about the horrors of the camps, but he kept insisting that the system could not be condemned outright.

VI

Evgeniya Ginzburg was one of the most evocative chroniclers of the Gulag. A Bolshevik believer from Kazan, she was arrested during the purges on trumped-up charges of being a member of a secret terrorist organisation. Her dark tale of the 1930s, not officially released in Russia until 1990, chronicled the horrifying degeneration of society and human behaviour during the purges. Ginzburg recounted how she was informed upon by former comrades, subjected to hours of meaningless questioning by interrogators, their eyelids red from the long nights of work, and psychologically scarred by the endless screams and groans of torture from neighbouring cells. She was spared the death penalty, but sentenced to a long stint in the Gulag, arriving in Magadan a decade before Olga had, in a similarly gruesome ten-day voyage by boat. Once in Kolyma, she met many of those who had interrogated her, themselves devoured by the beast they had previously helped to feed.

Ginzburg was eventually sent to the women's Gulag at Elgen, and Panikarov offered to take me there to show me the ruins of the camp. Oleg drove us along a deserted road, following Panikarov's directions at repeated un-signposted turnoffs, for two hours until we reached the spot. The ruins were unimpressive: there was a mound of planks that had once been the barracks, strewn across the ground like a cartoon wooden house after it had been blown down by the big bad wolf. Panikarov led me through some knee-high grass to show me where a small section of the original barbed wire fence was still visible, gnarled and rusting. There was no sign, plaque, or any other memorial to what had once gone on here.

Ginzburg wrote of seemingly endless winters in which the skin peeled from her face, and brief but equally unpleasant summers when the women were tormented by Kolyma mosquitoes, 'bloated, repulsive insects that reminded one of small bats'. It was hard to match the scene before my eyes with the images I had in my head from her memoirs: the women spreading snow on their tiny daily bread ration in a vain attempt to soften it up, the Georgian woman who speared her eye clean out of its socket when a branch got caught in the unwieldy machinery the inmates used to fell trees, those who went blind from the brightness of the snow, and those who hanged themselves rather than face more charges when inside the camps. There was nothing to remember them by here.

A couple of miles from the ruins of the camp was a later settlement, built during the 1970s and also named Elgen. More than two thousand people had lived here in the 1980s, in gingerbread cottages and five-story apartment blocks. There had been a school, and shops, and a youth club. Now, the buildings stood empty, the windows smashed out and the doorways throttled with giant weeds. The people had gone, and they were never coming back. There were just five living beings in Elgen now: a married couple who ran a meteorological station, and their three angry dogs, which launched themselves at the car as we drove by, sprinting after us growling as we drove through the sorry, long-deserted streets. The abandoned concrete buildings were a *perestroika* Pompeii. If the ruins of the Gulag at Elgen gave little hint of the horrors that had gone on at this spot, the ruins of the adjacent town were a much more eloquent reminder of a collapsed system, a collapsed country.

On the way back from Elgen, Panikarov directed us to take an unmarked turnoff from the road, and we arrived at the site of one of the few memorials in the region to those who died in the 1930s. The small monument, a chunk of roughly hewn stone, was around a mile from the location of a major NKVD prison, where those who were exiled to Kolyma in the 1930s and then re-sentenced to death for harsher 'crimes' in 1937 and 1938 were held. They had been marched to this spot from the prison and executed by firing squad. Panikarov was one of those who organized the monument's unveiling in 1991, a matter of weeks before the Soviet Union came tumbling down. A barely legible etching on the monument paid tribute to 'tens of thousands' of people who were shot during the terror at the site, though it is now thought the number was lower. There may be documents in the archives that shed light on the exact number, but they were still secret. Of the prison, nothing remained.

We stood in the rain looking at the monument. It did not receive many visitors, being so far off the beaten track. Coins and a few plastic carnations were scattered at the base, and had clearly been there for some time. But someone had come in spring, apparently, and adorned the monument with several flags bearing the St George's ribbon and the slogan: '9 May: 70 years of victory'. It seemed a grossly inappropriate touch to me. In one deft movement, it turned the victims into martyrs; people senselessly executed for imaginary crimes into those who had done their own small part to help precipitate the Great Victory.

Alongside the monument there was a small booth with a picnic table, and Panikarov announced he had brought something with which to remember the dead. He produced a length of processed sausage and a bottle of vodka. We had one plastic glass between the three of us. Panikarov poured me an oversized shot, which I did my best to gulp down.

I asked him about the victory flags, and about the whole idea that the Gulag was somehow a necessary component of the war effort.

'It was a cruel system, but if you think about it, how else would you get this gold? During the war, five hundred tonnes of gold was mined in Kolyma. If we hadn't mined all that gold, maybe we wouldn't have won the war. Yes it was cruel, and I don't want to justify it, but how else could you tame this territory?'

Had he always thought that way, I wondered? Of course not, he said, taking a superhuman slug of vodka. 'But look at the photographs of Elgen in 1936. They had sheep, cows, horses. They had fields of wheat.

It was great. And now you've seen with your own eyes what is there. Which do you think is better? Everything's gone to shit now. It's all the fault of Gorbachev and Yeltsin.'

'But Gorbachev was the reason you were able to pursue your interest in the Gulag, the reason you were allowed to start work on a forbidden topic,' I said.

'Gorbachev is a bastard!' he yelled, his face contorted in genuine anger and rivulets of vodka running down the crevices of his chin. 'We would all have been better off if he hadn't started his stupid *perestroika*. What an incredible country we had, and now it's all gone. Bastard!'

In reality, Gorbachev had never wanted to bring down the Soviet Union; his *perestroika* was a doomed attempt to save it. Even the Americans had tried to preserve some form of union; George H. W. Bush, in a speech made in Kiev in 1991, called on the non-Russian republics to retain a democratic federation with Moscow. The system rotted from within, no longer able to satisfy the basic needs of its people and brought down by an alliance of striking miners, hungry workers, and angry intellectuals, not to mention the restless imperial periphery. But in this new narrative, the miserable 1990s were not seen as a consequence of the Soviet failure, but bundled together with the *perestroika* period as a kind of nefarious outside plot to bring down an otherwise perfect country.

I liked Panikarov; the way he had built up his collection was quietly impressive, and there was something almost charming about his irritable demeanour. It was hard to argue over the legacy of the Gulag with someone who had devoted so much time to studying it; a man who quite literally lived with the Gulag. But his views were certainly a sign of the times. A person who had spent half his life memorializing the camps, cataloguing the crimes of the Stalin era and defending the memory of its victims, had over time come to believe the camps had been somewhat justified after all. He now saw his work less as uncovering the awful crimes of the period, and more as paying tribute to those who suffered while the country pursued a difficult but necessary course, en route to its historic victory in the war.

The three of us—Panikarov, Oleg, and I—sat in silence, each thinking his own thoughts, passing the plastic cup between us until the vodka bottle had been fully drained. From far below, in the ravine,

I could hear the whooshing of the fast-flowing river, into which it is believed that the NKVD agents tossed the corpses of their victims after executing them.

VII

Written in the 1960s, but not published in the Soviet Union until *perestroika*, Vasily Grossman's novel *Everything Flows* features a dream-like trial of Stalin-era informers. The accused demolish the prosecution, asking how they could possibly be any more guilty than everyone else: 'Like us, you participated in the Stalin era. Why must we, who were participants, be judged by you, who were also participants? Why must *you* determine *our* guilt? Do you not see where the difficulty lies? Maybe we really are guilty, but there is no judge who has the moral right to discuss the question of our guilt.'[10]

Later, when the Soviet Union collapsed, the same objections were raised against suggestions of real trials for leading Soviet bosses. Who was fully innocent? Who was untainted enough to preside over a trial? In a Venn diagram of victims and perpetrators, the overlap between the two circles would be considerable. Take those like Nechiporenko, the man whose file from 1937 I had read. It was very unlikely he was guilty of the crimes he was accused of. And yet, he was still a cog in the system. Had he never rejected an application from a student to study at his university, because of their class background? Had he never taken part in denunciations of colleagues before he himself was arrested, or perhaps just stayed silent while others did the denouncing?

Of course, there are different levels of complicity; keeping quiet to save one's own skin and performing multiple executions were moral transgressions of very different orders. But many of the men who carried out the criminal orders of the NKVD, sentencing innocents to death and pulling the trigger in basements, were not necessarily vile sadists either. There were enthusiasts among them, but also careerists caught in a spiral of worsening violence. 'Working in the NKVD was prestigious,' the historian Nikita Petrov, who studies the security apparatus of the period, told me. 'At the start of the 1930s, when there was poverty and famine, you got a nice uniform and were fed well. People didn't know that within five years they'd be sentencing thousands of people to death.'[11]

There were martyrs during the Stalin era, and there were monsters too, and between the two extremes there were many varying shades of guilt and of innocence. But almost everyone was at least partially a victim, almost everyone at least partially a perpetrator.

For Petrov, the important issue in dealing with the Stalinist past was not to launch court cases or file criminal charges against individuals, almost all of whom were long dead anyway. 'We don't need to call them all criminals, but we need to recognize the criminal nature of the organization and the criminal nature of the state at that time,' he said.

For Putin, this was a red line. While he never went so far as to justify the terror, he also never called it out as a crime. For someone who fetishised statehood, it was impossible to allow that the state itself could be criminal, especially a state that less than a decade later would win victory in the ultimate war. Putin said explicitly that while Russians should remember the terrible pages of their history, 'nobody must be allowed to impose the feeling of guilt on us'. In other words: it's our dirty laundry, and we will deal with it how we like.[12]

Many countries have glossed over the darker spots in their history and the character flaws in their heroes, from Central European narratives on local complicity in the Holocaust, to Japanese memories of militarism. I certainly do not remember learning much about the darker sides of British colonialism in my school history lessons. Probably, some level of distortion and wilful amnesia are inevitable parts of any country's historiography. But the Russian case of forgetting, when so many of the country's citizens had family members who had been affected by the crimes of the state just a couple of generations previously, took things to a different level.

There were only three museums in Russia devoted entirely to the camps and repressions: Panikarov's apartment in Yagodnoye, a former Gulag site in the Urals,[13] and a new museum that opened in Moscow in late 2015. Many city museums had a section on the Gulag, but the way they presented the facts was largely down to the mood and opinions of the individual directors. 'You can either put up a big portrait of Stalin and note construction achievements, or you can put up death rates and haggard faces. Unfortunately more often than not, it's the former,' said

Galina Ivanova, a historian who had researched the Gulag for twenty-five years and would become deputy director of the Moscow museum.

Ivanova was refreshingly frank about the Gulag. She had no cautious approval for awful methods in a difficult time. Economic studies had shown clearly that forced labour was ineffective economically, she said. Progress would have come quicker if tens of thousands of highly qualified specialists had been allowed to work in their natural fields and not rotted in the Gulag for years, not to mention the large number of specialists who were shot in the purges. Sergei Korolev, who went on to become the chief scientific brain behind the Soviet space project that sent Yuri Gagarin into orbit, was imprisoned for six years in 1938, some of which he spent labouring in the Kolyma camps. It was hardly the most effective use of his talents. And even in the cases where prisoners mined huge quantities of gold, it was inappropriate to glorify the slave labour, she said. 'You shouldn't make heroes out of prisoners, even if they really did achieve major feats.'

The Western impulse when mulling Russia's failure to come to terms with Stalin's crimes has been to compare them to those of Hitler. But it took the collective German consciousness decades to come to terms with the Nazi past, Ivanova said, and perhaps now Russia would also be able to face its demons, twenty-five years after the Soviet collapse. The Moscow museum, with modern exhibits, a cinema hall, and a memorial garden of saplings brought from the earth of different Gulag sites, was an attempt to start that process, but it was a drop in the ocean. Millions of children across Russia with schoolteachers like Larisa in Magadan would get a very different view of history.

Still, Ivanova was right that the German ability to feel *betroffen*—to experience a sense of shame, guilt, and embarrassment over the crimes of the past, and in doing so to receive absolution from them—did not come about overnight.[14] The Nuremberg trials were largely seen as occupiers' justice, and it was only later, when the immediate scars of the war had healed and the full horror of the concentration camps percolated into the collective consciousness, that the shame began. It was the sheer evil of the Holocaust, more than any other war crimes, that eventually came to haunt the German imagination and provide for repentance. For all that Kolyma was appalling, it was not Auschwitz. There was also an age factor, as a new generation of Germans in the 1960s demanded answers about the Nazi past from their elders. Germany's path to remembrance would doubtless have been very different had Hitler died undefeated, to be replaced by more moderate Nazi leaders who ceased his bloodiest policies but forbade discussion of them for a generation, in the same way that happened with Stalin.

A more interesting comparison with Russia is Spain. Franco ruled the country for nearly four decades until he died in 1975, and most of the violence came in the early years of his reign. This meant that when it came to the transition to democracy, the really grievous crimes were long in the past, as with the Soviet case. In Spain, an informal agreement was made, the *Pacto del Obido* (Pact of Forgetting), which meant there was no inquiry into past bloodshed and nobody was barred from serving in the new government. There was a 1977 amnesty law, but the pact of forgetting was never formalized or even much discussed. It was simply accepted by all sides that dredging up the bad blood of the past was inadvisable. The writer Jorge Semprún, a member of the Republican exile who was minister of culture between 1988 and 1991, said: 'If you want to live a normal life you must forget. Otherwise those wild snakes freed from their box will poison public life for years to come.'[15]

But the Russian experience was fundamentally different to the Spanish one. The Spanish forgetting had the clear goal of moving on and entering the European family. In Russia too, the broad idea was to unite the nation, but the ultimate aim was not to transcend the pain of the difficult history, but to retain glory for those bloody years, and ensure legitimacy for the successor state.

VIII

On my last night in Yagodnoye, I bade farewell to Panikarov, whose parting shot was to give me a final lecture on Western lies about the Gulag before he traipsed back home in the rain, a bottle of vodka tucked under his arm. The apartment Oleg and I had rented was chilly—the heating had not yet been turned on for the winter—and full of mosquitoes. Oleg was keen to get started on the litre bottle of vodka he had brought from Magadan, so I sat with him in the kitchen and took a couple of shots, before making a tactical withdrawal to the small bedroom to type up my notes. When I emerged an hour later, the bottle was almost finished, and Oleg was in tears.

'It's six years since my wife died, and every day I drink,' he sniffed, looking at the floor and slurring his words. 'She was so wonderful, so beautiful, she was the most perfect woman in the world. I never appreciated it then, but now I can see it so clearly.'

Oleg had met his wife at the power station. She was a shift manager while he was just an ordinary worker, but he managed to win her heart, and they married. They had two sons together, but then she was diagnosed with cancer, and died a slow and painful death six years previously. During their relationship, he hinted, there had been great difficulties: arguments, drama, recriminations. But once she was gone, he realized what he had lost.

I decanted what was left of the vodka into two glasses and proposed a toast to her memory, but he was inconsolable. I gave him a hug. And then, as if from nowhere, the weepy Dr Jekyll disappeared and an angry Mr Hyde emerged. He pushed me away and dried the tears from his eyes.

'What are you doing here anyway? You think people here have nothing better to do than talk to you? Why did you come here? Your America is trying to destroy the world. Iraq! Syria! Libya! And now Ukraine! You fucking scumbags, Putin is the one man standing up to you all. He's been remarkably restrained so far, but as far as I can see, America won't understand unless we fuck you up a bit. There will be war, and then you'll understand the great Russian bear has awoken! Fucking Americans!'

I made a token attempt to counter his claims, and pointed out that in any case, I was British and didn't much like recent American foreign policy either.

'Aha! Britain! You got rich from stealing the wealth of colonies! Not like Russia, Russia became great due to our own hard work!'

He was furious now, and made to stand up. While he wasn't looking, I surreptitiously removed his hunting knife from the table and slipped it into a drawer. But I needn't have worried; he was too far gone. He stumbled to the couch and passed out. The television was still on, humming ominous news about Russia's Western enemies as usual, drilling it into the subconscious mind of its viewers. I turned it off, and lay in bed awake for several hours, unable to block out the sound of Oleg's loud snoring and the reedy whining of the mosquitoes.

The next morning at breakfast, Oleg looked in amazement at the empty vodka bottle. 'Ever since my wife died, I've not been able to stop drinking,' he said, sheepishly. 'She was so wonderful; everyone respected her. She was a shift manager at the power plant.' I gently reminded him that he had already told me, and he was shocked. He remembered nothing.

We packed to leave Yagodnoye, and set off to drive an hour further down the Kolyma Highway to Susuman, from where I was due to fly back to Magadan. Like everywhere in Kolyma, Susuman had seen better days. There used to be twenty thousand residents, now there were just a few thousand. The airport's once-grand terminal building was strewn with weeds, half fallen down, and inhabited by a drunk man who howled like a wolf when Oleg and I walked in to enquire if we were in the right place. We eventually found the new 'terminal', a sky-blue shipping container marooned on one side of the small airfield. Oleg bade me farewell with a hug.

A man with a handlebar moustache processed my ticket while smoking a cigarette. 'We used to have three flights a day from here. There was a proper terminal, a waiting area, and even a shop. Now it's all fucked,' he said, matter-of-factly. There were only three flights a week now, and even then they were mostly empty. As the antiquated Antonov propellor plane, which felt like a flying minibus, juddered its way over the empty, desolate hills towards Magadan, I thought about Oleg's tears for his wife. Reading between the lines, the relationship had not been easy. It sounded like they had spent much of the time fighting. But from the vantage point of loss, people romanticized what they once had; they forgot the negative points and remembered the positive ones.

It was not unlike the memories of the Soviet past, I thought. Most of those who had found a new purpose in life since the Soviet Union's passing had little desire to see it return. They remembered a time of queues, of boredom, and of a lack of consumer goods. The middle class of Moscow and other big cities enjoyed the prosperity of the Putin oil boom, and strived for modern Russia to become less like the Soviet Union, not more. But for those who had tough lives—and they were the majority, especially in places like Magadan—it was a different story. Our views of the past are always coloured by our present circumstances.

The post-Soviet period had been traumatic not just for people like Oleg and Panikarov, living in the country's most remote corner, but for almost every Russian. It was hardly surprising that now, people were receptive to dwelling on the victory—the Second World War—and not on the painful points. It was basic psychology. For the war narrative to make sense, there could not be heinous crimes standing at the very foundation of the country, a trail of needless bloodshed leading up to and accompanying the victory that was its most famous achievement. Thus it was better not to speak of the Gulag and the purges, or at least to 'contextualize' them in the correct manner.

Not old enough to remember the Stalin period, and insulated from its horrors by an older generation of people like Olga Gureyeva who knew to remain silent about what they had been subjected to, people did remember the 1970s and early 1980s, and felt that those were better times than the present. Like Oleg with his wife, the combination of temporal distance and current unhappiness made it easier to romanticize that earlier time, and to see its passing as a great tragedy, or even a betrayal.

These feelings, while explicable, had been seeded and needled by the endless propaganda churned out by the television and government messaging. The traditional models for a societal transition out of dictatorship presupposed choosing one from reckoning or reconciliation. Putin's initial goal had been reconciliatory, to use history as a centripetal force to bring the nation together. But it was reconciliation without the hard work and discussions required to move on. Instead, it helped create feelings of victimhood and martyrdom, which would explode in 2014.

PART TWO

Curating the Present

5

The Olympic dream

I

Insulated against the gentle chill of a Black Sea winter's evening by a dark overcoat with matching fur trim, Vladimir Putin cast his eyes around the Fisht Stadium and allowed himself a faint smile. It was the seventh of February, 2014, and this was the moment he had been building up to for seven years—the opening of the Winter Olympics in Russia's coastal resort of Sochi. Perhaps, it was the culmination of a quarter of a century of waiting, since that moment in Dresden when he had realized the Soviet superpower was helpless to protect him.

I took my place in the press box to watch the opening ceremony. An all-male choir gave a rousing *a cappella* rendition of the Russian national anthem, with a bombastic orchestra joining for the chorus. There followed a sumptuous panorama of Russian history on a massive scale. Directed by the editor-in-chief of Russia's main state television station, this was the government-approved version of Russia's glorious yet troubled past; a collection of the proudest moments from a tumultuous history, put on display for the world to see. It began with inflatable replicas of bears, samovars, and the brightly coloured cupolas of St Basil's Cathedral floating through the arena in concentric circles, accompanied by baggy-trousered Cossack acrobats, pogo-sticking warriors, and thousands of dancers clad in psychedelic updates of Russian folk costumes. It was a whimsical and alluring portrayal of Russianness. Into this primeval Russia emerged the modernizing tsar, Peter the Great, ready to conjure St Petersburg from the swamps of the north.

Next came Natasha Rostova's dance from *War and Peace,* visualized as a stadium-sized ball with hundreds of dancers twirling in unison. The lights dimmed on the sharply dressed aristocrats, and the dainty music faded out to jarring, frantic string chords, the merest hint at the blood-shed of the Revolution and Civil War. The chords were replaced by the pulsating drive of 'Time, Forward!' the soundtrack to a film about early Soviet industrialization. A life-sized locomotive, electricity pylons, and construction planks all came flying into the stadium, an almost erotic display of pumping pistons and industrial might, forming an airborne collage reminiscent of a suprematist art work.

For once, the Second World War was absent, due to Olympic regula-tions banning the use of war imagery, and there was certainly no space for the purges, the famines, or the Gulag. On this occasion that seemed fair enough: opening ceremonies are meant as celebration, after all, not introspective self-examination. Danny Boyle's quirky, self-deprecating 2012 London ceremony avoided much direct reference to Britain's colo-nial legacy, presumably lest it look like either dubious romanticization of the imperial past or self-flagellation.

What was most revealing about this officially sanctioned excursion through Russia's history was where the chronology ended. We were treated to a crisp, vivid rendition of the Khrushchev-era thaw, the brief period of Soviet optimism in the late 1950s and early 1960s when life became more liveable, consumer goods became more plentiful, and the Soviets put the first man in space. Marching pioneers in pristine white uniforms and bright red cravats heralded Yuri Gagarin's remarkable 1961 achieve-ment. And then, nothing. That was it. The history was over, giving the impression that there was nothing to be proud of in the entire past gen-eration, fifty-three years of blank slate since Gagarin's 108-minute flight. Then again, what were the options? The stagnation of the Brezhnev years combined with the disastrous military incursion into Afghanistan? The brief intellectual excitement of Gorbachev's *perestroika,* which was quickly subsumed by economic and social misery? The advent of 'robber capital-ism' and the parcelling off of the country's prime assets to the oligarchs? Clearly, none of this would do. It was an extraordinary indictment of the country's recent history. Modern Russia was twenty-three years old, and yet there was no place for even a token nod to the new country coming into existence, let alone for glorifying any of its achievements.

In a way, the final event in this journey through Russian history was the opening ceremony itself. Tsarist Russia had its empire-building and its sumptuous aristocratic balls; Soviet Russia had heady industrialization, superpower status, and victory in the space race; and now Putin's Russia had the Olympics, a symbol of its return to the 'top tier' of nations that its president had called for fourteen years earlier.

Putin had initially been lukewarm on the idea of hosting the games in Sochi,[1] but once convinced of the idea, he took to it with zeal, and before long it became one of the defining goals of his presidency. In 2007, voting to determine the host city of the 2014 Winter Games took place in Guatemala City. Putin flew in and implored the delegates to back the Russian bid. For the first time in his presidency, he spoke English in public, in a six-minute speech. There was something unusually vulnerable about Putin speaking the unfamiliar language, with exaggerated mouth gestures and a cartoon Russian accent. 'Ai vent skiing zerr seeks or syeven viks ago, and ai know: rrreel snow eez garantid!'

Talking up Sochi to those present, he promised a marvellous show were Russia to be awarded the games, using a supplicant tone rarely heard before from Putin, and certainly never heard since. When Sochi beat South Korean city Pyeongchang by just four votes, Olympic officials hinted that it was Putin's personal touch that had swung the day. 'This is not just a recognition of Russia's sporting achievements, but it is, beyond any doubt, a judgement of our country,' Putin said, shortly after.

Channelling Peter the Great, who ordered his new capital city to be built on the spongy marshland of the north, and the Politburo's megaprojects to tame the steppe and the taiga, Putin ordered a brand-new winter capital to be constructed on the crumbling remains of Soviet Sochi. When I first visited the town in 2005, it did not even have a proper sewage system, and the nearby mountains had little in the way of winter sports infrastructure, save for a few terrifyingly creaky cable car routes and poorly maintained ski runs. The task was huge: the creation of a whole new resort complete with roads, tunnels, railways, ski runs, and modern hotels.

II

Even back in 2007, relations between Russia and the West were thorny. That year, Putin gave a speech to the Munich Security Conference denouncing the 'unipolar' world order that had risen up after the Soviet collapse. 'This is a world in which there is one master, one sovereign. This is pernicious not only for all those within this system, but also for the sovereign itself because it destroys itself from within,' Putin told the audience of international politicians in Munich.

But for all his frustrations, in 2007 there was still hope that things could improve. Putin said repeatedly that the Olympics would be proof that Russia was a reliable partner, and could be an important centre of power in a new, multipolar world. It was a message not only to the outside world, but also to Russians themselves.

Events in Georgia the next summer punctured any residual optimism, however. The charismatic, impulsive president Mikheil Saakashvili wanted to move his small post-Soviet nation out of the geopolitical and historical shadow of its giant neighbour to the north, and into the orbit of the EU and NATO. Aspirational EU flags flew from every govern-ment building in Tbilisi, and to emphasize the point, a Museum of the Soviet Occupation opened in the Georgian capital. When Saakashvili met Putin, the Russian president lectured him that the museum was an outrageous twisting of the countries' common Soviet history, especially given that Stalin himself had been Georgian.[2] Saakashvili, for his part, likened Putin's geopolitical bullying to a brash Russian oligarch ruining the atmosphere at a luxury holiday resort. 'That's the way they behave in international politics, because they believe that money brings power,' Saakashvili complained to me when I interviewed him in May 2008, as we rolled through Tbilisi in his armoured motorcade. 'There should be some concierge out there telling them to behave.' Three months later, Saakasvhili ordered an assault to reclaim Georgia's breakaway territory of South Ossetia. Russia invaded and routed the Georgian army in a mere five days.

The war with Georgia alarmed many, but not everyone in the West liked Saakashvili, and although Russia had been angling for an excuse to invade, it was clear that he had fallen into Putin's trap and made the first move.[3] This, combined with the accession of Dmitry Medvedev to the presidency in 2008, gave liberals inside Russia and many politi-cians abroad hope that the country's trajectory could gradually change. Medvedev spoke in a different register to Putin. He too wanted a great Russia, but his rhetoric was of cooperation and harmony rather than rivalry and conflict. Barack Obama's administration launched a 'reset' of relations with Russia in 2009, in the hope that gradually, the relationship could improve. The next year, Medvedev travelled to the United States, where he visited Silicon Valley, and Obama took him out for a cheeseburger in Washington, DC.

But Putin remained the real centre of power in Russia, and in 2011 he announced he would stand in the 2012 elections and return to the presidency, stymieing the liberals in government and society who hoped Medvedev would stand for a second term and slowly morph into a truly independent political figure who could gradually and gently redirect Russia's course. Large numbers of Muscovites came out to protest Putin's planned return and a rigged parliamentary vote in the months that followed, surprising both the authorities and the opposition leaders, who had been used to organizing gatherings at which police outnumbered the few hardy protesters.

Putin's previous agenda had been largely free of hard ideology, and was instead focussed on *stabil'nost'*, steadily improving economic prosperity and gradually improving the self-confidence of the country and its people. This was no longer sufficient as the growing middle classes, who jetted to Paris and London for weekends, demanded more in the way of political freedoms. The solution was to pit the majority of Russians against this uppity minority. When he returned to the Kremlin in 2012, Putin implemented a newly conservative and aggressive agenda, meant to rally the populace around its leader in the face of threats from foreign influence and opposition politics. The Church became more prominent, and state television propaganda hurled out invective about Westernized liberals trying to impose alien values on Russia. One notorious law banned 'homosexual propaganda among minors', essentially making it illegal to be gay in public, prompting outcry in the West. Pride in Russia's history, and particularly the Second World War narrative, became even more sacred pillars of the regime.

This was the atmosphere in which preparations for the Winter Olympics continued. In the run-up to Sochi, Western media coverage focussed heavily on the deteriorating political situation. Two days before the Olympics started, at *The Guardian* we published an open letter from more than two hundred writers, including four Nobel Prize winners, criticizing the backsliding on human rights and freedom of expression in Russia during the build-up to the games.

As the big opening arrived, the coverage remained sceptical. Twitter jibes from bemused journalists checking into their unfinished Sochi hotel rooms went viral. My hotel, which had been booked months before at huge cost to *The Guardian*, was still being finished when I arrived. The 'hotel', part of a soulless new quarter of cheaply built five-story identikit blocks, had no reception and no heating. It was impossible to do any work as there was no Internet and no mobile phone reception. My icy room at least had a door, unlike those provided to some of my colleagues, but for the first three days I was woken up at 6am by a fire alarm. I had stayed in far worse places than my room in Sochi, but that was not the point. Russia had spent billions on an Olympics that was meant to showcase Russia's greatness, and was making life extremely uncomfortable for the few hundred people whose job it was to transmit that greatness to the world. It was Putin who had continually linked the Olympics to a newly great Russia, demanding the country be judged on the games. Now, officials did not like the verdict when people did indeed judge, based on the inadequacies.

Once the games got under way, things improved. Russia's Olympians swept the medals table, leading to an outpouring of popular pride and patriotism. A country that had enjoyed precious few victories to celebrate since the Second World War was a nation of winners once again.

But while the Olympics served their purpose for internal consolidation, the international perception of the event was a different story. Russian officials were convinced that the media attacks were not based in fact but were part of a sinister plot, dictated by a West determined not to allow Russia to have its moment in the spotlight. When it later transpired that the medal success came on the back of a state-directed, audaciously sinister doping programme, in Russia the evidence was dismissed and the allegations chalked up to more Western sour grapes.

From my seat in the press box at the opening ceremony, I looked across to where Putin and Thomas Bach, the International Olympic Committee president, were sitting. There was hardly a single Western leader around them. China's Xi and Turkey's Erdoğan were the big names; otherwise Putin had to make do with the company of former Soviet leaders such as the Belarusian Alexander Lukashenko and the

Turkmen despot Gurbanguly Berdymukhammedov. The Americans, to rub salt into the wound, sent a delegation that included a number of gay athletes, in protest at the 'gay propaganda' law.

Ukraine's president Viktor Yanukovych, whose capital city was in the grip of protests, sat glumly through the opening ceremony, forlornly waving a Ukrainian flag and sitting next to an empty seat. Yanukovych had infuriated millions of Ukrainians by rejecting a trade deal with the EU in favour of closer ties with Russia. Putin's intelligence services told him the violence in Kiev had been stoked by the West, possibly with an eye on using the country as a future launchpad against Russia. As skiers took to the slopes in Sochi, the global news cycle was instead dominated by footage of epic clashes between protesters and Yanukovych's riot police in snowy Kiev. This was not the party for Russia's readmission to the ranks of great nations that Putin had planned.

Two and a half weeks after the opening, the same stadium held another flashy, high-budget show: the ceremony to close the games. By then, dozens of protestors had been killed in the Ukrainian capital. That same night, as news came that Yanukovych had fled Kiev, Putin held a meeting with his most trusted advisers, which went on until dawn.[4] He told them to begin investigating possibilities for the seizure of Crimea.

6

Ukraine is not dead yet

On 21 November 2013, ten weeks before the Olympics began in Sochi, Yanukovych reneged on signing the deal with the EU. The journalist Mustafa Nayyem posted on Facebook that those who were horrified with the president's decision should gather at Kiev's Maidan Nezalezhnosti—Independence Square. Many young Ukrainians had seen the treaty as the first step on the way to EU membership and a different future for Ukraine. On the first evening, a few hundred people turned up, but the next evening there were more. A week later, ten thousand came to protest, and a small number camped out on the square overnight. In the early hours of the morning, Yanukovych's riot police brutally dispersed them, and footage of the violence went viral online, causing outrage and functioning as a powerful recruiting tool for the nascent movement.

The protest mood escalated rapidly. I arrived in Kiev late on 30 November, a few hours after crowds had surged into City Hall and occupied it, turning it into a temporary protest headquarters. One group of protesters set about building makeshift defences for the newly seized building, while others doled out tea to those cold from spending hours outside on Maidan. Those who had come from outside Kiev bedded down in the grand main hall to get a few hours of sleep. A few evenings later, just as it felt as though the mood of insurrection might be on the wane, a group of protesters with a truck managed to tear

Kiev's most prominent statue of Vladimir Lenin from its perch. The Soviet leader was decapitated as he fell.

By the time I made it to the scene, Lenin was prostrate and headless, and exhilarated youths were hacking away at his granite torso with mallets, pocketing the shards that came loose as souvenirs. The gathered crowd sang the national anthem, which begins with the words, *Ukraine is not dead yet.* A bit later, a few young men made off with Lenin's head in a pickup truck. Yanukovych's family-run kleptocracy had little to do with the ideas of Lenin, but it was as if the protesters were casting off both the current unpleasant regime and the last remnants of the Soviet past simultaneously.

Inside City Hall, which already felt like a refugee camp as hundreds of people took advantage of the warmth to sleep in shifts, a large black-and-white portrait of the wartime Ukrainian nationalist leader, Stepan Bandera, appeared above the central entrance. With Lenin cast away, it was a symbolic changing of the guard.

In Ukraine, history was dangerous ground, most of all the memory of the Second World War, in which Ukrainians found themselves on both sides. Soviet Ukrainians fought and died in their millions for the Red Army, but Bandera's nationalists fought against the Soviets, initially alongside the Nazis, in the hope of creating their own Ukrainian state. Bandera's appearance at the protests reopened old history battles, not only between Russia and Ukraine but inside Ukraine itself. For some Ukrainians, Bandera was a patriot and a hero, for others he was a Nazi and a scoundrel. No amount of government myth-making around the war could bring the whole population together; in fact, each time a government tried, it only served to heighten divisions.

On the surface, Maidan had very little to do with history. The initial trigger was Yanukovych's back-pedalling on the EU agreement, and more broadly, it was a general howl of protest against the corruption that permeated his system, itself merely an even more bloated and blatant version of the appallingly crooked oligarchy that had been robbing Ukraine since independence. It was, as it came to be termed later, a *revolyutsiya gidnosti*, a revolution of dignity. But the historical debates would never be very far from the surface. The buzzwords were Russia, the EU, corruption, and democracy, but behind them was a duel between Lenin and Bandera. It was not about their actual deeds or beliefs; instead, the historical figures represented two competing ideas of what should replace the Soviet Union in Ukraine. It was a debate that had been newly energized nearly a quarter of a century after the collapse.

II

Ukraine, with a population of forty-five million, was more heterogenous than any of the fifteen countries that emerged from the Soviet collapse except for Russia, and it defied easy categorization. In the west were the spires and cobbled squares of Lviv, and other handsome towns in the central European tradition; in the south the bustling cosmopolitan port of Odessa and the Soviet beach resorts of Crimea; in the east the smokestacks and mine shafts of the Donbass region and its biggest city, Donetsk; and in the centre was Kiev, the cradle of eastern Slavic history and culture. Independence in 1991 followed centuries of attempts to carve out some kind of Ukrainian state, but there was no consensus about what contemporary Ukraine should look like, or who its heroes should be. The vast majority of people who lived within the country's borders felt 'Ukrainian', but there was a very broad spectrum of belief about what exactly that meant.

The debates on the origins and interactions of the Russian and Ukrainian peoples go all the way back to Vladimir the Great, the tenth-century ruler of Kievan Rus', who was baptized in Crimea and converted his people to Orthodox Christianity. Both Ukraine and Russia claim Vladimir as a founding father, and the early Kiev state as their antecedent.

Kievan Rus' was obliterated by the Mongol horde, and much later the principality of Muscovy began gathering lands and transforming into the Russian state, while on the wild Ukrainian steppe a loosely governed Cossack polity, the *hetmanate*, flourished. In 1654, its leader Bohdan Khmelnytsky pledged allegiance to the Russian tsar, though the relationship between Moscow and the western periphery remained a fraught one.

The concept of a separate Ukrainian ethnos took hold in the nineteenth century as ethnic nationalism began to sweep Europe. Ideologues looked back to the brave Cossack outlaws as proto-Ukrainians, but the idea of Ukrainians as a real 'other' was dismissed in Russia, where it was believed all eastern Slavs were Russians. The Ukrainian language, seen as a peasant dialect dangerously popularized by the poet Taras Shevchenko and others, was scorned and suppressed. An 1863 tsarist decree supported the view that Ukrainian as a language 'has not, does not, and cannot exist',[1] and was followed a decade later by another decree that forbade this supposedly non-existent language from being used in any publications. Russia refusing to take Ukraine seriously as a separate entity would become a recurring theme of history.

III

At the end of the First World War, the Ukrainians missed out in the Versailles distribution of sovereignty. Most of what is now Ukraine was incorporated into the Soviet Union, while a chunk of what is now western Ukraine passed from the collapsed Austro-Hungarian Empire to Poland.

The decade leading up to the Second World War is almost as critical for understanding the recent clash between Moscow and Kiev as the history of the war itself. In Soviet Ukraine, after a brief flourishing of Ukrainian identity in the 1920s,[2] a devastating, unnecessary famine during Stalin's collectivization drive caused millions of deaths, in what became known as the *Holodomor*. The few first-hand accounts of the *Holodomor* that survive make for gruesome reading. First came the absurd grain targets sent to the region from the centre; if the officials did not fulfil them, they would be considered wreckers themselves. Brigades of enthusiastic party officials and volunteers descended on villages and farms, requisitioning grain stocks, then personal supplies, before smashing up homes looking for anything that might have been hoarded.

The weak died first, but as the winter of 1932 set in, famine spread more widely. People went hunting for rodents, cats, and eventually other humans, as delirium from hunger took hold. There were cases of mothers cooking and eating their children[3] and of crazed, starving peasants killing and eating friends and fellow villagers.[4] The winter of 1932 brought heavy snows and left many villages isolated and their inhabitants locked away for months, with whatever pathetic supplies they had managed to scrabble together. When those who had survived emerged, they went from house to house and found emaciated corpses and the stench of death.[5]

Vasily Grossman, in his novel *Everything Flows*, wrote unforgettably about scenes from the *Holodomor*. Grossman lived in Donetsk, working as an engineer, in the early 1930s, and witnessed the famine first-hand. He wrote of the bodies of starved children, stacked on carts, 'faces like dead little birds with sharp beaks', and of men, women, and children crawling like animals with their last strength to find their way to bigger towns in the forlorn hope of finding food. Thus, millions of peasants were condemned to death in a country where there was not an acute food shortage. The official Stalinist line was that the collectivization drive was being sabotaged by Ukrainian nationalists and bourgeois wreckers. The hideous truth was kept from those who did not witness it.

By the spring of 1933, people were dying in eastern Ukraine at a rate of more than ten thousand per day.[6] Behind those sterile numbers, as ever, were hideous scenes: the 'enormous wobbling heads, stick-like limbs and swollen, pointed bellies' of starving infants, as seen by Grossman; the silence of whole villages, their entire populations dead from famine despite living on some of the most fertile soil in Europe.

A distant predecessor of mine, Malcolm Muggeridge, Moscow correspondent of what was then the Manchester *Guardian*, wrote that the famine was 'one of the most monstrous crimes in history, so terrible that people in the future will scarcely be able to believe that it happened'.[7] Instead, thanks to Soviet obfuscation and Western acquiescence in the lying, people in the future would often not even know about it. The tragedy took hold in the consciousness of Ukrainian nationalists, who saw it as an ethnically targeted crime, and it became part of their already sizeable grievance against Moscow. But in the lands where the mass murder actually occurred, there was less remembrance of what had happened in the quiet, peaceful villages. The area was resettled by migrants from Russia after the deaths, altering the demographics of the region permanently. 'Earth like that doesn't stay empty and unpopulated for long. How could it?'[8] wrote Grossman.

IV

As Soviet rule was visiting famine on the east of modern-day Ukraine, in the western part, under Polish rule, a Ukrainian nationalist movement emerged. The OUN assassinated the Polish interior minister in 1934 and called for the proclamation of an independent Ukrainian state.

Stepan Bandera, a fiery orator with an uncompromising devotion to the cause, was imprisoned by the Poles in 1934, but escaped from prison in 1939 and took charge of the more radical wing of the OUN, which felt it could use Nazi support to help realize its long-held dream of Ukrainian independence.

The literature produced by the Bandera wing of the OUN during 1941 leaves little doubt as to the fascist nature of the movement. One document referred to *odyn narod, odyn provid, odna vlada*, a Ukrainian version of *ein Volk, ein Reich, ein Führer*.[9] The OUN members greeted each other by shouting 'Glory to Ukraine!' and giving a fascist salute with the right hand. A document from May 1941 announced the OUN's enemies as 'Muscovites, Poles, and Jews' and proscribed 'terror for enemy aliens and traitors'.[10]

When the Germans entered Lviv on 30 June 1941,[11] members of the OUN proclaimed Ukrainian independence, something their Nazi allies had no intention of supporting. The independence declaration coincided with a pogrom of Lviv's Jews, a community that had lived in the city for centuries. Photographs from those days show Jewish women stripped and humiliated by baying crowds. A survivor recalled a man wearing a traditional Ukrainian shirt, beating Jews with an iron cane. 'After a while, he beat only against the heads. With every hit he wrenched off strips of skin. He put some people's eyes out, wrenched off ears. When the cane broke, he immediately took a large charred piece of wood and smashed my neighbour's skull. The skull broke and the brain splattered in all directions, also on my face and clothes.'[12] It was the first of many pogroms in Lviv; later, almost all the remaining Jews were dispatched to Belzec, a Nazi extermination camp in eastern Poland where up to half a million Jews were killed. Only seven people are known to have survived the camp.[13]

Bandera himself remained in German custody for most of the war, with the Nazis keen to keep him out of Ukraine given their utter lack of interest in his ambitions for Ukrainian independence. Later, many nationalist fighters joined the Ukrainian Insurgent Army (UPA), which fought both the Nazis and the Soviets. But the fascist links of parts of the independence movement were real, and became an important bone of contention seventy years later.

After the war, the Soviet Ukrainian republic was expanded and homogenized; Moscow took control of Lviv and the surrounding area. For the first time, all the Ukrainians were brought together in one 'state', even if the state was a constituent part of the Soviet Union, and the east and west had very different historical and cultural backgrounds. The Soviet authorities deported hundreds of thousands of western Ukrainians to the Gulag after the war, to cleanse the territory of supposed hostile elements. Some were guilty of war crimes, others were simply 'guilty' of fighting for the Ukrainian cause, while many of the deported had done no fighting at all, like Olga Gureyeva, whom I had met in Magadan. Bandera himself died in Munich in 1959 at the hands of a KGB assassin.

In the decades after the war, Bandera was portrayed by the Soviet Union as evil, and a fascist, not because of his beliefs about Jews and Poles, but because he opposed Soviet power. The Soviet war narrative downplayed the Holocaust and the murder of Jews in eastern Europe; the 'Soviet people' as a whole were the victims of fascism, regardless of ethnicity. Being fascist meant being anti-Soviet: that was Bandera's biggest sin.

In the long run, this served to strengthen the resilient Bandera cult. Many of the anti-Semitic and openly fascist writings of the OUN were rewritten or destroyed after the war, and the image of Bandera and his followers as heroic nationalist crusaders was passed down the generations among Ukrainian emigres, as well as around kitchen tables inside Soviet western Ukraine. When *perestroika* arrived, and Ukrainians could finally air all their negative emotions about Soviet power, it was natural that those who were denigrated by the hated Soviets should now be reinstated as heroes.

v

On 14 October 1990, a monument to Bandera was opened in Staryi Uhryniv, his birthplace, and the same day in Lviv, crowds pulled down the local monument to Vladimir Lenin. The Bandera monument was blown up twice in the next six months, presumably by Soviet agents, but each time it was rebuilt. As Ukraine won its independence, a Stepan Bandera Street and monument appeared in Lviv, while in Kiev and the eastern parts of Ukraine where the Soviet tradition of celebrating victory in the 'Great Patriotic War' was deeply entrenched, Bandera monuments were never erected, and the Lenins remained standing.

The east-west divide was only one of many fault lines in modern Ukraine, but there was no getting away from the fact that the country's different regions had divergent attitudes to the Soviet past. When Ukrainians were asked in a 1991 referendum if they wanted the Soviet Union to remain as 'a renewed federation of equal sovereign republics', just 16 per cent in Lviv said yes, compared with 85 per cent in Donetsk.[14] In 1993, a leaked CIA report predicted potential political unrest in Ukraine between the nationalist west and the pro-Russian Donbass and Crimea.[15]

For the first decade and a half of Ukrainian independence, these differing Ukraines coexisted peacefully within the borders of a single country. In the west, the Bandera cult became further entrenched, while in the east, a more positive view of the Soviet period combined with exposure to Russian media ensured that a majority of people bought into a Moscow-centric version of history. Soviet-style, bureaucratic presidents were in charge, and the central government allowed Ukraine's different regions to freelance their own historical narratives, while the oligarchs and politicians concentrated on plundering the economy.

In meetings between Yeltsin and Ukrainian president Leonid Kuchma during the 1990s, Kuchma repeatedly confessed he was not a 'real Ukrainian', according to a Kremlin source of mine, who on occasion was present. 'I am from Ukraine, I consider myself a Ukrainian, but those people in the west, those are the real Ukrainians. One day, they will come to power, and then everything between our nations will be different,' Kuchma apparently told the Russian president.

Moscow's nightmares turned real after the Orange Revolution in 2004. Yanukovych, an uninspiring candidate from Russian-speaking Donetsk, won a rigged vote, and the protests forced a rerun. Viktor Yushchenko, whose face had been disfigured by a poisoning attempt most people suspected was Russia's doing, won the new vote with promises of a new type of politics.

Following a frequent trajectory of revolutionary leaders, enthusiasm among the population soon turned to broad disillusionment, as the Orange coalition descended into infighting. Yushchenko did little to fight Ukraine's endemic corruption. In an attempt to stall the decline in support, he turned to memory politics to shore up his western Ukrainian base, and encouraged a campaign to publicize the terrible events of the *Holodomor*, so long suppressed by the Soviet regime. After decades of Soviet cover-up, modern-day Russia now conceded there had been a famine, but Russian school textbooks glossed over it in the same way as the purges and the Gulag: there was a vague sense that something bad had happened, but it was not something worth dwelling on and certainly not seen as a crime committed by a Moscow regime against the periphery. It was all part of the great modernization of the Soviet Union, without which the war victory would have been impossible. Ukrainian historians argued that the lands were specifically targeted *because* of their Ukrainianness, and the famine was thus a genocide. 'Hunger was selected as a tool to subdue the Ukrainian people,' said Yushchenko.[16] Given that famine also occurred in the Russian and Kazakh Soviet republics, others suggested the ethnic factor was not the primary motivator, whatever Yushchenko might claim. Among Western historians, there were differing views on the issue.

In Kiev, there was an openness about the crimes of the Soviet period that was refreshing in comparison with the Russian attitudes to the same events. But ultimately, the presentation of the facts was still politicized. Adjudging the exact number of deaths in the *Holodomor* is impossible due to the paucity of records, but a number of serious historians put the figure between 2.5 and 4.5 million. Yushchenko, however, publicly claimed that up to ten million died. It looked as though he wanted to brand the tragedy as 'worse' than the Holocaust, with its six million victims.

When I visited the *Holodomor* Museum in Kiev, a sizeable complex opened in the centre of town, a video explicitly compared the two massacres. Everyone knows about the Holocaust, complained the film, but what about the *Holodomor*? 'Mankind has *never* seen a more efficient extermination programme,' visitors were informed by the plummy British voice doing the narrating. Archive footage, of the limp corpses of Jews being tossed into ditches during the Holocaust, was used to emphasize the point that while this might be bad, the *Holodomor* was much worse.

This desire to 'outdo' the Holocaust seemed even more distasteful in light of the other side of Yushchenko's memory politics, which involved the lionization of the wartime Ukrainian nationalist movement. In 2007, Yushchenko posthumously gave Roman Shukhevych, who had been the UPA's military commander, the Hero of Ukraine title, the country's most prestigious award, 'in recognition of his special contributions to the national liberation struggle for the freedom and independence of Ukraine'. Yushchenko claimed Shukhevych had fought both the Nazis and the Communists, but this was disingenuous. Shukhevych was one of the authors of the Bandera-led OUN faction's blueprint for action, written in 1941, which called for the removal of all non-Ukrainians currently living on Ukrainian territory, and for the liquidation of 'Polish, Muscovite, and Jewish activists'.[17] He became a high-ranking officer in *Nachtigall*, a Nazi-organized battalion of Ukrainian nationalists, who wore German uniforms and carried German weapons. Soldiers of the battalion took part in the Lviv pogroms and other massacres of Jews. In late 1941, the soldiers were reorganized as the 201st Ukrainian *Schutzmannschaft* Battalion and sent to fight Soviet partisans in Nazi-occupied Belarus.[18]

As the tide of the war began to turn, many grew frustrated with the Nazis, both because it no longer looked so clear-cut that the Germans would win the war, and because the Nazis had made it clear that ambitions for an independent Ukrainian state were a pipe dream. Shukhevych and men from the *Schutzmannschaft* Battalion, along with thousands of Ukrainian police who had deserted, swelled the ranks of the UPA, which would be implicated in the massacre of thousands of Poles.

In Yushchenko's Kiev, talk of the darker side of the nationalist movement was dismissed either as a Soviet myth, or as a necessary and fleeting alliance to which there was no alternative. Before he left office in 2010, Yushchenko gave Bandera the Hero of Ukraine award as well.

The selective memory regarding the bloodier pages of western Ukrainian history was deeply entrenched. During an interview with Andriy Sadoviy, the progressive, liberal mayor of Lviv, he handed me a souvenir badge adorned with the recently designed city logo: five cartoon spires, lined up like shortbread fingers. In the centre was the clock-tower of the town hall, and on each side two prominent Lviv churches of different denominations.

'This is a sign of how many religions we have here, of what a diverse and tolerant place we are,' he said. I enquired as to why there was no synagogue pictured. 'Ah yes, we have some Jews too,' he said dismissively. I later repeated the question to a friend who had worked for the Lviv city council, and he bristled. 'It's nothing to do with anti-Semitism. The logo was designed for the 750th anniversary of Lviv in 2006, and at that point there was no synagogue in the city.' It seemed a weak excuse. Jews had helped define the city for almost 700 years of the 750 that were being celebrated; the fact that due to the Holocaust, synagogues no longer had a physical presence in Lviv seemed an insufficient reason to excise them from the city's legends.

At the spot in central Lviv where the Golden Rose synagogue had stood until it was destroyed by the Nazis, I found a 'Jewish restaurant', in which diners were invited to dress up in big hats and Hasidic locks, and engage in the 'Jewish tradition' of haggling over the bill. Plans were under way for a proper memorial complex on the site, but had long been stalled, leaving the dubious restaurant as the only monument to Jewish heritage in a city that had been one-third Jewish before the war.

Despite all this, Ukraine was not a nation of raging anti-Semites. Many people were simply unaware of the real scale of the Holocaust on their lands, and the auxiliary role Ukrainian nationalists had played. Soviet indifference to the Holocaust was at least partly to blame. There were around a thousand Holocaust massacre sites across Ukraine, where Jews were shot or bludgeoned to death one by one, unlike the industrialized slaughter further west. Only half of them were marked in any way at all; of those, many had nothing that noted the Jewishness of most of the victims,[19] a legacy of the Soviet requirement that 'the Soviet people' were the true victims of the war, regardless of their ethnicity. But modern Ukraine was not doing much to redress the balance. By Ukrainian law, in schools there was a single lesson about the Holocaust, one hour taught to those in the final year of school. In towns where fully two-thirds of the pre-war population had been Jewish, there were no memorials to the victims.[20]

At stake was not just memory of the Jewish history of western Ukraine, but also the very idea of what modern Ukraine was, and whom it included. Either Ukraine was a political nation, in which patriotism for the country as a political entity, rather than ethnic nationalism, would be the driving force behind national cohesion, or it was a nation state, the homeland of the ethnic Ukrainians. In the search for a post-Soviet identity, Ukrainian 'patriots' tended towards the latter. As in Russia, difficult pages of the past that might contradict the glorious national narrative were unwelcome, and were either denied or simply ignored.

After so many decades of suffering under Soviet rule and centuries in which a Ukrainian state never quite materialized, this impulse was understandable. The *Holodomor* was a real, awful tragedy, and after four decades in which there was no possibility for honest investigation or discussion, there was a lot of catching up to do. It was only natural that Ukrainians wanted to focus on their own tragedies, and to prove their status as victims of Moscow's ruthless policies. It was also true that to condemn the wartime Ukrainian nationalists was easy enough with the benefit of hindsight; many of those men aiming to realize their long-held ambition of an independent state in the midst of the Second World War had few good choices. But the willingness to overlook the more complex aspects of Ukrainian history, and to lionize the wartime nationalist movement while overlooking its dubious elements, would prove just as problematic as the selective memory around the war in Russia.

VI

As Yushchenko made Bandera a Hero of Ukraine in 2010, in the eastern city of Luhansk, local authorities erected a monument to the victims of the UPA. Within the boundaries of the same country, there were now monuments both celebrating the movement and commemorating its victims.

Yanukovych, the same man who had been ousted by the Orange Revolution, won the 2010 election more or less fairly, due to disillusionment with the Orange leaders. In the south and east, his electoral support base, people also despised his corruption but voted for him simply because he was not a nationalist. One of the new president's first moves was to rescind the Hero of Ukraine titles given to Shukhevych and Bandera by Yushchenko. When pressed on the *Holodomor*, he said it had been a 'tragedy', but stopped short of calling it a 'genocide'.

Yanukovych's biggest problem was that he had no overarching idea. He rejected the divisive rhetoric of the Ukrainian nationalists, but he had no attractive, softer version of Ukrainianness up his sleeve. All that seemed to matter to him was lining his own pockets. Even the oligarchs who supported him and benefited from him found his extreme avarice distasteful. An Odessa-based businessman, Vadim Cherny, told me in 2013 that under Kuchma, Ukraine had been a 'normal liberal black economy': corrupt, but with a complex scheme of kickbacks and obligations to ensure that at every rung of the ladder there was a piece of the profit. 'Now, it's all concentrated at the top,' he complained of the Yanukovych era. 'It's impossible. Before, the kickbacks were 20 per cent, 30 per cent, that is normal and fine. Now they are 90 per cent. How can you do business with that level of corruption?'

In foreign policy, Yanukovych also seemed to be after the best deal for himself. Both Russia and the EU had trade deals to offer Ukraine: the EU wanted Yanukovych to sign a free trade agreement that dangled the vague possibility of membership in the bloc at some unspecified point in the future, while the Russians had their own Customs Union. A number of post-Soviet states had joined, but the bloc needed Ukraine if it was to be a serious Eurasian player to rival the EU. Both sides demanded exclusivity, putting the bumbling Yanukovych in a difficult position.

For Russia, Ukraine was a special bone of contention, even more sensitive than Georgia, the Baltics, or any other post-Soviet nation. Western attempts to court Ukraine were seen as outside meddling in what should be a family matter. Back in 1993, the Russian ambassador to the United States had said relations between Russia and Ukraine should be 'identical to those between New York and New Jersey'. The United States should treat events inside the former Soviet space as they would the contents of a black box, he told the Americans.[21]

But Ukraine was now an independent country, and a large section of its population and elite wanted closer ties with Europe. Western Europe might have been hampered by a tangled bureaucracy and uninspiring politicians, but the boredom held a powerful civilizational aspiration for many post-Communist states: to become a *normal country*, where laws functioned, politicians were not corrupt, and power changed through elections. In the post-Soviet world, Russia had precious little with which to counter the European offering. 'Russia has two policy tools when it comes to its neighbours: the big stick and the little stick,' I was once told by the late Alexander Rondeli, a droll Georgian political analyst. 'Maybe, one day, they will discover the existence of the carrot.'

The debate on whether Russia or Europe held the key to future prosperity for Ukraine was rehashed each year at a conference held at the Livadia Palace, on the picturesque Crimean coastline. A tsarist summer retreat since the mid-nineteenth century, Nicholas II had the original palace knocked down and the current one erected in 1910, as the old building reminded him too much of his father's death. Less than a decade later, Nicholas had been executed and tsarism was gone. In February 1945, the Livadia was the venue used for the conference to decide the fate of post-war Europe, as Stalin, Roosevelt, and Churchill met and bargained over borders. It became known as the Yalta Conference, named after the town a couple of miles down the coast from Livadia.

The Yalta Conference was the archetype of great power politics: three men poring over the map of Europe and jockeying to keep influence over as much of it as they could. Stalin found the scolding of smaller countries over the sweeping decisions made by the great powers at Yalta to be absurd. 'It was ridiculous to believe that Albania would have an equal voice with the three great powers who had won the war,' he said.[22] Horse trading and grand gesture were key, as the three men decided the fates of millions of people and drew up new borders in Europe. At one point, Roosevelt mentioned to Stalin he believed a good martini should be served with a twist of lemon; the next day Stalin had a lemon tree dripping with two hundred lemons delivered to the American leader's lodgings.[23] Putin would have been delighted if politics still worked the same way.

Now, the Livadia was rented out for two days every September by the Ukrainian oligarch Viktor Pinchuk, who had become fabulously rich by buying up major industrial assets from the state (being married to the then-president's daughter did him no harm in this pursuit). Now, in an effort to gain a reputation as a respectable businessman and statesman, he held an annual conference for which every year, international politicians and thinkers came to Livadia to discuss the future of Ukraine and the world. The biggest names came for cash—Tony Blair and the Clintons were frequent guests—others came for the lavish dinners and excellent wine. On the last night of the conference each year, there was a party on the Black Sea shore, with free-flowing champagne, succulent canapés, chefs in white toques slicing whole spit-roast lambs, and international musical acts flown in to keep everyone entertained.

Greying politicians felt they were discussing important thoughts about the future of Europe and the world by day, then in the evening could get sozzled on high-quality Chablis and dance the night away, sometimes in the company of glamorous Ukrainian women half their age.

I attended the gathering several years in a row, and with each passing year, the debate on Ukraine's future became more and more bad-tempered. In 2012, Andrei Kostin, a close Putin confidant and the head of one of Russia's biggest banks, told the Ukrainians they would be foolish to sign a free trade agreement with the Europeans. That morning, a number of EU politicians had lectured the Ukrainians on the importance of rule of law, and insisted that eventual EU membership was a transformative societal goal.

Kostin, with all the finesse of a spurned lover drunkenly yelling at his departing ex that she was going to regret this big time, told the Ukrainians that nobody in Europe truly cared about them. While the EU might offer them laws, Kostin said, only Russia could offer them love. Europe was offering a 'marriage of convenience', whereas Russia felt a visceral, historical love for the country. From the back of the hall, Arseny Yatsenyuk, a former foreign minister who would go on to become a Maidan protest leader, shouted at Kostin that the suffocating, strings-attached love that Russia offered made Ukraine feel like a prostitute. 'We want to be just partners, not lovers,' he said.

A year after Kostin's passive-aggressive entreaties, at the 2013 Livadia summit, Kiev and Brussels were on the cusp of finally signing the historic free trade agreement, years in the making. Russia had become ever more outspoken in its opposition to the deal, but the Europeans were adamant that this was a bilateral treaty, and declared any three-way discussions between Brussels, Kiev, and Moscow to be inappropriate and unnecessary.

Moscow did not take these snubs kindly. Putin was bemused by Western leaders lecturing him that in the twenty-first century there was no such thing as a sphere of influence. The same leaders had little trouble meddling in countries thousands of miles away from their borders, as Iraq had shown. Putin wanted respect and privileges in his backyard, Russia's former imperial lands.

At Livadia that year, the sole Moscow representative, Kremlin adviser Sergei Glazyev, appeared to be inhabiting a different reality to everyone else at the conference. Amid the self-satisfied optimism of the Europeans, Glazyev issued ominous warnings for Ukraine's future if the country signed the agreement. Petro Poroshenko, a former minister and future president, gave Glazyev a public dressing-down. It was the imperious and obnoxious behaviour of the Kremlin and men like Glazyev that had pushed Ukrainians so firmly towards Europe in the first place, Poroshenko said. There was warm applause, but Glazyev merely smirked, and calmly repeated his talking points over the jeering. One stunned Eurocrat couldn't believe his ears. As we drank espressos in the Livadia's elegant Moorish courtyard, which Pinchuk had hung with vast Andreas Gursky prints from his collection, the politician let rip about Glazyev to me: 'What a fucking clown! Who does he think he is, coming here and speaking like we're all living in the nineteenth century?'

Later, I spoke with Glazyev in one of the Livadia's side rooms, walking past the very same circular table at which Stalin, Churchill, and Roosevelt had sat in 1945 as I made my way to the meeting. Glazyev, with quiet menace, said the Ukrainians were about to make a terrible mistake. The only way for Ukraine to balance its trade was to sign up to a customs union with Russia, he said, and suggested that by signing the EU deal, Ukraine would violate its friendship and non-aggression treaty with Russia. Moscow could potentially cease to recognize Ukraine's current borders as legitimate, and the country could fragment under the weight of its regional differences.

'It's not only a Ukrainian case. It happened in Europe several times. We had good decisions like in Czechoslovakia, and bad decisions like in Yugoslavia. So I think it's in our common interest to avoid social unrest and political conflicts. We should be very careful.' If Ukraine signed the deal, said Glazyev, there would be economic upheaval, inflation, social unrest, and a massive political crisis.

I asked him about a potential scenario in which Ukraine signed the agreement, and there were protests here in Crimea, where much of the population was pro-Russian. Could Russia intervene? 'We don't want to use any kind of blackmail. It is not our style,' he said, smiling mischievously. Russia recognized Ukraine within its current borders, he added. 'For now.' I thought I had probably pushed him a bit far with my implausible scenarios; at the time, the idea that Russia could really seize Crimea seemed fanciful to most observers.

At the party on the beach that night, Glazyev cut a lonely fig-ure. I watched from afar as he walked in, slipped over to the canapé table, and slunk out again without sharing a word with anyone, as the Europeans danced the moonlit night away.

They should have paid a little more attention to his messaging. In the end, Yanukovych never did sign the deal with the EU. After two meetings with Putin in the subsequent weeks, he shocked Brussels by announcing he would take up a generous offer of loans and aid from Moscow, and was putting the deal with the Europeans on ice. EU offi-cials were stunned, and wondered how Putin had turned him. Was it with graphs showing how Russian trade embargoes would destroy Ukraine's economy if the deal went ahead? With threats of military moves in Crimea? With some more personal form of blackmail?

In Ukraine, many were so incensed with Yanukovych's unexpected decision that they began protesting. The Maidan movement would topple Yanukovych less than three months after his U-turn on the EU deal. And when that happened, everything that Glazyev had predicted (or was it threatened?) would come to pass.

VII

Maidan was exciting and inspiring, especially for Moscow-based jour-nalists like me, used to working a region where it was accepted wisdom that protesting was a fool's game that could never lead to any real pol-itical change, however miserable with their lot people might be. Here was a genuine, dynamic, and spontaneous movement. A hardy core of activists set up residence on Maidan, building a tent camp complete with soup kitchens, a first aid centre, and daily history lectures. The protesters constructed huge barricades of snow around the square's per-imeter and reinforced them with wooden planks, to stall any storm by the riot police. At night, it felt like a medieval army encampment on the eve of battle: flags fluttering in the icy breeze above the barricades, crackling bonfires, and bubbling cauldrons of borscht.

The freezing temperatures and the increasingly violent response of Yanukovych's riot police did not deter the crowds. On Sundays, when the numbers swelled to tens or even hundreds of thousands, an extraor-dinary cross section of society seeped into Maidan from its numerous arterial streets: men and women, old and young, Russian speakers and Ukrainian speakers, Kiev intelligentsia and simple folk from the villages of western Ukraine. It felt warm and unifying; it was obvious these people were the good guys and the riot police staring them down were the bad guys. Every hour, day and night, those present would sing the haunting, plaintive national anthem.

It was easy to get carried away with the revolutionary enthusiasm, but there were occasional flickers of something more sinister. The red-black flags of the UPA, the Ukrainian Insurgent Army, became a frequent sight alongside the yellow-blue modern flag. The old chant *Glory to Ukraine!* with the response *Glory to the heroes!* became common currency, albeit without the fascist salute that had first accompanied it. Sometimes it was followed by *Glory to the Nation! Death to Enemies! Ukraine above all!*

Of course, language, slogans, and iconography change meaning over time; most of those shouting *Glory to Ukraine* had no inkling of its dubious history. The phrase became a way to express a healthy patriotism. Those who shouted it, and those who were happy to see a portrait of Stepan Bandera hung alongside the slogans about European integration, were rarely followers of the OUN's race philosophy. They probably didn't even know about it.

Most of my Kiev friends shrugged when I asked them about Bandera. They spoke both Russian and Ukrainian, were modern and progressive in outlook, and desperately wanted the country to become fairer, more democratic, and West-looking. They were not particular fans of Bandera, but neither did they find his presence problematic. If nationalists wanted to bring their symbols to the protest, let them; it was good to see patriotic spirits on the rise, they said. Bandera was a symbol in the same way Lenin was: by this point both Bandera and Lenin stood for symbolic attitudes to the past and thus the future, rather than representing the ideas the leaders had espoused in their lifetimes. But whichever way you looked at it, Stepan Bandera was an unlikely icon for those claiming to be of a progressive, European bent.

There were increasingly moments on Maidan when I felt uneasy. One night, a well-drilled group of young men marched by, sticks in hands. They looked ready to inflict violence. A few days later, a group of Maidan supporters captured one of the *titushki*, the hired thugs paid to disrupt rallies, and dished him out some of his own medicine, shoving his face into a bio-toilet and forcing him to sing the national anthem on his knees.[24] In late January, I met one of the leaders of Right Sector, a new grouping of nationalists calling for a more violent approach to Maidan. Andriy met me in a cafe on the second floor of a shopping mall in central Kiev. A couple of heavies stood by looking out; Yanukovych was still in power, and radical protest leaders risked arrest or kidnapping. He spoke quietly and with malice in his voice, and his aims were very different to those of most people I had spoken to on Maidan.

Andriy had little interest in forcing Yanukovych to sign the EU accession agreement: 'For us, Europe is not an issue; in fact joining with Europe would be the end of Ukraine. Europe means the death of the nation state and the death of Christianity. We want a Ukraine for Ukrainians, run by Ukrainians, and not serving the interests of others.'

I had brought a Ukrainian friend with me to translate, as I had suspected, correctly, that Andriy would insist on speaking Ukrainian with me rather than Russian. She was young and progressive, and shared Maidan's pro-European leanings. I left feeling queasy from his angry nationalist rant, and asked her what she thought. 'Oh, I don't agree with most of what he said, but he's very passionate,' she said, approvingly.

Right Sector and those who shared their views were not in a majority on Maidan. They were not even a sizeable minority. One of the first people to be killed by the riot police's bullets was of ethnic Armenian origin, reflecting the diversity of the protesting masses. The flickers of extreme nationalism were lost in an overwhelming sense that something inspirational was happening. But even at the very peak of the protests, only half of Ukrainians polled across the country said they broadly supported the goals of Maidan.[25] This was partly to do with the reporting by oligarch-controlled television, which supported Yanukovych until the last minute, but it nevertheless pointed to a divided country.

Yanukovych was a useless democrat; he was also a useless autocrat. He specialized in crackdowns that were brutal enough to radicalize more Ukrainians into action, but not brutal enough to subdue the revolutionary impulses with fear. He was held in contempt by Western leaders for his undemocratic impulses, and by Moscow for his unwillingness to take them far enough. In late February, the clashes escalated from bricks, Molotov cocktails, and police batons: both sides began using bullets, and nearly a hundred protesters were killed. Realizing the game was up in late February, Yanukovych packed up several truckloads of goodies from the trashy, vast estate he had built with his pilfered millions, and got the hell out of Kiev. The revolution had won.

One of the first things the interim government did after Yanukovych fled was to propose repealing a law that gave special status to the Russian language in majority Russophone regions in the east. The move was sensibly torpedoed by acting president Oleksandr Turchynov, but as a statement of intent and priorities it was unmistakeable. The country was in chaos, law enforcement was absent from the capital, and yet one of the interim government's first attempted acts was a symbolic, linguistic one.

Progressive Kiev residents told me it was ridiculous to make a fuss about the language issue. It was true that even in Kiev, more Russian could be heard on the streets than Ukrainian. If there was a language under threat in Ukraine, it was Ukrainian, not Russian. But that was easy to say when you were part of the metropolitan elite. For those watching gingerly from Donetsk or Crimea, the initiative looked menacing, especially when refracted through the propaganda lens of Russian television.

At St Michael's, a pale-blue baroque cathedral up the hill from Maidan, volunteers set up a field hospital to treat wounded protesters. Surgeons performed operations under the frescoed domes to remove bullets from the injured. The response to a call for help on social media had been overwhelming. Boxes of dressings, medicines, and anti-burn creams were stacked high in one of the church's antechambers, showing the level of solidarity among Maidan's supporters. At the church, I met Stas, a psychologist who had come to offer counselling to protesters, to help them overcome the trauma of the violence they had witnessed. I suggested to him that the riot police, too, would be in need of counselling when the mess was over. After all, they had been standing in the cold for weeks on end, and in the endgame of the protests had been attacked with Molotov cocktails and other weapons. Many of the rank and file were just ordinary lads carrying out their orders, rather than cold-blooded killers, I ventured. But Stas was in no mood for sympathy. 'I would be willing to give them counselling, but only when they're in prison,' he said.

This palpable mood of defiance, along with the murmurs about language laws, the red-black flags, and the portraits of Bandera, alarmed many Ukrainians who were disturbed by an exclusive nationalism. Nobody liked Yanukovych, but many Ukrainians did not much like the Maidan ideology either. For sure, the views of many in eastern Ukraine were still influenced by decades of Soviet and then Russian propaganda, but slapping them around the face with Bandera was not the best way to deal with that. There was a chance to build a modern, tolerant Ukraine based on a soft idea of Ukrainianness that rejected both the Soviet past and the more virulent forms of exclusive Ukrainian nationalism. That, indeed, was what most of the people on Maidan wanted. But the willingness of the bigger crowds to close their eyes to the influence of the fringe was dangerous. Of course, Russian television had a field day with the radical, violent element, and blew it out of all proportion. But that did not mean it wasn't there. In the south and east, people worried that this time, the post-revolutionary government could follow through on the more nationalist version of Ukrainianness that Yushchenko had not managed to implement in full. Now that so many protesters had been killed on Maidan, in the name of a Russian-speaking president from the east, locals there feared the nationalists would surely be out for revenge.

In Moscow, Putin realized he had lost his man in Ukraine for good, and with Maidan triumphant, Russia risked losing its foothold in the country for a generation. A Ukraine on track towards integration with the EU, and even worse, NATO, would be an unthinkable strategic disaster for Russia. There was the security of Russia's Black Sea Fleet, based in Sevastopol in Crimea, to think of, and also a visceral anger about the triumph of street protests in a country so close to Russia.

But underlying these of-the-moment concerns was the broader context. Two countries that had been seeking to define themselves for a quarter of a century had created dangerously incompatible versions of history and contemporary *raisons d'être*. Maidan offered up a radical new approach to Ukraine's future, both intellectually and strategically, but based it at least partially in wartime rhetoric that was divisive. Putin, in addition to his strategic concerns, could not countenance a Ukraine in which the Soviet period was viewed as an occupation, and the glorious Russian war narrative was turned on its head.

7

The Crimea gambit

I

With Maidan victorious, I joined the crowds as they broke into Mezhyhirya, Yanukovych's estate outside Kiev. There was both marvel and anger as people discovered how their leader had lived: the over-wrought palatial interiors of the main residence, the garage packed with vintage automobiles, the petting zoo with ostriches and llamas in residence, and the ersatz Spanish galleon moored on the president's private lake. I spent two hours walking through the sprawling grounds and still missed half the attractions.

As the capital was celebrating the realization that the corrupt Yanukovych was gone for good, detachments of well-organized, heavily armed men appeared in Simferopol, capital of Crimea. They seized control of the airport and the parliament. Local pro-Russian politicians insisted the men were 'self-defence squads', analogous to the groupings that had sprung up on Maidan, and ready to protect the people of Crimea against a potential incursion from the fascist-inspired, Bandera-worshipping hordes newly empowered in Kiev. It was fairly clear, despite the lack of insignia on the soldiers' uniforms and the strenuous denials from the Kremlin, that the men were Russian soldiers in the flimsiest of disguises.

Of the many issues Moscow had with Ukraine, Crimea was the most explosive. Crimea had been the Soviet riviera, a shimmering peninsula of verdant forests, rocky hills, and miles of pristine coastline, hanging down into the Black Sea by the thinnest of threads, a four-mile-wide isthmus linking it to mainland Ukraine. From Anton Chekhov's time onwards, Crimea was portrayed in literature and cinema as a luscious land of ripe fruits, sweet wines, and scandalous sexual liaisons.

The peninsula had seen its fair share of misery too—brutal Civil War clashes, the Nazi occupation and the wartime deportation of the indigenous Crimean Tatars. But these memories died quickly in a land where hardly anyone could trace their roots back more than a couple of generations. After 1945, Crimea was repopulated by Russians and Ukrainians from provinces decimated by the war. An estimated 90 per cent of all the post-war residents were newcomers,[1] proving conducive to the curation of collective historical memory.

Crimea was part of the Russian republic within the Soviet Union, until Khrushchev handed it over to Ukraine in 1954. It was an administrative transfer within the boundaries of a single state, but assumed momentous significance when the Soviet Union collapsed and Crimea ended up part of newly independent Ukraine. The Soviet Black Sea Fleet had been based at Sevastopol, and in 1992 there were serious deliberations in Moscow over whether to declare Khrushchev's act null and void and reclaim the peninsula. In the end, Yeltsin decided such a move would be too belligerent, and Ukraine retained Crimea. In 1997, Russia arranged an agreement to keep its contemporary fleet there, and the lease was later extended to 2042. Many in Crimea considered themselves ethnic Russians and were naturally more sympathetic to Moscow than to their new homeland, Ukraine.

A few days after the first appearance of the 'little green men', as locals had taken to calling them, I took the overnight train from Kiev to Simferopol, Crimea's scruffy but charming capital. I arrived in a city that was brimming with anger and possibility; there was a defiance that what had happened on Maidan did not represent the feelings of Crimeans. The Crimean division of the Berkut riot police had returned home, fleeing the capital in Yanukovych's wake after three months staring down the protesters on Maidan. In Kiev, the men faced calls for prosecution; in Crimea, they were given a heroes' welcome as the defenders of the constitutional order.

In central Simferopol, the ironically named Hotel Ukraine gradually filled up with consultants from Moscow. There was talk of holding a referendum on 'Crimean independence' in May. The date was swiftly brought forward to the end of March, then again to mid-March. Someone was in a hurry to split Crimea off from Ukraine, but still the Kremlin denied all involvement.

Much later, a retrospective Russian television dramatization of the Crimea events showed buses of frothing, violent Ukrainian nationalists entering the peninsula ready to massacre locals. But in reality, there was never any genuine threat, though the idiotic rhetoric in Kiev around the Russian language issue helped suggest that one could materialize. One group of angry young men I met, 'the people's defence force of Sevastopol', talked conspiratorially to me about how they had neutralized a number of terrifying and nefarious Ukrainian subversive operations. But when I pressed them on the specifics of the plots, the worst story they could muster was the arrival of a group of Ukrainians by train to Simferopol with bicycles and Ukrainian flags. The activists had hoped to ride through Crimea displaying Ukrainian symbols and showing their support for Kiev; the defence force had rounded them up and put them back on the train. It hardly sounded like the vanguard of a fascist onslaught.

Crimea's history had a special place in Russian military lore: Sevastopol saw a punishing 349-day siege during the nineteenth-century Crimean War, and an epic battle with the Nazis eighty-five years later. Many residents were linked to the Russian military, or were descendants of Soviet officers. It was the perfect place to wheel out the Second World War rhetoric that had been brewing in Russia itself over recent years. The presence of radical Ukrainian nationalists in the new government in Kiev, and the Bandera portraits on Maidan, added an extra element to the narrative.

Billboards went up across Crimea that portrayed the referendum as a stark choice: on the left-hand side, a map of Crimea in the red-and-black colours of the UPA, with a fat swastika in the middle; on the right, a red-white-and-blue Russian Crimea. Armed irregulars, manning the checkpoints that sprang up on the roads leading into major cities, wore balaclavas to hide their faces and orange-black victory ribbons to show their allegiance. The ribbon was almost as common a sight as the Russian flag during those days in Crimea, showing that people were pushing for an idea of a common history as much as they were backing Russia itself. In Lviv, 1945 was the beginning of hated Soviet rule, and 1991 the great liberation; here in Crimea, 1945 would be restored as the biggest celebration in the calendar, and 1991 was the tragedy.

II

In *The Island of Crimea*, a subversively counterfactual novel written in 1979 by Vasily Aksyonov, the Bolsheviks never won control of Crimea after the Russian revolution. The novel imagined Crimea as a Russian-speaking capitalist hub away from the Soviet mainland, something akin to Hong Kong or Taiwan. It painted a seductive if satirical picture of capitalist Crimea as an extraordinary land of glimmering highways, racy nightlife, and culinary delights. Prime Crimean oysters were sent by the planeload each day to Rome, Nice, and London, while 'the juiciest stayed behind and were served at the innumerable tourist restaurants'.

But if in the late Soviet period it was tempting to conjure up an imaginary Crimea of capitalist plenty, when capitalism actually arrived, it was disappointing and painful. After twenty-three years of living with the extreme corruption of post-Soviet Ukraine, by 2014 it was the Soviet past that people were wistful about.

'We were used to good infrastructure, our people got to travel a lot, and we had a relatively free intellectual life,' Sergei Kiselev, a professor at Simferopol's leading university, told me. 'That was why when it all collapsed, and we had the pain of *perestroika*, the bandit capitalism of the 1990s, and the mess of the Ukrainian state, it was so painful.'

Idealized memories of the Soviet past played a major role in the events that unfolded in 2014. There was certainly a national element to what was happening: many people had always thought of themselves as Russians, not Ukrainians. Especially in Sevastopol, home of the Black Sea Fleet, most people felt little connection to Ukraine. But without the intense propaganda it is unclear a majority would have been in favour of full accession to Russia. There was perhaps a small percentage of people who were passionately pro-Ukraine and a larger percentage who were passionately pro-Russian. But the great majority were fairly apathetic.

For sure, the nationalist slogans on Maidan, and the way they were transmitted on Russian television, helped create a separatist mood. Putin's Russia, with its cult of the Second World War and great power aspirations, was a stronger and more alluring national idea for many Crimeans than the one offered by Kiev. But far more important than any national or ethnic indicator was a vaguer, existential notion. There was a faint, often intangible longing for a past, if not for the actual Soviet past then at least for the sense of meaning that went with it. March 2014 was the first time anyone had taken a demonstrative interest in the fate of the people in Crimea for a very long time, and that in itself meant a lot.

A case in point was Vladimir, who had signed up for one of the local 'self-defence battalions'. He was born in 1964 in Soviet Belarus, and grew up in an orphanage, having never known his parents. After finishing school, he did his military service in a tank battalion, and in 1985 decided to join the army professionally. He was transferred to the military academy in Simferopol. By the time he had graduated into the Soviet armed forces, the country he had planned to serve was on the verge of collapse.

'Until the Soviet Union fell apart, I didn't even think along the lines of different countries or nationalities, and suddenly, it was all gone. And I turned into a nobody overnight. I had no idea what the point of life was; there was no sense of why you were raising your children, what the point of anything was.'

Vladimir, like millions of others, looked at the post-Soviet settlement with indignant confusion. The Soviet Union was no paradise, but everyone was in the same boat, and the rules were clear, he said. Actually, in the 1980s many ordinary Soviets had resented the obvious privilege afforded to the members of the ruling elite. But the redistribution of wealth and resources that came afterwards was so grotesque that it was easy to see why people like Vladimir remembered the Soviet period as one of utopian equality. 'Some guy who has never done an honest day's work in his life is driving around in a million-dollar car,' he complained. 'But guys who toil all day down a mine can't feed their families. What sort of life is that?'

Vladimir went into business, setting up a shop that sold furniture. It did not go well. It seemed that everyone was trying to make a fast buck off everyone else. Loans were not repaid, promises were broken. Protection money had to be handed over to gangsters. 'I got the sense that if you didn't con someone, it meant you were a loser,' he said. 'I realized business wasn't exactly for me.'

Vladimir hoped that rejoining Russia would put an end to the confusing and thoroughly unfair two decades that Crimea had gone through as part of Ukraine. He loftily described his sense of purpose as he signed up to the self-defence battalions, guarding against a threat that would never really materialize. 'I collected my rucksack, a knife, and various other important things, and I said to my daughter: "Your old man will be able beat off five or six people, but who knows what will happen after that. If I end up dying, know that I died happy."'

III

Men like Vladimir provided useful cover for the Russians, but the real action was coordinated by the highly trained 'little green men'. The key potential flashpoints for the Russians were the numerous Ukrainian bases on the peninsula. The Ukrainian military was underfunded, poorly trained, and had been run for two decades by generals far more concerned with skimming off as much money as they could than with creating any kind of adequate fighting force. Nevertheless, there were still thousands of armed men who had sworn loyalty to the state of Ukraine to be dealt with. This could not be left to the self-defence brigades. To avoid bloodshed, the threat would have to be neutralized by the Russian Army itself, even if Moscow was still insisting they were not there.

I headed for the port town of Feodosia, where I had heard a detachment of Ukrainian marines was coming under pressure to surrender. Outside the base, there was a gathering of angry locals, who said they were there to keep those inside under siege, and make sure no food or refreshments made it into the base. I slipped past them, and with the help of a Ukrainian journalist managed to sweet-talk my way onto the base. Inside, the marines told me that the public Russian denials of involvement were absurd. Just that morning, a serving Russian general had visited the base and told the men they must either leave Crimea or defect to the Russian Army; he had been greeted with jeers and insults, but promised to return that afternoon. I hung around in the hope I could join the meeting, but when the Russians came back, they were furious a journalist had been let onto the base, and said they would not begin their meeting until I was kicked out. Before I left, though, one of the Ukrainian marines conspiratorially beckoned me to pass him my dictaphone, and thus an hour later I received a clandestine recording that showed exactly how the Russians were putting pressure on Ukrainian soldiers.

The first voice on the tape introduced itself as Lieutenant General Igor Turchenyuk, deputy commander of Russia's entire southern military region. He would later end up on an EU sanctions list for his role in the takeover. He was courteous and just a tiny bit sheepish, appealing to the Ukrainian officers' sense of military duty. He told the men he had served in Central Asia, Hungary, and the Russian far east during a long career that began in the Soviet Army. Most of the Ukrainians in the room were too young to have served then, but they were nevertheless descendants of the same army, he said. He was, he told the men, of Ukrainian extraction himself, hence his Ukrainian surname. Turchenyuk told them he was there on the orders of Vladimir Putin, to protect the Crimean people, and said the officers must lay down their weapons. The voices in the hall grew unruly. Was this an invasion? From whom, exactly, did the weapons need to be protected?

An angry voice piped up: 'Look me in the eye like a real officer, and tell me what status you think my battalion has. Am I a terrorist? A separatist? Am I threatening anyone?'

'We have an order to carry out,' the general repeated again and again. 'We are all military people here. We have been given the order.'

'Imagine if I came to some base of yours in the Urals, having come from a superpower, hypothetically imagine it. I show up, surround you, and tell you these words. What would you think? Put yourselves in our shoes. You are talking nonsense.'

Many of the men said their families had received threatening anonymous text messages in recent days, telling them they should either defect to Russia or leave Crimea. But the officers said they would not give up their weapons and would not leave their base without a fight. At the end of the discussion, one of the junior officers asked to speak, and in a voice cracked with emotion, addressed Turchenyuk: 'I was born in the Soviet Union, like all of us sitting here. When the Soviet Union collapsed, you reconstructed everything. You had so many problems in your country but you started to rebuild it. I always looked towards Russia as to an older brother, a helper. I was always inspired by your heroism in wars, we always looked to you as our defenders. We could always rely on help from you in any situation. Nobody could ever imagine that there would be such chaos in our country. And how did you react? In the weakest moment for our country, you took advantage, and started to support strange people, separatists. Now you have lost all the international authority that you had built up so well. Do you not think that your behaviour will destroy not only our country, but your country too?'

Turchenyuk floundered in his reply, saying he could not comment on the political leadership as it was outside his remit as a soldier. As for Russia, he said, it was not true the country had lost its authority: 'Look at the Olympics. It's no coincidence that the last Olympics we had were in 1980, when the Soviet Union was at the peak of its powers. Now the international community has again given Russia the Olympic games. Not every country is entrusted with such preparation, maintaining security and so on! I watched television today and I also saw all these foreign politicians judging us. I know all of this. Whether they are right or not, that's a question for those people who are commanding us. We are simply carrying out the orders that our leadership gave us. Please understand me properly. I am a soldier, just like you, and no more.'

Turchenyuk left the base having failed to make any progress with the marines.

At the Belbek airfield in southern Crimea, the Russians were forced into more aggressive tactics. Well-equipped soldiers in unmarked olive green uniforms swarmed around the perimeter of the base, and a detachment of them came inside, seizing most of the territory save the buildings where the Ukrainians were holed up. The brigade's commander, Yuli Mamchur, made it clear from the outset that there would be no capitulation, and demanded that his men be given access to their weapons cache, which the Russians had seized. A tense standoff ensued.

When I arrived, a group of tracksuited locals was guarding the entrance to the base. They gave me what was already becoming a standard lecture about the Western media, called me a 'homosexual liar', and threatened to beat me up if I didn't get lost. I gave up, but returned half an hour later and found they had gone, so slipped through the entrance to the base and walked up the hill to the main part of the airfield. Abandoned, rusting Soviet fighter jets were visible on both sides of the path. The current Ukrainian brigade stationed at the base was a fraction of the size of its Soviet antecedent.

Major Vladislav Kardash, a deputy squadron commander who had previously represented Ukraine in UN missions in Iraq, Sierra Leone, and Sudan, was in no doubt that the men surrounding the base were not locals. They were not even regular troops from Russia's Black Sea Fleet. They were elite Russian special forces troops, flown in specially, he was certain.

The Ukrainian soldiers were patriots of their country, but their heroes were not the Maidan's heroes. They were mainly Russian speakers, and they were proud of their regiment's history. It had been formed as a Soviet regiment during the Second World War, and fought in air battles with the Nazis over Crimea. Mamchur knew how important the Second World War was to the Russians, and hoped it could provide a common language. He ordered his men to march, unarmed, towards the Russians, holding aloft both the Ukrainian flag and the brigade's Second World War banner. No Russian soldier would dare shoot at the descendants of a Soviet war regiment, he was sure.

The men advanced slowly towards the enemy, holding aloft the crimson Soviet banner as a medieval army might have marched with an icon of Christ. The Russians looked panicked, and screamed at the men to stop, but the Ukrainians kept walking. The Russians shot into the air, and one of the Russians screamed that if the Ukrainians advanced any further, he would shoot them in the legs. Still the Ukrainians marched. Eventually, they were within spitting distance from the furious Russians, who did not carry out their threats. Mamchur raised a hand and told his men to stop, and the Russians shouted for calm, promising negotiations. Bloodshed had been averted, perhaps because of the flag.

Later that day, the Ukrainians again marched on the Russians. This time, the locals who had earlier shouted abuse at me took part in the standoff. Five of them formed a line on the tarmac. Behind them was a group of the heavily armed Russian special forces, and even a couple of Russian military vehicles. The five local hoodlums were the thinnest of cover stories to mask the presence of the Russian military, who according to the Kremlin's official line, were not there.

Major Kardash and the other Ukrainians at Belbek were caught in the middle of an unsavoury historical conflict. 'I'm also unhappy about the nationalists in Kiev,' he said. 'I'm disgusted by their fascist symbols, and I'm worried about what they're saying about the Russian language. But we're saying that openly, and then the Russians come here and call *us* fascists!'

Kardash could not get his head around the fact that Russian soldiers had stormed his base and fired their guns. 'Except the Nazis, nobody has ever fired a shot here,' he said, in disbelief.

The officers at Feodosia and Belbek made brave stands, but they were not in the majority. At many of the bases, after a token period of holding out, most of the rank-and-file soldiers defected to the Russian Army. Some of them were happy to serve a country to which they had always felt a link; others simply did not want to leave their homes and families. Most of the officers from Feodosia would be escorted to the border with mainland Ukraine a few weeks later; in the absence of any kind of support from Kiev, their words about not giving up their base without a fight were empty ones. Mamchur, the commander at Belbek, was briefly taken hostage by the Russians and then dispatched to mainland Ukraine when it became clear he would not defect. He later became an MP. By 21 March, less than a month after the military operation began, the Russian flag had been raised at 147 Ukrainian military facilities in Crimea.[2]

IV

It was obvious from the encounters at the Ukrainian military installations that the Kremlin was directing events in Crimea, but with the operation shrouded in secrecy, it was only much later that I was able to piece together exactly how Putin had coordinated the operation.

On 23 February 2014, soon after Yanukovych had hotfooted it from Kiev and gone into hiding, a delegation of high-ranking Russians called on Leonid Grach at his office in Simferopol. Born in mainland Ukraine in 1948, Grach came to Crimea in 1967 for his military service and fell in love with the peninsula. The climate, the mentality, and the quality of life were all different to other places in the vast Soviet motherland, and Grach settled in Crimea, working first as a factory director and then entering the ranks of the local party leadership. By the time the Soviet Union collapsed in 1991, Grach had risen to become first secretary, the top party boss for the region. He stayed in politics during the 1990s, but by 2014 he was long retired, with the reputation of a charming if eccentric old Communist. His office was sparsely furnished, with a cheap desk and a bronze bust of Lenin. A small oil painting depicting a pensive Vladimir Ilyich perusing a newspaper was hung on one of the white walls.

The visitors from Moscow included Oleg Belaventsev, a top aide to Russia's defence minister, who would later become Putin's representative in Crimea. They had arrived in the peninsula to help spirit the fugitive Yanukovych out of the country and get him to Russia. But the men had another, top-secret, matter to discuss. Surprising discussions were going on in the Kremlin, they said: the plan was for Crimea to separate from Ukraine and declare itself independent. At this point, the testimony of Kremlin insiders suggests Putin had not yet decided whether Russia would actually annex Crimea, but it was clear the option was under consideration. Would Grach be interested in becoming prime minister of either a Russian-protected 'independent' Crimea or a Russian-annexed region of Crimea?

Separately, a high-ranking acquaintance in the FSB called Grach from Moscow to say an FSB delegation was in Crimea and wanted to meet with him. The men appeared at his home with a special secure telephone; the Russian defence minister was on the line and repeated the offer. Grach was to organize a meeting of locals the next day and declare a split from Ukraine, making it look spontaneous.

Much later, when I visited the office with the two Lenins, Grach recounted the tale, as his assistant brought in cups of instant coffee and stale square biscuits. Grach had always been of the belief that independent Ukraine could only prosper in coalition with Russia; a book he had published in 2007 finished on that very conclusion. In fact, he remained devastated the Soviet Union had ever collapsed. In the 1980s, he had supported Gorbachev's reforms in principle, and understood the need for freedom of thought and exchanges of opinions, but he rued the speed of change. 'Once you've opened all the stable doors you should be prepared for the fact that the horse might not run in the direction you want it to,' he told me, wistfully. For him personally, it was a shock to the system; he had been the most important person in the region, and then he was swept aside in an instant.

Now, the Kremlin was giving Crimea a chance to integrate with Russia. Despite his Ukrainian roots, Grach had no doubts: he accepted the proposal made by his high-ranking visitors without hesitation.

There were lots of different groups of Russians in Crimea, freelancing for various competing interest groups in or close to the Kremlin, before the official line was laid down. By the next day, Grach was already out of the picture, discarded in favour of two local Russian nationalists, perhaps because they would make more easily manipulable partners than the eccentric and dogmatic old Communist. He would not be the man who led Crimea's glorious 'homecoming'.

As the Russian operation to seize Crimea continued, Grach, perhaps bruised by being shunned for the top job, began to speak out against Russia. It was not that he had suddenly become a fan of Ukraine; he still supported the 'historical process' of Crimea's return to Russia, but he felt people did not quite realize what they were voting for. 'I had to tell people that they need to be absolutely clear that they're not returning to the Soviet Union; they're returning to a Russia that is even more corrupt than the Ukraine they've left.'

v

The Crimean Tatars, who had a very different view of history to the Russian majority in Crimea, were an even bigger problem for Moscow than the Ukrainian bases. Like the Kalmyks and the Chechens, they had been deported on Stalin's orders during the Second World War. Unlike most of the other deported nationalities, the Crimean Tatars had not even been permitted to return home to Crimea during the Khrushchev era—the beautiful coastline villages where many of them lived had been turned into resort spots for the Soviet elite, and the Crimean Tatars remained in Central Asia until 1989, amounting to four and a half decades of exile. There were those who were deported as babies and returned to Crimea as grandparents. For them, the war involved a national tragedy of appalling proportions, while 1991 marked the end of the regime that had oppressed them and the start of new hope for a future back inside Crimea.

By 2014, the Crimean Tatars made up just 13 per cent of the population in Crimea, but they had a good claim to be the 'indigenous' inhabitants. The Tatars saw Kiev as much less of a menace than Moscow, and were by far the most vocal opponents of the annexation. As with the Chechens, the years scattered like human dust in towns and villages across Central Asia had somehow served to create a keener sense of nationhood and unity, rather than dilute it.

In the days before the referendum, Mustafa Dzhemilev, a Soviet-era dissident who now headed the *mejlis*, the Tatars' informal parliamentary body, received a phone call asking him to fly to Moscow for negotiations. When he landed in Moscow, a fleet of limousines with flashing blue lights sped across the tarmac to the plane, and he was driven out of the airport without so much as clearing passport control. He was whisked into town, dodging all traffic, to a grand building where the recently retired leader of the Russian region of Tatarstan, Mintimer Shaimiyev, was waiting for him.

Shaimiyev, the former local party boss, had organized a referendum on full sovereignty for Tatarstan in 1992, and 62 per cent voted for independence. But in the end, Yeltsin devolved enough power to Shaimiyev to keep the local elites happy, and the region remained part of Russia.

Now, two decades later, Shaimiyev wanted to give Dzhemilev the message that the Crimean Tatars, too, could flourish under Moscow's rule and benefit from the Kremlin's cash. After a brief chat, he ushered Dzhemilev up to the third floor of the building and showed him into a sparsely furnished room. In the centre of the room, there was a table, bare except for an old-fashioned white telephone. Vladimir Putin was on the end of the line, and he had a deal to offer.

Putin told Dzhemilev that if the Crimean Tatars endorsed Russian rule, Moscow would do more for them in the first few months than Ukraine had managed in twenty-three years of independence. He insisted that all the social and economic problems of the Tatars would be solved, and even offered financial help for those who still remained in Central Asia and wished to return. But Dzhemilev, a tough and wily old dissident, was no Kadyrov. He told Putin he would be happy for any help Russia could give the Crimean Tatars; after all, as the successor state of the Soviet Union, Russia had a moral responsibility to help soothe the wounds caused by the deportation. But this should only be done as part of a treaty between Russia and Ukraine, he said, and after Russia had removed its occupying troops from Crimea. There would be no deal.

'We won't just be on the side of whoever gives us the most money,' Dzhemilev told me a year later, as he puffed away on Marlboro Lights at his apartment in Kiev, where he was living out a second exile, having turned Putin down. 'We have our principles.'

VI

Events in Crimea moved inexorably towards Russian annexation, a conclusion that had gone from unthinkable to inevitable within the space of a couple of weeks. Shortly before the hastily organized referendum, I went to interview Sergei Aksyonov, the obscure Russian nationalist leader who would take over as the Kremlin's governor of Crimea once the annexation had been completed. (He was no relation to Vasily, author of *The Island of Crimea*, though the correlation was a juicy coincidence, especially given that the novel ends with the Soviet Union annexing Crimea.)

According to the official narrative, Aksyonov was the leader of the spontaneous uprising onto which Russia later latched, though in reality he was the man the Russians had selected to run the show for them once they had discarded Grach. Local MPs were rounded up by the 'little green men', frogmarched into Simferopol's parliament, and told to vote for Aksyonov as the territory's new prime minister. He then announced a referendum on Crimean 'independence', and said the subsequent independent country would immediately ask Russia to swallow it up. It was a remarkable rise to prominence for someone who, until the Russian intervention, had been a political nobody. Aksyonov had a reputation as a petty bandit, with close links to the criminal gangs who had run business in the peninsula during the 1990s, when he had gone by the nickname 'the Goblin'.

We met inside the government building his men had taken over, in the heart of Simferopol. He was an hour late, which a secretary put down to there being 'so many visitors from Moscow'. He had closely cropped greying hair, a tall, stocky frame, and wore a permanent look of something between confusion and irritation, perhaps because he had hardly slept during the recent days of drama. As we spoke, an aide bustled in and out with decrees for him to sign. Men armed with rifles, pistols, and knives patrolled the corridor outside.

I asked Aksyonov about the men in military fatigues currently blockading Ukrainian military bases, and the men who had seized control of the parliament to allow him to be sworn in. He chuckled, and told me they were all locals, exactly the same as the protesters who had been on Maidan in Kiev. On Maidan, I pointed out, there had not been people in top-end military fatigues with state-of-the-art weaponry. 'They are all locals, they took the uniforms from military depots here, we just haven't had time to sew on Crimean flags,' he said, with a smirk.

I knew he was lying, and he knew that I knew he was lying. He was a cynic, probably deeply corrupt, and a poor politician, as his rule after the annexation would show. But Aksyonov's reasons for supporting the annexation were not entirely mercenary. He was from a military family; both his parents were born in Russia, but his grandfather, a Soviet officer, was sent to Moldova to serve, where Aksyonov was born in 1972. He had always wanted to join the army, and even though the Soviet Union was tottering on its last legs by the time he finished school, in 1989 he entered the military academy in Simferopol.

'We were the last class ever to graduate from the institute. We finished in 1993, and they told us: the Soviet Union is over, you have to take an oath to Ukraine. If you don't want to be part of the Ukrainian Army, you can resign. It was a dark moment for me.' He had signed up to serve his country out of patriotic motives, and by the time the training was over, the country had ceased to exist.

He mourned its passing. 'There were a lot of good things in the Soviet Union: there were social guarantees, stipends for students, pensions. There was no big divide between rich and poor. And then after that, all the rulers were just interested in lining their own pockets. The rich got richer and the poor got poorer.'

Aksyonov had by all accounts taken enthusiastic part in this unfair free-for-all himself. In both Russia and Ukraine, few people who rose through the worlds of business or politics in the 1990s could claim to have a spotless record. Politicians like Aksyonov, and indeed Putin, manipulated political messages about the 'unfair 1990s' even though they themselves did extremely well out of the period. But I often wondered if such rhetoric was entirely born of cynicism, or if perhaps they were working through thoughts about their own role in the events. Just because Aksyonov, like Putin, had done well out of the chaos and disorder of the 1990s, it did not necessarily mean his revulsion for it was fake.

I asked Aksyonov why he was so against Ukraine's plans to sign a trade agreement with the European Union, expecting the usual answer about Western imperialism, or the trade agreement being cover for an eventual NATO takeover. His reply surprised me. The two decades since the collapse of the Soviet Union had destroyed the country's economy, he said. No Ukrainian businesses could compete on the European market, and once the agreement was signed, big European companies would flood Ukraine with cheap goods and hammer the economy even further. Crimea, just like the rest of Ukraine, needed time to recover its true potential before it could be exposed to European realities. And this went for the people as well as the businesses: 'Imagine when people find out they have to follow all the same laws as in Europe, have to stop at red traffic lights, let pedestrians cross the road! We are not mentally ready for that yet! We would need twenty years to readjust, to develop to that level!'

Slightly flustered at the implication of what he had said, he quickly recovered himself, insisting he did not mean to suggest that Russia was any less advanced or civilized than Europe. It was a brief but revealing glimpse of a frequent duality: a mix of bravado and insecurity.

Two days later, on 16 March, Crimeans went to the polls. Crimean Tatars and many pro-Ukrainians boycotted the vote. The only observers were a motley bunch of far-right European politicians: an odd choice to endorse a vote that was supposedly about repelling fascism, but then the Kremlin's rhetoric had long equated 'fascism' with 'Russophobia'. These men were supporters of Russia, and thus by definition must be against fascism. Six of them held a surreal press conference on the eve of the vote in which they spent an hour ranting about the evils of American hegemony, and congratulated the people of Crimea on their choice before they had even made it.

The official results, enthusiastically endorsed by the observers, showed an 83 per cent turnout, with 97 per cent of voters saying yes to becoming part of Russia. A later report by the Kremlin's own human rights council suggested the figures were more like 50 to 60 per cent support for Russia on a turnout of between 30 and 50 per cent.[3]

Whatever the real figures, Aksyonov declared Crimea independent. A concert on Simferopol's main square that evening drew thousands of people, some of them drunk and bellicose, some of them happy families with genuine, warm smiles. One man burned his Ukrainian passport, as the Russian national anthem reverberated around the square, and 'Crimea is Russia' was beamed onto the administration building with green lasers.

Two days later, on 18 March, Putin gathered the entire Russian elite in the Kremlin to announce the formal annexation of Crimea. The whole operation had been swift, ruthless, and largely bloodless. It was less than a month since the Sochi Olympics had drawn to a close and Yanukovych had fled Kiev. Putin told those gathered in the lavish Kremlin hall that the Crimea issue was 'of vital, historical significance' to all Russians. Later that evening, he and Aksyonov appeared at a rally on Red Square to cheering crowds. Tied to the neck of his overcoat, Aksyonov wore the orange-black St George's ribbon, symbol of victory in the Second World War.

VII

Putin's speech in the Kremlin was one of the key moments of his long rule over Russia. It was more than a justification for the specific Russian action to seize the peninsula; it was the culmination of a decade of his personal frustration and a quarter-century of Russian irritation at not being listened to. Even if the move would change irrevocably the tone of relations between Russia and the West, many believed it was worth it. Back in 2005, Putin's top strategist Vladislav Surkov had complained about relations between Russia and Europe: 'We are not enemies, but merely competitors, and this is what is so difficult to take. If you're an enemy you can die heroically on the battlefield; you can go head to head, there is something heroic and marvellous. But to lose out in a simple competitive race, that just means you're a loser.'[4]

Better a return to the adversarial sparring of the Cold War than an uneven and humiliating friendship, went the logic. That was a more fitting state of affairs for a first-tier nation: no more would Russia pander to what it saw as the obnoxious meddling and criticisms of the West; instead, the natural state of confrontation had won the day, and Russia could fight on its own terms.

Putin made great play of Crimea's historical Russianness and the need to right the wrong of Khrushchev's transfer of the region to the Ukrainian SSR back in 1954. But the real issue at stake was the need to show Russia as an assertive power, one that would not be pushed around, and that was willing to act decisively when it felt its interests threatened.

The Russians became the largest diaspora nation in the world when the Soviet Union collapsed, Putin said. Ethnic Russians across the Soviet republics woke up one morning and found themselves separated from their mother country. Their parents or grandparents had been sent there in internal Soviet transfers, and now found themselves viewed as remnants of an occupying force in the very places where they had grown up. The Russians had become a diaspora without leaving their homeland, said Putin. 'And what about the Russian state? It humbly accepted the situation. This country was going through such hard times then that realistically it was incapable of protecting its interests.'

Now, however, Putin's Russia was powerful enough to right that wrong, at least in the special case of Crimea. But instead of acceptance, the rest of the world accused Russia of violating international law, Putin said incredulously. 'It's a good thing they at least remember that there exists such a thing as international law—better late than never!'

Putin railed about the Western recognition of Kosovo's independence against the will of Belgrade. The Western nations, he said, were fuelled by 'amazing, primitive, blunt cynicism', distorting international events in their interests, 'calling the same thing white today and black tomorrow'.

He complained that after the 'dissolution of bipolarity' that followed the Soviet Union's collapse, there was no longer any stability in the world, as the Americans ran things according to their whims, seeing no need for consultation. The Americans ignored the UN and international law, believing 'that they can decide the destinies of the world, that only they can ever be right'.

It was absurd to compare, as Putin did, Kosovo, which became an independent nation after a sustained campaign of ethnic cleansing, and Crimea, which was gobbled up by its bigger neighbour on the basis of theoretical and greatly exaggerated threats. Equally, whether or not the US invasion of Iraq was illegal had no bearing on whether or not the Russian annexation of Crimea was illegal.

And yet Putin had a point. The behaviour of the United States and its allies in the aftermath of 9/11 made it much easier for Russia to dismiss the moral high ground of American politicians. In the post–Cold War world, the US *had* been free to act more or less as it pleased, with few checks or balances. An illegal war in Iraq with awful human costs and terrible longer-term consequences did not result in international sanctions against George W. Bush, Tony Blair, or their respective countries. Why, then, should the largely bloodless annexation of Crimea have those same countries crying like hyenas? Putin had complained about American exceptionalism in Munich back in 2007, and many times since. Now, he had done something about it.

As well as the general howl of protest against American unipolarity, the Crimea gambit also addressed the specific strategic concern of preventing Ukraine from tilting decisively towards the West and potentially kicking Russia's Black Sea Fleet out of Crimea. Putin had said it was unacceptable for Yanukovych to be toppled, and now he had proved that he meant it.

Putin was convinced that the Maidan protests had been funded and provoked by Western intelligence services. In a situation where Russia was now demonstrably weaker than its supposed adversary, this led to an angry insecurity in which Russia was an aggressor because it feared it would otherwise become a victim. A new military strategy adopted by the Kremlin in December 2014 included in the list of threats to Russia the installation of anti-Russian regimes through coups in neighbouring countries, and the promotion of violent regime change in Russia itself.[5]

Despite the Western sanctions and economic downturn that followed, the annexation of Crimea proved popular with the electorate. Putin's approval ratings soared to an all-time high of 86 per cent. This was partly, of course, due to the belligerent, selective reporting of Russian television stations. But there was also something real and tangible about the return of Crimea for many Russians, a balm to a wounded post-imperial nation that had not been given many opportunities to feel like winners over the past generation.

Putin dismissed the sanctions as part of a sinister and long-standing policy aimed at weakening Russia. 'The policy of containment was not invented yesterday,' he said in December 2014. 'It has been carried out against our country for many years, always, for decades if not centuries. In short, whenever someone thinks Russia has become too strong or independent, these tools are quickly put to use.' It was deft messaging, lumping in the current Western policies on Russia with all previous assaults on the country, implicitly including the Nazi attack in 1941.

With time, it became clear that 2014 could be exploitable for Putin's Russia as a new celebratory date, a contemporary companion for 1945. It had not, in the end, been the year that Russia had successfully hosted the Olympics and been welcomed back into the international family. Instead, it would be the year in which Russia finally stood up for its interests and forced the world to take it seriously.

8

The Crimean Tatars

I

In his Kremlin speech, Putin claimed Crimea had 'an enormous civilizational and sacral meaning' for Russia, comparing it to Temple Mount in Jerusalem. There were indeed grounds to suggest Crimea had historically been more Russian than it had been Ukrainian, but the millennium-long lineage of Russian Crimea claimed by Putin was largely a fiction. It is probable that Vladimir the Great, prince of Kievan Rus', was indeed baptized in Crimea in the late tenth century, but the territory did not then become Slavic. Instead, descendants of the Mongols mingled with various indigenous peoples of the peninsula, and eventually became known as Crimean Tatars. The Tatar khans ruled from Bakhchisarai, their alluring capital in the heart of Crimea's hilly interior. The Crimean Tatars were a force to be reckoned with, fearsome warriors in fur-rimmed spiked helmets, masters of their rugged horses and with a reputation for brutality in their raids for slaves and cattle. In 1571, a Crimean Tatar force invaded Russia, burning Moscow and taking tens of thousands of prisoners before retreating back to Crimea. They would not trouble the Russian capital again, but even as Russia expanded inexorably, the Tatars remained firmly ensconced in the Kirim ('the Fortress', from which comes the Russian *Krym* and the English Crimea), ruled by their khan, who was not a hereditary monarch but elected via the nobility. The khanate secured backing from Constantinople, and functioned as a protectorate of the Ottomans, Russia's main rival by the eighteenth century.

In 1782, Grigory Potemkin, Catherine the Great's erstwhile lover and the man in charge of her new provinces in what is now Ukraine, passionately urged the empress to annex the peninsula. The status quo was dangerous because the Ottomans 'could reach our heart' through Crimea, Potemkin warned Catherine. It was worth acting decisively to seize the peninsula while the Ottomans were weak, preoccupied with riots and plague, and the British and French were still distracted by the war in America, Potemkin told the empress. It was a similar pre-emptive logic to reasoning used in 2014: that Russia had to move decisively to prevent a hypothetical future NATO member Ukraine from kicking the Russian fleet out of Sevastopol and turning the Black Sea into a NATO sea.

Catherine was not immediately convinced. What about the international repercussions, she wondered. Potemkin told her it was naïve to think about such vagaries, given that nobody else did. 'There is no power in Europe that has not participated in the carving up of Asia, Africa, America,' he told Catherine,[1] much as Putin would later use Western misdeeds to justify his own flagrant violations of international law.

The first Russian takeover of Crimea used the carrot as much as the stick. In 1771, Shahin Girey, a Tatar noble who would go on to become the last of the Tatar khans, travelled to St Petersburg. Catherine invited him to watch dancing girls in a closed, exclusive circle, wooing him with access and jewels. It was the tsarist equivalent of the white telephone and Putin's financial offers to the Crimean Tatar leader Dzhemilev more than two centuries later. The next year Shahin Girey returned to the Russian capital, and left with 20,000 roubles, a gold sword, and a good disposition towards the Russians.[2] A few years later he was elected khan, and in 1783 gave up power under Russian pressure without a fight. He was kept under an honourable house arrest in St Petersburg, while the Tatar nobility were bought off with promises that their customs and Islamic faith would suffer no repression. Among later generations, the final khan became a byword for cowardice and collaboration. 'Nobody wants to be the second Shahin Girey,' Dzhemilev told me, explaining why he turned down Putin's offer of cash.

Relations between the Tatars and their new Russian overlords were initially cordial, but arriving Russian landowners seized much Tatar land, and by the turn of the century, there were stories of Russian soldiers amusing themselves by taking pot-shots with their muskets at mullahs during the midday call to prayer. The Russians also provoked ire among the locals for using headstones from Tatar cemeteries as building materials.[3] The relationship deteriorated to the extent that during the Crimean War in the mid-nineteenth century, the Tatars provided the allies (Britain, France, and the Ottomans) with logistical and intelligence support. They paid for it in a series of reprisals in the aftermath, and by 1867, around 192,000 Tatars had fled the peninsula for Turkey, out of a total population of 300,000. They left 784 deserted villages and 457 abandoned mosques.[4] Russian peasants flooded the region, and the aristocracy built palaces along its coastline, of which the splendid Livadia outside Yalta was one of many. Crimea's demographic makeup was changed forever, and it was really only from this point onwards that Crimea could in any way be considered 'historically Russian'.

II

A sizeable Crimean Tatar minority remained in the peninsula, and by the turn of the century had its own newspapers and secular, modernizing political leaders. *The Kurultay*, an informal parliament of Tatar leaders, gathered at the palace in Bakhchisarai in late 1917 and promulgated a remarkable constitution, which was certainly the most progressive in the Muslim world, and more progressive than many in the West. The constitution called for the creation of a Crimean Democratic Republic, in which 'freedom of identity, word, press, conscience, meeting, dwelling, union, protest' were guaranteed and the 'complete equality of women with men' was proclaimed.[5] The Bolsheviks arrested and shot the *Kurultay*'s reformist leader, Noman Celebicihan.

After the Civil War, Lenin's policy to allow nationalities to 'take root' meant the Crimean Autonomous Socialist Soviet Republic[6] was set up, as a unit with some devolved powers within the larger Russian republic. Even though Crimean Tatars by this point made up only about 25 per cent of the population, they were given a disproportionate number of leadership roles. Then, as elsewhere, there came famine, collectivization, and the purges, in which many of the top Tatar leadership were shot. There was a huge row-back on the early-Soviet promotion of localized national identities, not to mention a fierce campaign against Islam as part of the Soviet anti-religion policy. By the end of the 1930s there was not a single working mosque in Crimea; mullahs were labelled 'parasites' and deported to Siberia.[7] Tens of thousands of peasants were deported during the collectivization campaign, in a dress rehearsal for the wholesale deportation that would come a decade later.

Crimea was occupied by the Nazis for most of 1942 and 1943, meaning many more Crimean Tatars came into contact with them than did the Chechens. Nazi anthropologists believed the Goths who had once lived in Crimea were closely related to the Germans of South Tyrol.[8] The Nazis planned to repatriate them to Crimea, which would be renamed Gotenland.

Thousands of Crimean Tatars joined 'self-defence units' directed by the Germans, and there are reports of some taking part in massacres. But many Tatars who ended up fighting for the Germans hardly did so out of free will, having been captured and forced to fight. Thousands more were rounded up and sent to work in Germany as part of the *Ostarbeiter* forced labour system. There were also many Tatars active in partisan groups, fighting against the Germans, and thousands fighting with the Red Army at the front.

Elvedin Chubarov, a Tatar historian, admitted to me that there had been collaboration among Crimean Tatars, but said it was no more than among other nationalities who had experienced occupation. As with the Kalmyks, the Tatars had experienced a decade of famine and terror under Soviet rule, and many had high hopes for an occupying force they knew little about.

The Tatar deportation, which was launched on 18 May 1944, followed a similar pattern to those of the Kalmyks and the Chechens; the Soviet authorities already had the ritual set after so much practice. Early in the morning, every Tatar family was woken by a knock at the door and told to get ready for a long journey. Again the Studebaker trucks, again the cattle wagons and the seemingly endless rail journey towards Central Asia.

Even according to the NKVD estimates, 27 per cent of Crimean Tatars died either during the journey or in the first three years of exile; the Crimean Tatars' own accounts suggest the figure is actually 46 per cent.[9] The Tatars were scattered far and wide across Central Asia.

In the peninsula itself, Crimean Tatar place names were Russified—Karasubazar became Belogorsk, for example. Russians moved into Tatar homes, while the coastal Tatar villages were torn down and replaced with hulking great concrete *sanatorii*, Soviet spa retreats designed for the masses. Books published during the 1920s in the Crimean Tatar language were destroyed, mosques were blown up or turned into cinemas, and gravestones from Tatar cemeteries used as building materials.[10] References to Crimean Tatars were removed from the *Great Soviet Encyclopaedia*, and even mentioning the name was considered seditious. They were now 'Tatars who formerly resided in Crimea'. There was no such thing as a Crimean Tatar.

III

Mustafa Dzhemilev, the man whom Putin would attempt to seduce with offers of financial aid during the annexation, was born in November 1943, during the Nazi occupation of Crimea. He was six months old when he was deported along with his parents and the rest of the Crimean Tatars to Central Asia. Dzhemilev's family ended up in Gulistan, a dusty town on the Uzbek plains. It was thousands of miles away from the lush vegetation and shimmering sea of Crimea, both geographically and psychologically.

One of Dzhemilev's early, vivid memories was of the morning of 5 March 1953, when a voice came over the radio announcing that Stalin had died. Across the Soviet Union, there were tears and mourning, even among those millions of families who had lost relatives in the purges and the Gulag. But the Crimean Tatars were a close-knit group, and by and large they knew Stalin was responsible for their predicament. 'Finally, the dog has kicked it,' Dzhemilev's father muttered. The older generation knew what kind of public show would be required, and impressed on the children the need to affect mourning, to avoid raising suspicion and provoking potential retributions. A family friend paid a visit to the Dzhemilevs with a bag of onions, and told them to keep them peeled and on hand in case tears were required.

At school, the deputy headteacher made an impassioned oration about the death of the great leader and father of the nation. 'Now we are all orphans,' he told the children. He became so overwhelmed with emotion he could not even finish his speech, breaking off mid-sentence, and scurrying out of the hall with tears streaming down his face. Dzhemilev remembered his father's words and the bag of onions, and assumed the teacher must be faking it. 'I followed him out of curiosity to the classroom where he'd shut himself away, and looked through the doors, and there he was, beating his head against the wall and letting out great peals of grief. He really was devastated. Everyone was crying, except the Crimean Tatars.'

During Khrushchev's thaw, the Chechens, Kalmyks, and other deported nationalities were allowed to return to their homelands, but the Crimean Tatars were neither pardoned nor allowed home. The absolution from the stain of collaboration finally came in 1967, but the decree that rehabilitated them also proclaimed that they had 'taken root' in Central Asia and thus there was no need for a return to Crimea.[11]

Dzhemilev heard so many stories about the land from which he had been deported as a baby that it became an obsession. He read everything he could about Crimea at the library in Tashkent, and became ever more active in the dissident movement, exchanging memos with other activists in cities across Central Asia on how best to advance their national cause. He was jailed for the first time in 1966, shortly after leaving university: he refused to do his military service, saying he would not fight for the country that had stolen his homeland. He received five more convictions over the next two decades, including one sentence of hard labour.

The transcripts of Dzhemilev's 1976 trial in Omsk, for the 'dissemination of knowingly false fabrications that defame the Soviet state and social system', are notable both for the absurd nature of the proceedings and for the courage and moral clarity that shines through in his words. He was sentenced to two-and-a-half additional years in prison despite the blindingly obvious flaws in the trial. His 'last word' was a searing indictment of the court, the Soviet system, and the KGB,[12] and he vowed to continue a hunger strike that had already been going on for nine months, during which time he had been force-fed.

Dzhemilev told me the hardest moment during his multiple prison terms was an incident in 1985 in Magadan, nearly five thousand miles away from Crimea. The Gulags in the desolate eastern outpost had long ceased to function, but the city still operated a prison meant for particularly recalcitrant offenders. Dzhemilev was taken to the chief warder, who adopted a hostile tone with him: 'It's time for you to sign this paper and recant all your stupid anti-Soviet views. Crimea Shrimea! You need to become an ordinary Soviet man. Otherwise you're never getting out of here, and you'll never see these guys again,' he said, pointing to a photograph of Dzhemilev's wife and son he had placed provocatively on his desk.

'This was hard. The end of the century was approaching, Gorbachev would soon be talking about democratization and *perestroika*, and inside the prison it felt like 1952,' Dzhemilev recalled, dragging on yet another cigarette. 'I still don't quite believe it but I said to him: "Look here. You're nobody, you're a lackey. You'll do what you're ordered, and if you're ordered to kiss my shoes, you'll do that, so don't portray yourself as the master of my fate. And as for your Soviet power, it will soon collapse, and you'll all run like rats and find somewhere to hide. And I will see those people in the photograph again, I promise you. But God willing, you will never see your children again."'

For his outburst, Dzhemilev was sent to the 'pressing chamber', a cell containing four hardened criminals who did the guards' bidding in return for tea or other privileges. 'They set about me like wolves,' he remembered. But he had befriended a Georgian mafia authority who was also serving time in the prison and respected Dzhemilev for his principled stance. The mafia—thieves-in-law as they were known at the time—were the only people more feared by the other inmates than the prison authorities.

'Suddenly this voice cries out in a thick Caucasus accent, "Chamber number six! Listen up!" and the guys stop instantly and there is total silence. "Yes Goga, speak," they say, meekly. And he calls out, "You've got a political in there. Touch a hair on his head and it'll be curtains for you." They all backed away. There was no defence against a thief-in-law in jail. "Everything's fine Goga, we're not touching him!" came the cry. That was a pretty close call.'

As the Soviet Union entered its death throes, tens of thousands of Crimean Tatars flooded back to the peninsula, nearly half a century after they were kicked out. In 1991, the Tatars held a second *Kurultay*, mimicking the one that had proclaimed the ill-fated Crimean Democratic Republic in 1917. Dzhemilev was elected chairman of the *mejlis*, the Tatar governing council.

For the Crimean Tatars, 1991 was a date of great celebration. But still, their problems were substantial. According to the best estimates, they had lost around 80,000 houses, 34,000 plots of land, and 500,000 heads of livestock during the deportation.[13] They returned with nothing. Even if their old family houses were still standing, they had no legal recourse to repossess them. Many of the villages had simply been wiped off the map and replaced with tourist infrastructure. The Crimean Tatars seized land, illegally or semi-legally, and built temporary settlements. By the end of the 1990s, a World Bank study found that only 20 per cent of these settlements had electricity, 30 per cent had running water, and none had proper sewage systems.[14] They were refugees in their own homeland.

IV

The casual traveller to Crimea today would have little idea of the tortured history of the peninsula's original inhabitants. At the vast, sprawling holiday resorts on the coast, there is no mention of the Tatar hamlets that had been destroyed to make way for them. There is no museum of the deportation, and no proper monument. Without knowledge of the horrific history of the Tatars, it was hardly surprising that locals were resentful of tens of thousands of new arrivals, suddenly appearing and claiming the peninsula as their own.

I wondered if at the khan's palace in Bakhchisarai, the historical seat of Crimean Tatar power, there might be something to remember the deportation and the other sorry episodes in their history. The white-walled fortress is now a museum, and visitors can tour the former living quarters of the khans and their harems, decorated with exquisite carvings and ornate stained-glass windows. The guide told me that the beautiful 'crying' fountain, an intricate marble and gold structure about which Alexander Pushkin penned famous verses, had previously been located in a different room. 'After the Russians took over, they moved everything around and messed it all up,' she grumbled to me, conspiratorially. I asked why on earth the Russians had done so, before realizing she was referring to the Russian takeover of 1783, not that of 2014.

At the back of the palace, a space had been cleared and a set of stone steps led up to a series of memorials of a much newer vintage. The numbers 1941 and 1945 were emblazoned on each side of the stairway. Inside the enclosure, there were several monuments to brave soldiers and peaceful civilians killed by 'fascist butchers'. The ensemble was topped off by a mounted Soviet tank, from the battalion that had liberated Bakhchisarai from the Nazis in 1944.

The heroic Soviet war effort and huge losses sustained in Crimea certainly deserved commemoration, but this seemed a grotesque historical perversion. In the ancient Tatar capital, in the seat of power where the Crimean Tatar khans had ruled for centuries, monuments had been intruded, memorializing the very same war during the course of which the entire Crimean Tatar nation had been deported. Amid the war monuments, there might at least have been space for something to commemorate the deportation, but there was nothing.

The memorial complex was a Soviet creation, and I wondered if at the main history museum in Simferopol there might be something newer that would be more instructive on what had happened to the Crimean Tatars. There were, unsurprisingly, several halls devoted to the war effort, including a field tent into which visitors could climb and imagine themselves out on the front lines, and walls adorned with portraits of young Communist activists, their hair swept back and their eyes filled with fiery enthusiasm. One exhibit showed the shawl of Vera Geiko, a local partisan volunteer. She had scrawled on it: 'My life is ending, tomorrow I will be shot. Long live the USSR! Death to fascists!'

I asked the kindly babushka watching over the exhibit if there was anything on the Crimean Tatars, and she pointed me in the direction of a small glass case in the far corner of the room. The exhibit reproduced the official Soviet deportation decree in full, which stated that during the war many Crimean Tatars betrayed the motherland and were 'particularly noted for their beastly attacks on partisans'. There was no commentary on the decree, save for a small piece of paper in the bottom corner of the exhibit, which gave the caveat that many Crimean Tatars were deported 'without proof of their guilt'.

A history teacher in Simferopol told me he had never taught any of his students a class on the deportations, under either the Ukrainian or Russian school curriculums. So it was that schoolchildren in a region where within living memory the entire population of one of the area's founding ethnic groups had been deported would learn absolutely nothing about the events. In 2008, Anatoly Mogilev, then the leader of Ukrainian Crimea, publicly referred to the Crimean Tatars as 'Hitler's henchmen'.[15] Many Crimeans regarded the deportation as a soft punishment for the disgrace of collaboration, rather than a terrible crime that bordered on genocide. The simplified war narrative meant there was no understanding why some Crimean Tatars might have been amenable to Nazi messaging in 1942, after a grim two decades of Soviet power.

V

As Putin was offering Dzhemilev and others financial incentives, the uncooperative majority were targeted with fear tactics. A number of Tatars went missing during the annexation; one was found dead two weeks later, with signs of torture on his body. In the early months, pressure was put on Crimean Tatar media outlets, the main source of independent information about what was going on in the region.

Ilmi Umerov, who had been the mayor of Bakhchisarai since 2005, decided to stay in his post for several months after the annexation, but by August 2014, when preparations were under way for Russian local elections, he felt he could no longer serve a regime he believed to be an occupying force. He went to see Aksyonov, Crimea's leader, and told him he was resigning. Aksyonov tried to persuade him to change his mind, Umerov told me.

'I told him I thought Russia was an occupying force, that this was an annexation, and that these authorities were illegitimate. He told me not to be an idiot, and just to hold my tongue for a while and take the cash. He said this is forever, so you need to find a compromise, a way to cooperate with us and keep existing.'

Umerov ignored the advice, becoming an outspoken critic of the government and Aksyonov's regime. A few weeks after we met, FSB agents came to search his home. A year later, in the summer of 2016, his house was raided early in the morning by heavily armed special forces, and he was summoned to face the absurd charge of calling for the undermining of Russia's territorial integrity. Crimea was part of Russia now, and suggesting you believed it should still be part of Ukraine carried a potential jail sentence of five years. The court incarcerated him in a mental asylum for three weeks, in order for him to undergo forced psychiatric assessment, an echo of a dark Soviet practice.

As for Dzhemilev, a month after the phone call in which he rejected Putin's offer, the Tatar leader was travelling to Kiev when he was handed a piece of paper by Russian border guards at the new 'border' with Ukraine. The document informed him he was banned from the territory of Russia for a five-year period. 'I laughed, and told them: "Ever since you let me out of prison in Magadan I've had no desire to visit Russia again. I only did so on the invitation of your Putin, so why bother banning me?"'

But according to Russian law, Crimea was now also Russia, and so two days later when Dzhemilev returned from Kiev, he was stopped at the border and told he could not enter. Around three thousand Crimean Tatars gathered on the other side in protest; the guards had to shoot into the air to quieten them down. The decision was binding, unless he changed his mind about working with the Russians, it was communicated to him through an intermediary. So now, he was stuck in his flat in Kiev, living out a second exile, a sad coda to his epic struggle to return to Crimea throughout the Soviet period. 'It's pretty easy, compared with the camps,' he said. 'I sit at home, and I have enough cigarettes. But it does make me angry. I was the head of the *mejlis* for twenty-three years and then you come on your tank and say I'm not welcome in my own homeland.'

In a final, vindictive salvo against Dzhemilev for not taking the deal, Russian state television aired an 'investigation' into him in summer 2014. He had never really been a dissident, the programme 'revealed', but in fact had been a petty thief and rapist, who had collaborated with the KGB and then persuaded them to change his criminal record to one of political dissidence.

Not every Crimean Tatar thought Dzhemilev an unequivocal hero,[16] but he was a man who had a long and proud history of standing up for his beliefs. He had preferred to spend years in prison than to go against his principles and stay silent during the Soviet years, and he had rejected Putin's offer of a deal that would doubtless have led to a very comfortable financial settlement for him personally. To smear him as a petty thief and a rapist was ludicrous.

A year after the annexation, I asked Dzhemilev in Kiev whether he regretted turning Putin down. Russia was clearly in Crimea for a long time, possibly forever, and the Tatars were a vulnerable minority who needed all the help they could get. Had he ever been tempted to take the money, take the deal? He fixed me with a pitying smile.

'We didn't put our homeland up for sale!'

VI

Not everyone agreed that resistance was the best path. Zaur Smirnov, who had been the deputy head of the *mejlis,* was one of the highest-profile Crimean Tatars to agree to work with the Russians. He joined the government's committee on interethnic relations, and had been in the job a year when I paid a visit to his office, in a shabby building on the outskirts of Simferopol in March 2015. Imposingly tall and dressed in a sharp suit, he had a Koran on his bookshelf and a picture of a thin-lipped Vladimir Putin hung above his desk. Born in Tajikistan, in deportation, he considered himself fully Crimean Tatar, despite the Slavic surname handed down from a Russian grandfather.

Smirnov was defensive, almost angry, as he answered my questions while doodling stick trees in his notebook. He laughed off the idea that most Crimean Tatars were pro-Ukraine. Ukraine had done nothing for the Crimean Tatars in the twenty-three years they had been ruled by Kiev, he said. The Tatars were pro-Ukraine mainly by default, purely because they were so suspicious of Moscow after everything the Soviets had done to them. 'It is hard to explain to our people that today the Russians are not trying to use Crimean Tatars like it happened before, like Ukraine did or the Soviets did,' Smirnov said with a sigh.

He insisted that working with the Russians was the only logical way to advance the interests of his people, and accused Dzhemilev and others in Kiev of being the real enemies. I asked him if he had lost any friends over his decision to collaborate with the Russians, and he became irate. He was welcome in any house, he said sharply, unlike the monsters who tried to direct the Crimean Tatars into a dead end from their comfortable homes in Kiev.

I suspected Smirnov genuinely believed he was doing the best thing for the Crimean Tatars. He wore a nice suit but his office was in an unkempt old building in a forgotten corner of Simferopol; it hardly reeked of the cash and privilege of collaboration. Indeed, with Russian rule clearly in Crimea to stay, as a small and beleaguered nation required to live in the shadow of its former oppressor, it was hardly the most illogical thing to suggest the best *modus vivendi* for the Crimean Tatars was to take the Russian money and use it to improve their lot. But Smirnov went further. He wanted the Crimean Tatars to stop complaining about their history.

'We shouldn't inject Crimean Tatars with a victim complex, because what was done before was a conscious policy to make us a nation of victims, always asking for something, always protesting. You can't build a nation on loss and victimhood.'

There was a kernel of good sense in his words: nobody likes a professional victim. But the underlying logic was perverse. It was hardly as though the Crimean Tatars were harping on about a centuries-old territorial dispute, or a massacre deep in the annals of history. Within living memory, the entire nation had been smeared, cruelly deported from its homeland, and kept in exile for a generation, before returning to a population who knew little of its struggles and were deliberately kept in the dark about the awful history.

Shortly after I spoke to Smirnov, Crimean authorities proposed canning the memorial ceremonies on 18 May dedicated to remembrance of the victims of the deportation. Dmitry Polonsky, the deputy prime minister, said the '18 May cult' of Crimean Tatars led them to have an inferiority complex. Instead, it was suggested the Tatars should switch their commemoration date to 21 April, the day on which Putin signed a decree that finally rehabilitated them: it was to be a happy celebration, not a glum wallowing in grief. Just in case anyone thought this was an optional suggestion, Crimean Tatars were banned from gathering at their usual spot on 18 May; the square was cordoned off and surrounded by police. In 2016, four Crimean Tatars from the town of Sudak were fined 20,000 roubles each for daring to wave the Crimean Tatar flag on 18 May. Such a gesture was judged to 'infringe the established order for the holding of political demonstrations'.

Amid all the voices braying that Crimea was Russian, or Crimea was Ukrainian, few in either Moscow or Kiev[17] had done even the most cursory research into the bleak history of the Crimean Tatars, who had been living in the region for centuries before either Russians or Ukrainians had settled there. Now, the Crimean Tatars themselves were being told to stop droning on about their painful history. It was a plea for wilful amnesia, for an acceptance that dragging up the crimes of the past was undesirable. It was just like Chechnya and the demand to be liberated, not defeated.

Smirnov made the comparison explicitly. 'Look at the Chechens, look at their leader Ramzan Kadyrov. They've gone through two terrible wars, with so much loss. But today the Chechen people are in renaissance. Knowledge of our history should not be to the detriment of the people; it should benefit people.'

The deal on offer was the same one as in Chechnya, and was very simple: take the cash, and forget the history.

9

Russian Crimea

I

When I returned to Crimea for the one-year anniversary of the annexation, I found that the realities of Russian rule had come as a sobering shock to many. It turned out that the Russian authorities were just as corrupt as the Ukrainians, but with an extra layer of bureaucracy. People were suddenly required to fill out sheaves of paperwork to register their cars, or to run their businesses—to do the things they had always done before without hassle. Pensions went up but so did prices, and Western sanctions meant credit cards did not work in the region and mobile reception was poor.

Oleg Zubkov, a businessman who ran a large safari park an hour out of Simferopol, had been such an enthusiastic supporter of annexation he'd promised to set his big cats on any Bandera fans who dared to enter Crimea. When Russian rule actually arrived, it made him miserable. Months before the annexation, he had proudly mounted giant lettering in the style of the Hollywood sign on a nearby hill. The house-sized letters spelled out 'LION PARK' and had cost him tens of thousands of dollars to import. But the new Russian authorities told him they violated a Russian law on 'the installation of large objects in public spaces', and ordered him to take them down and pay a fine. Later, two of his tiger cubs died when heating cut out during a weeks-long power cut. Almost all of Crimea's electricity came from Ukraine, and radicals had blown up the power lines. 'Under Ukraine things here were bad, but now Russia is here things are even worse,' he complained, as he drove me in a golf buggy around the safari park, which still contained dozens of lions but had no visitors. It was temporarily closed due to the ongoing spat with the authorities.

Many people felt similar disappointment, though few expressed a desire to return to Ukraine. The war that had broken out in eastern Ukraine by then was a marvellous retroactive propaganda tool for the Kremlin. If it hadn't been for the annexation, dozens of different people separately told me, Kiev would have launched a military operation in Crimea by now. Nobody remembered that the only threat from Kiev a year previously had been a few youths with Ukrainian flags on bicycles.

I caught up with Vladimir, the failed furniture salesman who had excitedly gone off to join the self-defence brigades during the annexation. I found him at the headquarters of the 'people's resistance force', just off Simferopol's main square. This was now an official body of around five hundred men, distilled from the ten thousand irregular volunteers who had signed up the year before. The men had been given smart khaki uniforms, with Russian insignia and shiny new 'People's Resistance' badges sewn into the upper arms. The wall in their office featured a laminated Putin photograph and a framed headshot of Stalin.

Vladimir was now the deputy commander of the force, and he suggested we go for coffee at Victory, a Soviet-themed retro cafe not far from the headquarters. He had a visible spring in his step as we walked the short distance to the cafe.

I asked Vladimir if he thought the Stalin portrait in the headquarters was appropriate, especially given Stalin's treatment of the Crimean Tatars. 'We don't love Stalin because he killed a lot of people, but because he killed a particular part of the population,' he said, as we sipped on our gritty coffees. 'In fact he didn't even really kill them, he just imprisoned them, and it was the segment of society that didn't want to unite around this great union. It was hard to create such a great country and even harder to keep it together. That's why your Margaret Thatcher was able to destroy it in 1991, together with that one,' he said, in a derisive tone and slapping his forehead to indicate Gorbachev's birthmark. Stalin's ruthlessness was the only thing that had made the Soviet Union great and kept it great, he said.

Vladimir was bursting with conspiracy theories. I kept asking about life in Crimea, but he kept wandering off on tangents. Did I believe in wizards? Did I know that the Queen of England has a stone made by Jews under her throne, which was what made her so powerful?

'I will never agree not to use the words "mother" and "father",' he said, apropos of nothing, as we were discussing Western sanctions on Russia. I inquired what on earth he was talking about, and he explained. He had seen a television programme that revealed how in Europe it was now illegal to call parents 'mother' and 'father'. Apparently, the 'gay lobby' had complained, and now by law Europeans had to refer to 'Parent one' and 'Parent two'. He was glad that with Crimea now a part of Russia, such indignities would not be visited upon him.

He had not seen much in the way of fighting during the annexation, he said, when I steered him back to the topic, but had still played a part. When I asked what exactly he had done, he smiled a knowing, secretive smile, and asked if I believed in talismans. I was expecting more cod mysticism, but his new talisman was something very real: a gun. He gave me a grin full of expectation as he withdrew it from under his coat to show it off, setting it down on the latticed retro tablecloth in front of me. It was a sleek, chrome pistol, which carried an engraving in fussy italics on one side: a personalized message of thanks to Vladimir for his courage during the events that reunified Crimea with Russia, from the Russian Defence Minister Sergei Shoigu.

Vladimir's quest for meaning in life had certainly been satisfied. The drifting, juddering uncertainty he had felt when the Soviet Union collapsed did not have much to do with the specific Ukrainianness of Crimea; it was more universal. But the Russian capture of Crimea from Ukraine had enabled him to overcome it. He had gone from a failed businessman, who could not find his place in the world, to someone who strutted the streets of his city wearing a smart uniform and carrying a personalized gun.

I asked him what specific things had changed for the better over the past year, and he paused for a moment, before responding that the best thing of all was the lack of stress when he turned on the television.

'Everyone is speaking Russian on every channel! I always felt alien everywhere. I travelled around Ukraine, went to Poland, I was offered money to go to Lithuania and work driving trucks, but I decided not to, even though it was good money. Who is waiting for me in Lithuania, in England, in Australia? Nobody. And then you turn on the television here, in your own home, and some bastard is speaking to you in Ukrainian. You can't understand what a relief it is now to turn on the television and only hear Russian.'

II

The day after I caught up with Vladimir, I joined a small group of people at Gagarin Park on the outskirts of Simferopol. They arrived in twos and threes, and slowly opened their coats and bags, looking sheepish yet exhilarated, revealing things they had long ceased to believe it was possible to display in public.

Two young women exposed sweatshirts featuring the Ukrainian trident, while others pulled yellow-blue flags from their bags. Alexander Kravchenko, a skinny youth with blond hair shaved at the sides and a Cossack-style ponytail, undid his black waterproof jacket to reveal a *vyshivanka*, the traditional Ukrainian shirt, embroidered with a red column running from the neck to the navel. The organizer of the event was Leonid Kuzmin, a soft-spoken twenty-four-year-old with a slight lisp and wispy facial hair. A history teacher with a somewhat nervous manner, he entreated those present not to make any political statements. Mainly, they obeyed him, though everyone knew that in the current climate, the very fact of the gathering was political. A short distance away, several police officers in navy uniforms kept an eye on things; one spoke conspiratorially into his mobile phone.

It was the 201st anniversary of the birth of the Ukrainian poet Taras Shevchenko, traditionally a day of celebration across Ukraine. Born a serf in the early nineteenth century, Shevchenko published *Kobzar*, his first collection of poetry, when he was just twenty-six. The series of musings on Ukrainian identity, written in the Ukrainian language, probably did more than anything else to create a sense of nation among the descendants of the Cossacks. Tsar Nicholas I had Shevchenko exiled for a decade over fears his poetry could provoke Ukrainian nationalism. When he died in 1861, a funeral procession accompanied his coffin down the Dnieper River from Kiev to Kaniv, where he was buried as a national hero, albeit of a nation that as yet had no state.

Shevchenko was reimagined as a proto-revolutionary by the Soviets, who erected monuments to the poet across the country, including one in Simferopol. Shevchenko was used as part of the unifying, 'Friendship of Peoples' nationalism that the Soviets promoted, but with the onset of conflict between Ukraine and Russia, he had regained his properties of fission over fusion. On the same day a year previously, a gathering at the Shevchenko monument was the last display of pro-Ukraine sentiment in a Crimea that was already mid-annexation. A few hundred pro-Ukrainians, who already realized there was no stopping the political process that had begun, sang folk songs and wept.

A year later, holding such a celebration had become much riskier. Russian law required official permission for all gatherings of two or more people, and the new Russian authorities in Crimea told Kuzmin he could not hold his gathering in the logical place, next to the Shevchenko monument itself. The black marble bust, with its head angled quizzically towards the ground, was 'busy', the police claimed. They gave him permission to hold the event on the other side of town. Many of the pro-Ukrainians who had attended the year before had fled Crimea in the intervening year; of those who had not, most presumably thought it was not worth the danger of raising their heads above the parapet. About thirty people showed up for Kuzmin's gathering, a pretty sorry turnout.

Kravchenko read some verses Shevchenko had dedicated to his fellow poet Marko Vovchok, which began as follows:

Not long ago beyond the Urals
I wandered and beseeched the Lord,
That our truth should not be lost,
That our words should not expire.

He was not much of an orator, and forgot some of the lines.

When they were done with the poems, which could hardly be heard over gusts of wind, there was a half-hearted cry of 'Glory to Ukraine', and Kuzmin declared the gathering over. We stood and chatted about life for pro-Ukrainians in the new Russian Crimea. About twenty minutes later, as we were getting ready to disperse, a few of the policemen walked over and informed Kuzmin and Kravchenko, politely and quietly, that they were under arrest.

Merely hinting Crimea belonged to Ukraine could make one guilty of 'separatism', and thus liable for a jail term of up to five years. In the end, the men were charged with the much lesser offence of 'breaking the established order of a public gathering' by displaying political symbols at a cultural event. A hearing was set for later that week.

The day of the trial, Leonid had some disturbing news to share. The headmaster at his school had called him into his office that morning and told him the education ministry had been on the phone. A person who organized pro-Ukraine demonstrations was not fit to teach Crimean schoolchildren. He was fired on the spot. He packed up his things and bade farewell to his colleagues at the school, where he had taught history for the past three years. Some of the teachers were openly hostile towards him; more discreetly, a couple of others approached and said *sotto voce* that they were sorry for what had happened. Nobody made any kind of public stand. In the space of a couple of days, Leonid had been arrested, summoned to appear in court, and lost his job. It seemed harsh punishment for reading a poem.

Inside the courthouse, the personnel had changed little since the takeover. Almost all the employees of the Crimean prosecutor's office, police force, and security services had gone over to the Russians. Moscow simply appointed a few top officials to oversee the transition, and flew in planeloads of officials on day trips, once a week for several months, to give training to the former Ukrainian civil servants.

The scene at the courthouse was familiar from the dozens of court cases I had covered in Russia: the light pink walls and prefabricated cheap wooden furniture; the aggressive hatchet-faced women controlling the visitor log, who just at the point when you became so exasperated with their obstinacy that you were on the verge of either rage or tears would suddenly become extremely friendly; the prosecutors strutting through the corridors in navy uniforms, carrying stacks of typewritten documents; and the queues of confused citizens shuffling around with sheaves of papers bearing intricate ink stamps.

The courtroom where the 'Shevchenko case' was to be heard was tiny, the size of a single bedroom. It had one small bench, with space for about five people to sit down, including all the witnesses. I managed to slip to the front of the queue and sneak in with one other journalist. Everyone else was told there was no space by two irritable bailiffs.

On the wall above the judge's chair was a sparkling new Russian crest, the double-headed eagle embossed in shiny gold on a scarlet background. Judge Natalia Urzhumova was announced by the sound of her cream stilettos on the distressed parquet floors, and wore a black judicial cape with embroidery and silver cuffs. She looked irritated. When I googled her later, I found a Ukrainian government decree appointing her to the position of deputy head of the court in 2005, and pictures of her attending legal gatherings in Kiev in subsequent years.

It was certainly an unusual case: the judge herself had served Ukraine for almost all her professional life, and was now about to try people for holding its flag. Adding to the absurdity was the fact that attached to the outer wall of the courthouse was a postbox in yellow and blue, embossed with the Ukrainian trident, which the new authorities had evidently not yet got round to removing. They were the same symbols that were being judged as 'extremist' inside the building.

Kravchenko's case was up first, and the first witness was a policeman, Officer Zaitov. He had been one of those guarding the gathering, and had written the report about Kravchenko's actions. Wearing a leather jacket and blue jeans, as he was off duty that day, he did not look happy to be in court.

LAWYER: When did you first see the defendant?

ZAITOV: I was ordered by the commanding officer to bring citizen Kravchenko into the station for a chat.

LAWYER: Did he have any extremist flags or clothing?

ZAITOV: I saw that he had a small yellow and blue ribbon pinned to his chest.

LAWYER: You said in your report that Kravchenko was displaying forbidden symbols. What did you mean? *(pause)*

ZAITOV: I think maybe I meant the ribbon.

LAWYER: So the yellow and blue ribbon is forbidden?

ZAITOV: I don't know if it is forbidden or not.

LAWYER: But you wrote the report, and said he was displaying forbidden symbols.

ZAITOV: I don't know if it is forbidden or not.

LAWYER: So why did you write that he was wearing forbidden symbols?

ZAITOV: I don't know if he was wearing forbidden symbols.

LAWYER: So why did you write that he was? *(long pause)*

ZAITOV: I was asked to write it. I don't know what I meant.

LAWYER: But you wrote that it was forbidden in your report! And because of your report the defendant is standing before you today! So, what did you mean? *(Very long pause)*

ZAITOV: I don't know.

LAWYER: No further questions.

Zaitov sat down next to me on the bench and stared at the floor. He was breathing heavily and looked distraught. Next up was the female police officer who had written the indictment based on Zaitov's report and her own further questioning. Unlike Zaitov, she surveyed Kravchenko with naked contempt. Everything about her bearing suggested she wanted to prove a point, and she seemed to relish the logical gaps in the case rather than be embarrassed by them.

LAWYER: You mentioned that he was displaying forbidden symbols. What did you mean?

POLICEWOMAN: It's there in the report. I based it on that.

LAWYER: But you must have asked Kravchenko, or Zaitov about what was meant? What forbidden symbols?

POLICEWOMAN: Provocations. There were provocations.

LAWYER: I'm sorry, I need you to be more precise. What are you accusing the defendant of doing?

POLICEWOMAN: Of saying provocative words. Provocative banners, flags.

LAWYER: What words? What flags?

POLICEWOMAN: Look, I don't know. They wouldn't just bring someone to a police station for no reason, would they? He must have done something wrong.

LAWYER: No further questions.

The judge declared the hearing over and withdrew to consider her verdict. The evidence had been so pathetic that even in the skewed Russian system I thought there was no way she could return a guilty verdict. Of course, there was a definite political subtext to the gathering, and doubtless Kravchenko and the others present wished Crimea had remained part of Ukraine. But it was also abundantly clear that none of them had broken any Russian laws, however they might be interpreted. The gathering had official permission to go ahead, the Ukrainian flag was simply not an 'extremist symbol' according to Russian law, and to suggest that a Ukrainian flag was not a relevant symbol at a gathering to celebrate the national poet of Ukraine was absurd.

The judge asked for fifteen minutes to consider her verdict but took over an hour. I wondered if was she having a crisis of conscience. She perhaps felt sorry for the weedy Kravchenko, who was clearly no bloodthirsty revolutionary. Perhaps she had made a call to whoever had ordered a guilty verdict: *Look, the police have really screwed this up. Nothing adds up, the charges are farcical, the lawyer has proved that what happened was not against the law, and what's more I've got a foreign journalist here. There's no way I can convict.*

Or, perhaps, she was just having her lunch. She found Kravchenko guilty and sentenced him to forty-eight hours of 'correctional labour', speaking in a monotonous mumble as she read out the sentence and making no eye contact with him. It later transpired that the maximum punishment the law provided for was only forty hours: presumably she was not yet fully up to speed with the exact provisions of the Russian legal code.

Kravchenko left the room with a wry grin. Next it was Leonid's turn, and his hearing proceeded in a similar vein, the police unable to back up the contents of their report, especially as Leonid had not even been holding or displaying any kind of flag or ribbon. The main incriminating factor was that he had stood 'near' a Ukrainian flag, and that as the organizer of the gathering, he should have told people to put their provocative flags away.

Unlike some of the higher-profile political defendants I had witnessed in Russian courtrooms over the years, Leonid did not use his final word to the court to make a barnstorming political speech denouncing Vladimir Putin, the Russian legal system, or the ridiculousness of being arrested for reading a poem. Instead, he had memorized elements of the laws he was accused of breaking and explained to the judge why he had to be found innocent, in a garbled high-speed stammer: 'According to paragraph 15, point 1a, of article 54 of the legal code of the Russian Federation, the police did not give me warning as an organizer that there were people at the gathering who were acting in a way not in accordance with the declared subject of the gathering, which means that I cannot be held accountable for breaking the aforementioned article in relation to my duties as organizer of the said gathering,' he said, all in one breath, with his hands shaking and his soft voice breaking up. He need not have bothered. He was quickly found guilty, and also sentenced to clean the streets for forty hours.

It was a petty case about a petty event and carried a petty sentence, but there was something profoundly interesting about the small gestures on display in the courtroom that day. Leonid was undoubtedly brave, though I wondered whether he might have been better off organizing the gathering at home. He had retained his pride and dignity, but lost his job. Not long after the trial, he was beaten up in the street, and when I met him a year later, he was working as a dentist's assistant, the only job he could find. Perhaps he could have done more good by quietly giving hundreds of Crimean schoolchildren a more nuanced view of history than they might receive from their other teachers, rather than losing everything over a half-an-hour public gathering.

As for the judge, there was no way she could genuinely believe the verdicts she had dished out to be legally sound, and it was hard not to feel insulted by the way she had listened carefully to all the arguments, asked questions, flicked through documents, and stood on procedure, only to throw it all out the window. Today, she was sentencing innocent men to sweep the streets; perhaps tomorrow, she would sentence people she knew to be innocent to spend ten years in a high-security prison in Siberia.

In the weeks after I left Crimea, I thought often about the court case. I thought of that angry glint in the policewoman's eyes, the same look of hatred and vengeance I would see so many times during the conflict in eastern Ukraine. I thought about the judge, and wondered what she said to her husband about the case over dinner that evening. Did giving verdicts that were not legally sound gnaw away at her conscience, or had she long ago accepted it as part of the job? But most of all, I thought of Officer Zaitov and his shame-filled eyes. They were the eyes of a man tortured by his small part in the farce, by being forced to stand face to face with the real consequences of the small compromises the system had demanded of him.

III

Aside from the human emotions and compromises on display, the court case was also a small cog in Russia's attempts to curate the present-day reality in Crimea. The Kremlin's justification for its annexation of the region was that the overwhelming majority of its residents wanted to be part of Russia. For a variety of historical, sociological, and financial reasons, many people did indeed want to be part of Russia, but it was nothing like the unanimous desire Russia claimed. In order to bring reality into line with the projection, even small displays of dissent like Leonid's had to be stamped out immediately. If you let twenty people demonstrate unheeded, tomorrow perhaps a hundred people would come out, and the week after thousands.

The day after the court case, I had an interview with Oleg Saveliev, the Kremlin's Minister for Crimea. I found him in a smart office in the centre of Simferopol, wearing a grey cashmere scarf knotted below the neck, a sharp suit, and an expensive watch. Parachuted in from Moscow, Saveliev's job was to liaise with the local authorities in Crimea and oversee the distribution of the huge amounts of money the Russians were pumping into the transition. The room had a large map of Crimea on the wall and smelled faintly of cigarette smoke. Saveliev doodled on a small notepad with MOSCOW. KREMLIN. embossed at the top in green, and conversed with a wry *I know your game* smirk on his face.

Anyone who spent time here would realize immediately that the locals wanted to be part of Russia, he said, but the Western press and governments twisted the facts to suit their own agendas. I agreed it was clear from speaking with people that a majority favoured union with Russia, though how much that was to do with the messaging they had received from their televisions was a separate issue. But what about the minority, people like Leonid, who had been arrested and had lost his job just for waving a Ukrainian flag? Was that really necessary?

Saveliev looked at me in disbelief.

'I don't know anything of the example you're talking about, but there is certainly no way they could have been arrested for waving Ukrainian flags,' he said. But that is exactly what they were arrested for, I protested. I had just been to the courtroom.

He eyed me with his sardonic glare and spoke to me with an angry edge: 'I'm sure you've seen this kind of thing many times. They probably agreed in advance to have cameras there, so they could organize a provocation, and then after that get the flags out. And what a great image, just what was ordered up by your editors. We all know how it works, don't we?'

IV

There was never much love for the Western press among Russian officials, but after events in Ukraine in 2014, anger and suspicion had reached Cold War levels, and Saveliev's anger was a refrain I had heard many times. In Moscow, I went to see Igor Nikolaichuk, a professor whose work involved ranking different countries by the 'level of Russophobia' in their media outlets. He had recently authored a 230-page report, entitled 'The foreign media and Russia's security'. It was filled with colourful graphs and pie charts, maps, and statistical equations. Austria had come out in first place, while the UK finished fifth in the anti-Russian stakes.

We met in a conference room at his institute, a big complex in North Moscow guarded by interior ministry troops. The institute used to be a top-secret department of Russia's SVR foreign intelligence service, but now functioned as a government-sponsored think tank. Nikolaichuk was eager to explain the methodology behind his studies: first of all, every single day of the year, all articles about Russia from the global press were collated and individually logged. Their tone was analysed and labelled as either positive, negative, or neutral. So far, his team had analysed more than 350,000 articles in total, he said. They then catalogued the results by country and looked at the macro data. This meant differences between, say, *The Guardian* and *The Daily Mail* became less important, and what came into focus was 'a picture of the state orders for forming opinion among the British audience'. I asked him what he meant by 'state orders', and he gave me a conspiratorial look. It was quite clear, he said, that there is a coordinated information policy at state level in every country. 'There has to be a way to form society's opinions. We do it here too. You call it propaganda, but it's actually called "special informational-strategic operations for forming mass opinions."'

He anticipated what he believed would be my next, naïve, question: 'What about freedom of the press, freedom of speech, journalistic ethics, and so on? Let's agree immediately that I won't discuss these issues because I don't think they exist. For me, what exists are the national strategic interests of a country and the resulting vector of its press, which forms opinions towards Russia.'

I asked how he thought these government 'orders' were carried out. Was I meant to receive daily briefings from MI6, or did I simply intuitively know how to please my masters, I wondered? Nikolaichuk said it was hard to say, because management of the media is 'one of the most closed areas of political life in any country'. When it came to internal politics, there could be honest debate, he believed, but on foreign policy matters, there was an 'elite consensus' and a strict line had to be taken by all media. In the case of reporting on Russia, the line was that 'Putin is the devil himself and Russia is the evil Empire'.

We spoke for another hour, mainly discussing Nikolaichuk's bizarre views about Angela Merkel's plan for a Fourth Reich, and the existence of a global shadow government that was attempting to break Russia into little pieces. I had a headache and made my excuses to leave. He thanked me profusely for coming to see him and insisted on writing a warm inscription to me on the inside front cover of his report—the same report that stated that my job was to blacken Russia on the orders of my political masters.

The discussion had been frustrating but it explained a lot. Nikolaichuk was by no means a key decision maker, but his reports were distributed around various ministries, and somewhere along the line, parts of them would probably appear in the red intelligence folders placed on Putin's desk.

The belief that all journalists were simply following orders was widespread in Russia, where the very idea that objective media coverage was theoretically possible was scoffed at even by well-read intellectuals. Given Putin's view that the Obama administration was working to overthrow him, it followed that the Western media must be working towards the same goal. Journalists like me were engaged as part of a sinister project to sabotage Putin's work to return Russia to the position of a respected first-tier nation. And if the negative media coverage of Russia was simply the result of naked national interests at work, the logical response was for Russia to fight back with media outlets that reflected its own national interests. Thus, working for Russian state television was 'no worse' than working for any other news outlet. Indeed, perhaps it was better: the United States and its various puppet states had dozens of channels telling their billion-dollar lies, while the plucky underdogs in Moscow were fighting the Kremlin's corner alone.

Speaking to hundreds of journalism students at a youth camp in summer 2015, the state television anchor Ernest Mackevicius told them he believed the definition of journalism had undergone a change during the events of 2014. 'You understand that for the past year and a half, we work as part of the government; we are basically soldiers. Because information today has become a very serious and effective weapon.'[1] Not to engage in its own media warfare would simply be a dereliction of duty on Moscow's part, he believed.

The main element of the Russian entry into what it saw as the global 'information war' was Russia Today, the Kremlin's English-language television station. The channel, launched in 2005, quickly expanded from its initial mission to show Russia in a more favourable light to a more ambitious goal: to show how broken the West was. Sometimes, the news stories from Europe and the United States were comically crass propaganda, while other times they were perfectly valid. They just happened to come from a Kremlin-funded channel that avoided covering similar stories in Russia. The channel's slogan, 'Question more', was curiously inapplicable to stories about its home country.

In 2013, I was among a group of foreign correspondents invited by RT to tour their newly opened Moscow studios and observe an interview with Putin to mark the occasion. We were herded into a corner of the studio where Putin and half a dozen RT correspondents were seated round a table, and ordered not to make a sound, let alone try to ask a question. The day felt like a way for the channel to laud its access and its finances over the Western media. In an age when media organizations across the world were closing bureaus, laying off correspondents and making cuts, RT was expanding furiously. In opening remarks, Putin told RT's editor-in-chief Margarita Simonyan that the goal behind setting up Russia Today had been 'to break the Anglo-Saxon monopoly on global information streams'. The mission had been completed successfully, Putin added.

The ingratiating, softball enquiries from the RT journalists around the table, during the subsequent interview, made a mockery of the 'Question more' slogan, but Putin was right about the success of the mission. In early 2017, US intelligence agencies reported that RT had been part of a multifaceted Russian operation to influence the US election in favour of Donald Trump. Quite how effective RT had really been at changing the opinions of Americans was a matter of some debate, but the very fact that such high-level discussions were taking place about the channel's influence was a win for Putin: this sort of meddling was exactly what he believed the West was doing in Russia, and exactly the sort of thing he believed a first-tier nation should be doing if it was to keep up with the Americans.

While sowing mischief abroad, the channel remained timid on domestic stories. An RT correspondent I had known for some years admitted to me, over drinks in the bar of our Simferopol hotel during the Crimea annexation, that he was unable to mention the obvious Russian military operation in the region on air. At the same time, the channel's anchors mocked Western correspondents for suggesting that Russian soldiers were active in Crimea.

A year after the annexation, a domestic Russian television channel made a major 'documentary' about the 'return' of Crimea to Russia. It was a thoroughly fictionalized account, involving dramatic reconstructions of events that had never happened, and leaving out most of the behind-the-scenes manipulation. The offers of cash to the Crimean Tatars or the threatening text messages sent to the families of Ukrainian soldiers would not make for good television. Instead, the Russian Army was portrayed as intervening heroically to save the helpless residents of the peninsula from massacre. It was in an interview aired as part of the documentary that Putin admitted for the first time that he had ordered the seizure of Crimea almost immediately after Yanukovych had fled, blowing away the previous Russian narrative that events in Crimea were a spontaneous uprising to which Russia had merely responded. But everyone had known that already: there were wink-nudge T-shirts on sale across Russia featuring Putin's face and various Crimea-linked slogans. A monument to the 'little green men' was constructed in Crimea. The lie was something to revel in; it was a celebration of the fact that Russia had got one over the West.

RT, of course, offered no apologies about its own failure to report on the presence of Russian troops and the mocking of Western media who did so. There was no inquest about the false reporting, no apology to viewers, and no undertaking to really 'question more' next time around. I later saw photographs from a Kremlin reception, in which the RT correspondent who had said he could not talk about the troops received a medal for his Crimea coverage.

'*Krym nash!*—('Crimea is ours') became the slogan of the year, yelled triumphantly by those who had a reason to be proud for the first time in a long time, and muttered with bitter irony by the minority of Putin's opponents, who were horrified at what had happened to Russia's standing in the world.

Andrei Kondrashov, the man who made the pseudo-documentary, said he had never been more proud of a programme in all the decades he had worked as a journalist. The events documented were momentous ones, he said, at an event hosted at a state news agency to mark its release: 'Crimea's reunion with Russia is the second most important event in Russian history, after victory in the Second World War.'

PART THREE

The Past Becomes the Present

10

Donbass: the spiral

I

In 2012, Alexander Khodakovsky was deputy head of the Donetsk region's Alfa team, an elite special forces unit inside Ukraine's SBU security services. Back then, I spent two weeks in Donetsk during the Euro 2012 football tournament, and watched England beat Ukraine in the city's impressive Donbass Arena. More than fifty thousand fans dressed in blue and yellow cheered on the home team, shaking the stadium with repeated chants of U-KRA-I-NA, and were despondent when Ukraine lost one–nil, after the referee incorrectly ruled out a perfectly legitimate goal for the hosts.

At the time, Khodakovsky was in charge of organizing security for the games in the city, positioning his sniper teams at key points across Donetsk and drawing up anti-terrorism plans with other regional security bosses. A lot changed for him in the two years that followed. After the Maidan revolution and the annexation of Crimea, separatist rumblings began in eastern Ukraine, centring on Donetsk. A motley group of locals comprising political consultants, hooligans, and a man who dressed up as Santa Claus for children's parties, declared the region independent from Ukraine. Khodakovsky was one of most serious local figures to join the rebel cause. The ultimate hope was for the region to be gobbled up by Russia, in the same way Crimea had been.

The very idea of a 'Donetsk People's Republic' sounded comical initially, but it soon stopped being funny as the region spiralled towards war. It was hard to believe that this was the same city where two years previously, the Ukrainian footballers had been greeted by a sea of yellow and blue. Now, just walking down the street wearing the colours of Ukraine could have you assaulted, or worse, as the atmosphere turned febrile.

Khodakovsky saw action on the front lines of the conflict, fighting against the armed forces of the state he had spent his whole adult life serving. His official title now was Head of the Security Council of the Donetsk People's Republic, and he was considered to be the number-two figure in the separatist authorities. His office was on the top floor of the former coal ministry, a Stalinist behemoth on Donetsk's Lenin Square. The long corridors had high ceilings and polished wooden floors; the offices were accessed through double doors painted white and embossed with octagons. It was one of the grandest buildings in Donetsk, a reflection of how important coal had been to the city during the Soviet period. In the top-floor stairwell, a gruff contingent of heavily armed men radioed through my arrival, and I was eventually ushered into a room where his secretary sat at a desk, a Salvador Dalí print on the wall behind her. Through another set of doors was Khodakovsky's office, adorned with Orthodox religious icons. Of medium but muscular stature, balding, and with something between stubble and a beard, he was dressed in a black polo shirt and olive green trousers, a pistol at the hip.

He spoke quietly, with confident diction, able to hold a civilized conversation about his actions and thought processes, unlike almost everyone else in the separatist movement. It was odd, being in this wood-panelled room having philosophical discussions about the conflict, when on the front lines and on the streets, the level of discourse rarely moved beyond shouted propaganda points.

In our first meetings, I suspected that his unusual frankness was a calculated strategy to appear trustworthy while remaining elusive on the really key questions. Later, I began to think he simply wanted an outlet to talk things over.

'We don't fully understand what we want,' he said, pensively. 'We understand that we need to take care of the people and repel the threat from Kiev. But then, what we saw as the threat is a subjective question. Some people might say you've conjured up your own imaginary threat and now you're fighting it. But then that's more of an ideological question than a practical one.'

II

Khodakovsky was born in Donetsk in 1972, to a mother from Vinnitsa region in the heart of Ukraine. She spoke Ukrainian as a first language, but her family moved to the Russian-speaking Donbass region for work when she was a child. His father was born in Snezhnoe, an hour's drive from Donetsk, in 1951, six years after victory in the war, and with Donbass still in ruins from the years of conflict and Nazi occupation. Khodakovsky's father had mixed origins: Russian, German, and Polish. But nobody paid much attention to ethnicity in Donbass, which had a history of drawing chancers and wanderers to its factories and mines. Almost every town in Donbass originated as a mining settlement, and most were mere villages before the advent of the Soviet industrialization drive. That meant the heritage of the region was not particularly Russian, or Ukrainian. It was Soviet.

Khodakovsky remembered life growing up in the 1970s and 1980s in Donbass as a tough grind. His father worked on the railways and his mother had a factory job, but they rarely had enough money to buy clothes for their son. As a twelve-year-old, he said, he wore his mother's old coat, much to the amusement of his classmates. The zip had broken, so she sewed buttons on for him. Jeans, the new craze from the West, were an unthinkable luxury. Aged fifteen, irritated that he could not afford a bicycle, he constructed one at home by welding together a rusting discarded frame he found with two wheels of different sizes. It looked like a circus bike. 'But even though life was hard, there was a kind of point to life, which I guess was built as much on being contrary as on any achievements,' said Khodakovsky. 'We didn't care what people in the West thought of us, and we took a masochistic pleasure in not caring.' He quoted Vladimir Mayakovsky's ode to his Soviet passport to me: *From my baggy trouser leg, I pull out the precious object. Read it with envy: I'm a Soviet citizen!*

As so often with Soviet nostalgia, I suspected this sense of purpose might have been magnified and intensified in the memory over time, but dozens of people said the same thing to me. Donbass was a tough land of hard work and long shifts; its factories, mines, and mills helped power the Soviet planned economy, acting as the backbone of a country that would put the first man in space and lead the progressive forces of the world. The name of the local miner Alexei Stakhanov, even if his feats were at least partially fictionalized, became a byword for heroic overachievement in pursuit of the Communist cause. The factories themselves were grimy, awe-inspiring, and unfathomably huge. The Azovstal steel plant on the coast at Mariupol stretched out for miles and provided scene after scene of industrial pornography. On a tour of the plant, I felt like I was looking at footage from a 1930s Soviet movie about the joys of heavy industry, or perhaps the backdrop to a chase sequence in a Bond film. I imagined 007 sprinting along the high, rusting galleys before dispatching a villainous Soviet agent into a vat of molten iron or a raging furnace below.

Across the Donbass region, there were towns built up in the Soviet period around these giant, polluting behemoths. In Konstantinovka, about forty miles from Donetsk, the fumes from the glass, zinc, and brick factories had made it hard to breathe; people sometimes had to scrape a brown lining from their apartment windows that accumulated from the acid rain. But there was near full employment during the Soviet years, and there was a pride in the output of the town's industrial enterprises. The glass factory was famous for making the red ornamental stars that topped the Kremlin towers in Moscow, and the glass sarcophagus through which the embalmed corpse of Vladimir Lenin peered out at visitors to his mausoleum. Later, it made hundreds of thousands of glass bottles, to be filled with sickly Crimean champagne and dispatched to weddings and birthday parties across the Soviet Union, from Tallinn to Dushanbe. When the country collapsed, so did the integrated economy, of which the Donbass factories had been a key part.

III

After finishing school, Khodakovsky was sent to do military service. It was 1990, and he was dispatched to a paratrooper unit based in Kostroma, not far from Moscow. In August of the next year, the men were told they were leaving on an unexpected trip to the capital. None of them knew what the mission was, though they assumed they were preparing for a parade of some sort; the regiment had always been one of those to take pride of place at parades. When they arrived to Tushino, a base outside Moscow, the commander addressed the men. If anyone present was not willing to carry out any potential order, he should take two steps forward.

'Nobody moved a muscle, though I think I wasn't the only one to have shivers run down my spine. It's one thing to have the usual army difficulties: not to get enough food or sleep, or get cold. But it's quite another when you're being sent off on military tasks for which you're utterly unprepared.'

The men would be required to take part in the storming of the White House, the seat of government in Moscow, where Boris Yeltsin was holed up in defiance of a coup of old hardliners who were determined not to allow the collapse of the Soviet Union. But two days later, Khodakovsky's unit was sent back to Kostroma. There would be no storm. The coup had failed, and with that the fate of the Soviet Union was all but sealed. Looking back on it with his current level of military expertise, he realized it would have been a bloodbath had they gone through with the storm. It was only later he grasped the momentous nature of those days. Hardly anyone had wanted the Soviet Union to collapse, he said, but its citizens were so passive that nobody fought to keep it alive, and it was felled 'like a big organism infected with a tiny virus'. There were no antibodies.

For Khodakovsky, the collapse of the Soviet Union was an original sin to which he kept returning in our discussions. 'I miss the Soviet period, in a moral and ideological sense. I am not saying I liked the totalitarian system. But the human and social relations. Everything was more ascetic and more human. Market relations just push people away from each other. There was something different in people before, something different in their spirits. We feel that we have lost something, and we want to get it back.'

Khodakovsky had dreamed of working for the KGB or the Soviet border guards, and had applied to the border guard academy in Alma-Ata, capital of the Kazakh SSR. But then the Soviet Union came tumbling down, and the Alma-Ata academy was no longer an option. So he returned to Donbass, now located in the newly independent nation of Ukraine.

If the late Soviet period had been hard going for ordinary workers in Donbass, the 1990s were much, much worse. Khodakovsky remembered a miserable diet, with goods scarce and little money to buy what was available. Hyperinflation meant that within a couple of weeks the meagre salaries people were paid became even more worthless. As a luxury, he could occasionally afford a brand of cheap Polish sausage made of offal and ground-up bones, that when fried would dissolve into a gelatinous mess. In the early 1990s, he and friends would travel around the region's collective farms, collecting half-rotten apples on the ground that had not been harvested. They turned them into juice: a rare source of vitamins.

While the majority of the population lived in genuine poverty, a tiny minority managed to use foresight, guile, and heavy weaponry to emerge from the period with riches. Across the whole of the former Soviet lands, there was a messy scramble for resources wherever there was something to steal. In those places where the potential rewards were particularly big, the violence was worse: the heavy industry of the Urals, the Pacific import channels in Vladivostok, and the factories of Donbass. There were bloody feuds and contract killings across newly independent Ukraine, but in Donetsk it was particularly bad. People came to business meetings with machine guns in the 1990s; there were shoot-outs in the streets with grenade launchers. A local journalist told me he remembered sitting in his Donetsk newsroom in 1994 when a police snap came over the wire about an assassination attempt in the centre of the city. A trailer truck with four people standing on the back had driven past the house of a man named Rinat Akhmetov and fired grenade launchers at the property. That was the first time anyone had heard of Akhmetov, who survived the assassination attempt. A year later, the city's most notorious mafia boss was less lucky. Akhat Bragin, a former butcher known as Alik the Greek, had risen to become the president of Shakhtar Donetsk football club and the owner of many businesses. He was assassinated in a bomb explosion at the Shakhtar stadium in 1995.

By the end of the 1990s, Akhmetov had become the city's most successful businessman. He liked to take evening strolls down Donetsk's central street, the journalist recalled, while two paces behind him, an aide would walk with a briefcase and security guards kept up a perimeter. The briefcase, apparently, was to block radio signals and prevent remote-controlled explosive devices from being detonated.

Over time, Akhmetov hoovered up many of the biggest factories and enterprises in the region, and became the richest and most powerful man in Donbass. He joined forces with Viktor Yanukovych, the future president, who had been a petty criminal in the 1970s, but rose to become king of the local political scene. As a double team, Yanukovych and Akhmetov were unstoppable, but it was still a dangerous time, as many businessmen met violent ends. In 2000, there were threats on Yanukovych's life and he went into hiding for three weeks in western Ukraine. Khodakovsky, by then a high-ranking security officer, was assigned as his personal bodyguard. 'It was just the two of us, and we chatted for hours each day. He didn't make a great impression on me. Everything for him was about power, money. He was extremely intellectually limited, though he had a slippery talent for ingratiating himself with the country's leadership.'

By the turn of the century, Akhmetov had successfully made the transition from a shadowy semi-gangster to a modern businessman. Like most oligarchs in Ukraine and Russia, he almost never gave interviews, relying on his smooth spokesman, a friendly but tight-lipped Scot named Jock Mendoza-Wilson, to deny anything you might throw at him. Akhmetov hired Western consultants to improve his corporate governance, and enjoyed welcoming Western diplomats into his box at the Shakhtar stadium, where he held forth with lengthy comparisons between Ukrainian politics and football tactics.

In 2011, Akhmetov paid £136,400,000 for two apartments in the One Hyde Park development in London and had them knocked into one, making it the most expensive property ever purchased in a city famous for the obscenely expensive abodes of the international oligarch class. A worker I spoke to at one of Akhmetov's plants in Yenakievo, who was paid around £100 per month, would have had to work for 113,000 years to earn enough money to buy the apartment. The work was so dangerous, and the pollution so great, that he would be lucky to last twenty. I had a hacking cough after spending an hour touring the plant, and a streaming nose for three days afterwards, so acrid was the air inside. Still, Akhmetov was considered a model boss in the Donbass region, financing the modernization of some of his plants and offering regular paychecks, however small they might be. Other bosses were much worse.

Akhmetov paid for the regeneration of the centre of Donetsk, transforming it from a polluted metropolis, with slag heaps piled up in its very suburbs, to a modern city with pedestrianized boulevards lined with trees and flower beds, and a world-class stadium for his beloved Shakhtar. The football club was given lavish funding to bring a contingent of talented Brazilians to Donbass, and became the strongest football team in Ukraine.

But outside the very centre of Donetsk, little of this beautification was visible. When my overnight train from Kiev pulled into Konstantinovka in the spring of 2014, the first thing I saw was GLORY TO THE COMMUNIST PARTY OF THE SOVIET UNION, announced in metre-high block letters daubed on the side of an apartment block adjacent to the station building. Little else in the sightline suggested glory of any kind. Nothing looked taken care of, and everything was either grey or a wild, out-of-control green. Women wheeled pushchairs past the half-ruined apartment buildings, along triffid-like grass verges unmown for years. Such dereliction was one thing in Magadan, isolated at the end of the world, but here in the heart of Europe it felt even more depressing.

Across the Donbass region, the landscape was dotted with the decaying shells of mining and heavy industry, built to service the integrated economy of a country that no longer existed. There were slag heap pyramids the height of apartment blocks, cooling towers that had not belched out their fumes for two decades, and factory carcasses with the windows blown out, abandoned like ruined temples to a forgotten God.

In winter, driving through Donbass was particularly depressing, a monotonous vista of greys and browns: naked trees and fields of withered brown sunflower stalks. Muddy water splashed up as the car dipped into potholes in the road, and buses drove past, the grimy faces of miners just about visible through the mud-caked windows. When it got really cold, locals had to hobble along pavements like penguins, trying not slip on the thick layer of ice that covered the asphalt.

In Konstantinovka, a splash of colour was provided by a vast, once-spectacular mosaic, the tiles of which covered the whole of one side of a five-story apartment block. It depicted rockets and spacecraft, and bore the legend GLORY TO THE CONQUERORS OF SPACE. Over the years, many of the tiles had fallen off, and the mosaic now looked like an almost-completed jigsaw puzzle. Underneath was an advertisement for a pawn shop: WE BUY GOLD. The contrast between then and now could hardly have been starker.

All over Konstantinovka, and indeed the whole Donbass region, cheaply printed flyers glued to lampposts solicited female hair. On various given days, women with hair longer than thirty centimetres were invited to come to a particular salon to have it all chopped off and sold, to traders who would pack it up in suitcases and take it away to sell as hair extensions in other parts of the world. It was one of the most depressingly personal things a woman could feel the need to sell; the very presence of the adverts seemed an affront to dignity.

Donbass was not the only part of Ukraine where people had suffered from the collapse of the Soviet Union. But while post-Soviet life was equally tough across the country, in the western part there had never been much of a belief in the Soviet order. There was Ukrainian nationalism and a sense of Ukrainian identity to fall back on when the Soviet Union collapsed. In Donbass, it was different. Most people considered themselves to be Ukrainians, but did not feel the new Ukrainian state offered them much.

Khodakovsky's Ukrainian special forces unit grew out of a Soviet unit: the officers had simply changed their uniforms in 1991. Most of them did not approve of Ukraine leaving the Soviet Union, but there was nothing they could do about it, Khodakovsky told me. 'We didn't quite understand our new motherland, and we didn't know how we should feel about it. We couldn't build our patriotism on Ukrainian nationalism; this was alien to us, we were internationalists. We didn't agree with the big decision to end the Soviet Union, but because we couldn't influence it, we just built our own world.'

The unit was a close-knit group of officers, and the men threw themselves into their work. There were specialists in different disciplines: paratroopers, underwater divers, hostage rescue experts. Khodakovsky directed his men in different practice scenarios: scaling buildings with mountaineering equipment, freeing hostages from an aeroplane, organizing sniper cover for major events.

Khodakovsky never thought about taking Russian citizenship. Donbass was his homeland, and Donbass was part of Ukraine. But he struggled to feel patriotism for the new country. The leadership of the SBU, the Ukrainian security service that Khodakovsky's unit was part of, was grotesquely corrupt. Privately, the men called their employer 'SBU Ltd.' Khodakovsky insisted to me that his unit was completely removed from the corrupt schemes that permeated all Ukrainian ministries and agencies, though I could not be sure he was telling the whole truth. Certainly, his revulsion for the corruption of the top ranks was genuine.

He kept returning to the quest for a more overarching sense of purpose during those years. 'I think the education of a real officer in a unit like mine was impossible without some kind of ideological basis. As an officer you have to understand that your service can end up with you having to sacrifice yourself, and you have to know what you would be sacrificing yourself for; not just for money, surely. A man should have higher motivations inside himself than just money. So we were always looking for ideas that would work for us.'

IV

In 2004, when crowds massed in Kiev for the Orange Revolution, Khodakovsky was called to the capital along with many of the other regional special forces leaders, in case violence broke out. He saw that those protesting were genuine and sincere, not the paid-for shills of Western intelligence agencies that the Kremlin claimed they were. Even though he was wary of the western Ukrainians, he respected their protest. But in Donetsk, politics remained different, more inert. Akhmetov and the regional elite directed the political scene; they told people what to think, where to demonstrate, how to vote. The Donbass oligarchs were used to turning the protest volume up and down in the region with the precision of a conductor bringing in different parts of an orchestra: here a media campaign, there a protest movement. The region's workers were 'mobilized' to vote for Yanukovych in 2010, ensuring the Donbass candidate got elected to the national post at last.

When Maidan began in late 2013, Yanukovych again turned to his Donbass support base. One day during the height of the protests, thousands of people were bussed from Donetsk to Kiev, to hold their own rally on a square just down the road from the protesters and show that the crowds on Maidan did not represent the whole of the country. It was a sorry sight: groups of middle-aged women standing around with little enthusiasm, holding flags and placards they had obviously been given and told to wave. They had travelled hours by bus to be there and it was quite clear they would have much rather stayed at home. Groups of youths from the east were handed tea and biscuits at an encampment up the hill from Maidan. They hung around, bored and shivering, until they were allowed to get back on their buses and make the long journey home.

I watched a Russian television cameraman marshal a group of women with flags into place behind his correspondent, who then delivered his piece to camera: 'Today, Kiev is again protesting, but this time it is in support of Viktor Yanukovych'. The cameraman gestured at the women to look more engaged. It was a pathetic parody of the genuine revolutionary enthusiasm among the Maidan crowd, and I giggled at the audacity of it.

In retrospect, it was short-sighted to dismiss these people as mere paid shills. It was testament to just what a useless, unsympathetic crook Yanukovych was that even his traditional supporters from his own heartland could not get enthusiastic about backing him. But just because they were not excited about Yanukovych did not mean they were ready to accept the imminent triumph of Maidan.

When the situation in Kiev became critical in early 2014, a group of twenty Donetsk officers, with Khodakovsky in charge, was sent to the capital. Khodakovsky despised Yanukovych, but also had little time for the protesters. 'Nobody who works in law enforcement wants to see public unrest,' he said, matter-of-factly.

He and his men were based in a room at the SBU headquarters on Volodymyrska Street in central Kiev, and he claimed they mainly stayed indoors, doing planning work. The only time they were sent on operation was on 18 February to help clear the Trade Unions House, the protest headquarters on one side of Maidan that burned to the ground that night. A few days later came the endgame of the protests and the mass shootings that killed nearly a hundred protesters. Investigations have not proved conclusively who started the shooting, though it seems clear that government troops were responsible for much of the carnage. Khodakovsky insisted that the initial sniper fire had not come from government troops, and blamed a shadowy third force supposedly at play. 'We were getting chaotic radio messages saying there were snipers shooting at both sides, and the sniper department from Crimea went to look for them. My team was sent to guard the presidential administration.'

The presidential administration was already deserted and the protesters were in control of the city, so Khodakovsky and his men returned swiftly to the SBU headquarters. The Crimean Alfa group had already left, and his Donetsk men were the last ones out of the building, from an initial Alfa contingent of around 240 people. As they left in the early hours of 23 February, SBU functionaries were burning sensitive documents, aware that in a matter of hours, the protesters would be inside. Twenty-three years after his paratrooper unit was told to stand down as the 1991 coup failed, Khodakovsky again watched powerless as the government he served dissolved before his eyes. He and his men boarded a bus and slipped out of Kiev, as the Maidan crowds marched jubilantly through the city.

In Donetsk, he had conversations with friends, associates, and ordinary people, to gauge the mood. Close associates of Yanukovych got out of town as quickly as possible, taking as much of their ill-gotten wealth with them as they could manage. 'It was clear that nobody from the local elite who would have been able to organize things was ready to do so,' said Khodakovsky. 'Everyone was terrified, waiting, fleeing. In the end, it was down to people like me, who were hardly in the first place on the social hierarchy, to take responsibility.'

At that time, Khodakovsky claimed, his only thoughts were to prevent the groups of radicals he had seen in Kiev from coming to Donbass. He imagined a government in which every ministry had a Right Sector member or other radical Ukrainian nationalist in charge. He knew how much anger there was in Kiev towards Donetsk, as the source of gangster politicians like Yanukovych, and wondered what Kiev's revenge would look like. He and others set up a number of checkpoints around the city, and launched a group he called the Patriotic Forces of Donbass, which would eventually grow into the Vostok Battalion of four thousand men. Khodakovsky would become the commander-in-chief.

A number of well-placed people told me that Akhmetov, for so long the King of Donbass, had initially helped fan the flames of protest, something the oligarch denied. But it made sense: as a known associate of Yanukovych, things could get ugly for Akhmetov with the new authorities. Having a manipulable separatist movement under his control, in the same way that he had always directed political activity in the region, would be an excellent bargaining chip with Kiev when it came to ensuring his financial and physical survival in the post-Maidan order.

Khodakovsky met with Akhmetov during the early stages of the revolt. 'He was pretty calm, he knew he had these huge interests and that everyone would have to bargain with him,' Khodakovsky recalled, with a chuckle. 'But it soon became clear to him that the tradition was broken, and we didn't want to negotiate. He was used to being able to manipulate things from the sidelines: he had a Soviet approach to politics. He thought the people were apolitical and the height of their political ambition was to sit with a bottle of vodka and criticize the leadership. But it turned out that both the form and the content of this new protest movement was different to what anyone had seen before. Suddenly he couldn't manage these crowds; he couldn't tell people to protest and then twenty minutes later order them home.'

Now, people were demonstrating sincerely. The atmosphere was more reminiscent of Kiev's Maidan, not the usual inert Donetsk paid-for protests, said Khodakovsky.[1]

v

In the early post-Maidan weeks, the emboldened separatist movement seized the local administration headquarters, and Donetsk was convulsed with twin sets of demonstrations: angry, pro-Russia marches and defiant pro-Ukraine meets, which also drew several thousand people. The town was split, largely along class lines. In general, the middle class, the university educated, and those who felt they had made something of their lives since the Soviet collapse, were horrified by the rebel movement.

Even if they did not subscribe to western Ukrainian nationalism, they thought of it as a better option than joining the 'Russian world' offered by the separatists, and realized that the Maidan's bark was worse than its bite. It was no coincidence that it was Donbass where the insurgency really took off, while similar projects, needled by the Kremlin, in student-heavy Kharkiv and intellectual Odessa found some support but not enough to succeed. Crudely put, it was a battle between those who had eventually emerged from the mess caused by 1991 with some success, and those who had not. In Donetsk, the latter group was able to form a critical mass.

Enrique Menendez was one of the organizers of Donetsk's pro-Ukraine marches (he had grown up locally; the exotic name was because his grandfather had been a Spanish Communist who fled to the Soviet Union after the Spanish Civil War). With a cherubic face, a shock of blondish hair and lots of ideas, Menendez ran a small marketing firm, and was proud of the nascent Donetsk middle class. The Donetsk team of programmers had won the 2010 Microsoft imaging cup for Ukraine, he reminded me every single time we met; his own company had been approved as a Google advertising affiliate.

Menendez had known Pavel Gubarev, one of the main organizers of the pro-Russia marches, for years. Gubarev had been declared 'people's governor' of Donetsk in the early days of the uprising. Menendez watched Gubarev's pro-Russia marches and saw angry working-class people, with hate and resentment etched into their faces. Menendez looked on in horror; he called Gubarev to ask what the hell was going on. 'I was naïve. I said to him, "Come on Pasha, what are you doing? Look at these people, they don't represent the intellectuals, the middle class, this isn't all of Donetsk!" He laughed, and he said to me: "What, your office plankton, Enrique? They are nothing. We've multiplied them by a factor of zero."'

Later, Menendez thought about Gubarev's strange expression: *we've multiplied them by a factor of zero*. In fact, he realized, for years the small wealthy class of Donetsk had been multiplying the majority of the population by a factor of zero: reducing their lives and opinions to nothing. They had been creaming off financial profits while accepting a tightly controlled political field, where ordinary people had no say in anything and Akhmetov was king. Nobody had paid any attention to the masses or tried to address their concerns. It was a classic process of social disenfranchisement that would come as a shock to people in other more established democracies in the years after. The Brexit referendum, and Trump's electoral victory, led societal elites to wonder whether they, too, had failed to pay attention to whole swathes of the population for far too long.

During March and April, Khodakovsky and his men travelled around the city in minibuses. They wore civilian clothing and hid weapons at secret locations. On 12 April, a suspiciously well-drilled group of men led by a former Russian FSB officer, Igor Strelkov, appeared in the town of Slavyansk, north of Donetsk. They seized buildings and announced a takeover of the town. It looked like the start of what the Kremlin had done in Crimea all over again. Leaked documents later made it clear that the Russians were indeed stirring up trouble, and providing support to those with separatist inclinations from the very beginning in Donetsk and the region.

But Khodakovsky insisted that the initial impulse was very much a local one. He was tired of seeing the pathetic, paid-for protests of miners and other workers that were put on in support of Yanukovych, damp squibs that made it look like the people of Donbass were passive. He wanted to show that Donbass had a real voice, and real concerns. "Of course, afterwards, people from Russia made contact with us. Of course we were used, we became puppets. But in the beginning, it was a genuine and natural thing.'

Khodakovsky's group became more and more emboldened, taking over government buildings and raiding Ukrainian Army bases. In some places, bases were seized at gunpoint; in others, the soldiers simply ran away. Those in charge were arrested; commanders lower down the chain did not know how to react, or how loyal their men would be to the state of Ukraine. Khodakovsky did a deal with some of the Ukrainian commanders, allowing the soldiers to leave with their personal firearms but leaving the main weaponry caches behind, adding to police and other weapons stockpiles the rebels already controlled.

One afternoon in early May 2014, I saw people gathering outside the seized local administration building in central Donetsk. They were just chatting at first, but word came that some Ukrainian marines were holed up in a hostel on the other side of town. The group set off, gathering new recruits as it weaved through central Donetsk, and gradually turned into something of a mob. The people became angrier and angrier as we marched. En route, someone saw a building flying the Ukrainian flag; a man raced inside and soon appeared at a second-floor window. He leaned out, and ripped the flag off its pole, to cheers. About two hundred strong by now, we marched past a McDonald's, where a cheerful young couple were sitting at one of the tables on the outside terrace in the spring sunshine. Ignoring the political turmoil unfolding in the city, they were opening up Happy Meals for their two young children.

From the marching crowd, a stout middle-aged woman with a bowl cut, whom I'd seen earlier exchanging pleasantries with a friend, suddenly turned to the family with a face contorted into anger, and yelled at the top of her voice: 'You fucking scum, shovelling that American filth into your gobs! Fuck you!' The family looked back, too confused to be scared.

We kept going until we got to the marines' hostel. 'They're in there, the swine! Get them! Kill them! Burn them!'

Luckily, the marines had scarpered. The place was empty, and the crowd eventually dissipated, disappointed. I tried to strike up a conversation with two of the women from the crowd but they hissed abuse at me when they found out I was a Western journalist. I knew these women: they were the kindly, fussy middle-aged women who would insist on feeding you another bowl of soup to make sure you left their home fully sated, however short they were on cash to feed themselves. And here they were baying for blood. It was a depressing sign of how easy it was to whip up hatred and fury.

In those chaotic early days, checkpoints began to spring up at regular intervals along the roads out of Donetsk and other towns in the region. Passing them was always something of a lottery. There was a fat, jovial former lorry driver who wouldn't let me go before he'd recounted his journeys through Europe for a good half an hour, and a skinny teenage boy in an Adidas tracksuit who waved his gun in my face and demanded cigarettes. There were angry men, friendly men, curious men, scared men, scary men, and men who were clearly itching for the chance to use their newly acquired weaponry. Occasionally, there were also women, usually in their early twenties. At one checkpoint, a man in shades puffed on a huge cigar while forensically searching the interior of every passing vehicle; at another, a teenager with a face full of vengeance called my driver Andrei a faggot and demanded money from him. It was hard to square the thoughtful, erudite Khodakovsky, speaking plainly and openly about the rebellion and its inadequacies, with some of the swivel-eyed angry youths from his battalion I ran into on the streets, shouting abuse and boiling over with anger.

Travelling after dark was ill-advised; at a twilight checkpoint stop, the American journalist Simon Shuster was pulled out of his car without a word and pistol-whipped, blood streaming from the back of his head where he'd been hit. The assailant's comrades pulled him away before he could finish what he had started. The next day a separatist authority phoned Shuster to say the man who assaulted him had been apprehended, and invited him to attend the retribution session planned for that day. He declined, and flew home to get a brain scan. It was a wild time, with uncertainty and malice hanging in the air.

My skull remained intact at least partly thanks to Andrei, who had a marvellous checkpoint manner, offering up chatty pleasantries and a beaming grin to whoever was poking a suspicious nose through our windows or waving a weapon in our direction. The minute we were safely past, his bonhomie would immediately disappear.

'Fucking low-class scum,' he would spit, without fail, every time he'd finished the verbose, tension-defusing routine he had down to a tee, and we had sped off. 'You were nobody, and now you've got a gun and you think you're somebody? Utter scum. Filth. Debris of society!' He would mutter away for a couple of minutes before composing himself again to deal with the next round of armed men.

As the separatist movement in Donetsk began to take root, Kiev appointed Sergei Taruta, a local oligarch, to try to bring order to the region. For a while, before things got really nasty, there was a dual authority in the city. The separatist government operated from the seized local administration headquarters, while Taruta and his team were holed up on the top floor of the Victoria, a high-rise hotel he owned that was now eerily deserted. Taruta, an urbane Jewish businessman with a passing resemblance to Woody Allen and a wry sense of humour, did not seem like the right man to find a common language with the angry street protests. One evening, one of his advisers agreed to give me a briefing on the latest situation, and asked me to come by the Victoria at midnight. By the time I got there, the sharply dressed adviser was already nearing the end of a bottle of whisky in the deserted top-floor restaurant.

'We're fucked, everything's fucked,' he said, in slurred but proficient English. 'My girlfriend just called, told me to fuck someone, anyone, anything. But I don't want to. What do you think?'

'Mmm, difficult,' I said, unsure whether to keep my pen hovering above my notebook.

I tried to steer the conversation back to the political situation. 'What are your plans? Are there any attempts to hold talks with the Donetsk People's Republic guys?'

'Yes! They stole one of Taruta's cars, so I've got to go and talk to the bastards tomorrow. Scary! Wish me luck.'

He poured another whisky.

'OK, and what about other issues? Are you going to talk to them about anything other than the car?'

'Fuck! Of course! Of course it's not only the car! They stole a load of fucking paintings as well!'

There were other, more serious, attempts at negotiations that were rebuffed by the separatists, who were sure of Russian support and did not want to speak to the Ukrainian authorities anyway. But as a first view of how the Ukrainians were attempting to resolve the situation, it hardly filled me with confidence. Taruta and his men, with their expensive whisky and designer T-shirts, seemed beamed in from a different planet to the people on the streets. They were the people who had done well out of the Soviet collapse. Those on the streets were the ones who had lost. It was not long before Taruta and his team fled Donetsk in fear of their lives. Most of Donetsk's middle class left too, terrified at what was happening to their home city.

II

War

I

On 8 May 2014, the day before Victory Day, I attended a modest banquet in the village of Ilyicha, about an hour outside Donetsk. The village, named after Lenin (his patronymic was Ilyich), was formerly a collective farm. Now it was run-down, sleepy and impoverished, but everyone always made an effort to put on a decent spread for Victory Day, even this year, with conflict looming over the region.

The village had only one surviving veteran, a wiry ninety-three-year-old man who looked pleased as punch to be basking in the limelight for the day, and half a dozen 'war children' in their seventies and eighties, who had lived through the Nazi occupation of Donbass. Two long tables were laid with delicacies that were luxurious by local standards—fat slices of sausage, cubes of bright-yellow cheese, and hunks of grilled chicken, to be washed down with brightly coloured fizzy drinks and, of course, generous shots of vodka. As well as the elderly, the cream of village society—several teachers, a doctor, and some local officials—were in attendance. The head of the village administration, a portly matriarch named Irina who greeted every arrival with a warm embrace, gushed how delighted she was that a foreign journalist had come to witness their humble celebration. It made a pleasant change from Donetsk, where the discovery of a foreign journalist tended to precipitate angry abuse about my putative anti-Russian lies. Irina was a benevolent whirlwind, and ushered me over to the heaving table with a smile. A few days later, she would organize the village's participation in the hastily arranged referendum on the creation of the Donetsk People's Republic.

Geopolitical concerns seemed a million miles away from the soporific, rural Ilyicha, but even here some of the villagers had signed up to the rebel cause. The Ilyicha resistance at this point was a ragtag group of local lads, who had received guns looted from the police headquarters of a nearby town and had set up their own checkpoint. Villagers complained that its location was inconvenient, as it disrupted movement from one side of Ilyicha to the other, so Irina had marched down the road and told them in her best *you very naughty boys* tone of voice that they should move it, which they promptly did. It all seemed a bit like a game.

As we were eating, another woman appeared, who introduced herself as the head of the local recruitment service for the Donetsk rebels. She had none of Irina's warmth, and hectored the room in a shrill voice: 'The fascists are coming! We fought them off in 1945 and we will fight them off again! Everyone sign up, and if you can't sign up then help support our heroic men! To victory!' We all chinked our vodka glasses.

I was sat next to seventy-eight-year-old Nadezhda, her sizeable frame now frail and stooped, her grey hair tucked underneath a bright turquoise shawl. She would have been about five years old when the war started. She was hardly able to walk and almost completely blind. I tried to help her with the food as she struggled with shaking hands. Suddenly, she grasped my wrist surprisingly tightly.

'Yura, is that you? Yura dear, have you come back?'

'No, I'm sorry. I'm a British journalist. I don't know where Yura is,' I told her awkwardly.

'Yura! But it is you! You were away for so long. And now you're back. Will there be another war?'

Our conversation was drowned out by the start of the musical part of the programme. I noticed a solitary teardrop cascade down the wrinkles on Nadezhda's face as the all-female choir sang an *a cappella* folk song. As the singing drew to a close I made to leave, offering my congratulations to all the elderly folk in earshot. But as I rose to get up from the table, Nadezhda again took hold of my arm.

'Will there be another war?' she enquired again.

'No, I don't think so,' I said.

'Are you sure? I am scared. On television it's war, war, war. Everyone is talking about war, and I am scared there will be another one. Let God stop it, please, nothing is worse than war.' She screwed her eyes up, trying her hardest to focus on me and work out who I was. She was shaking, scared, and confused.

'I'm sure. Everything is going to be just fine,' I promised, for want of anything better to say.

II

On the next day, Victory Day, it became clear to me that there really would be a war. Donetsk was a city on the brink. All the rhetoric around Victory Day I had watched build in Moscow over the previous years was coming home to roost. A parade meant to honour the war dead turned into a defiant show of military strength, and locals showered the 'defenders' of the would-be Donetsk People's Republic with flowers and affection in the central square. The men all had orange-and-black St George's ribbons tied to the ends of their Kalashnikovs.

A tragedy in Odessa the previous week proved one of the key moments in the spiral towards full-blown war. There still seemed a possibility that as much as half of Ukraine could split off and demand to join Russia, and while in Donetsk things were furthest advanced, skirmishes and fights were breaking out across a large swathe of the country under the banner of the orange-and-black victory ribbons. In Odessa, a group of pro-Russia thugs marched through the city, a pattern that had been recurring as trouble was stirred up across southern and eastern Ukraine. Having seen similar marches descend into violence elsewhere in the country, the Ukrainians in Odessa were prepared, and had a good number of football hooligans among their own number.

The pro-Russians, this time, had bitten off more than they could chew and were pursued through the town by the Ukrainians, with occasional fights on the way. They barricaded themselves inside the trade union building, but pro-Ukrainian protesters threw Molotov cocktails at the windows. A minority continued to do so even when it became apparent that the building was on fire and people inside were at serious risk of losing their lives.[1]

At least forty-two pro-Russians died in the building, a terrible tragedy by any measure. But in the spirit of drumming up support for the separatist cause, the deaths were smeared with a crude and inappropriate brush of historical comparison. Russian television called it a 'fascist massacre', and politicians in Moscow compared it to Nazi atrocities during the Second World War. Ukrainian authorities did not help matters, by appearing not to take the appalling loss of life seriously.[2] In Odessa, the awful event shocked everyone, and both sides pulled away from the brink. But to those already angry in Donetsk, it looked a confirmation of all the worst scare stories: if people did not organize the resistance, fascists would soon be arriving in Donbass to sow bloodshed here too. Outside the seized Donetsk administration building, now operating as rebel headquarters, people lit candles for the dead in Odessa, and sorrow quickly turned to anger and defiance.

Inside the building, the walls were plastered with photocopied pictures of Barack Obama and Ukrainian politicians, Hitler moustaches scrawled onto their faces in pen. A group of men draped in a huge St George's banner drove a car around the town blaring out war marches and waving a huge flag that had Stalin's face superimposed onto what appeared to be Rambo's body, and the slogan DEATH TO FASCISTS. Many people out on the streets were wearing the orange-and-black victory ribbons that were fast becoming the semi-official symbol of the Donetsk resistance.

The late-Soviet war cult had been particularly strong in Donbass, a region that had been decimated by the war. As a young child growing up in Donbass during the late Brezhnev era, Khodakovsky said his whole childhood revolved around memories of war and victory: 'All the most interesting films I watched were about the war; all the children's books I read were about the war.' He remembered being about fourteen, and finding a bundle of red fabric in the courtyard of a local factory with a group of friends. They cut it into the shape of a flag, pulled apart a spade to make a flagpole, and took turns to mount it on the balconies of their apartment block, pretending they were Soviet soldiers taking the Reichstag. His own childhood memories reinforced how powerful the war narrative could be. 'In the tsar's time people believed in the Church and the tsar. The Soviet period had its own clear ideological tenets. But in modern times, there is no consolidating ideology,'

Khodakovsky told me much later. 'But when you start talking about victory, all arguments end. It's a formula that works well, and I say this without irony or cynicism, but from the point of view of internal political tasks and consolidating society, it's an excellent device. After all, there's nothing else to use.'

In the Soviet and modern Russian war narratives, it was not just the victorious side that was painted with broad brushstrokes. The Nazis, too, appeared as a very generalized enemy; the specificity of their evil was rarely discussed. The official rhetoric about 'fascism' glossed over the leader cult, the militarism and the gas chambers, and stripped it bare to just one quality: the war against the Soviet Union. It was Hitler's attack on the Soviet Union that became the core essence of 'fascism' and the original sin of the ideology. The Holocaust was a side issue, a secondary crime of the Nazis after the invasion of the motherland. This made it easier to transpose the war narrative onto the present-day battle against enemies of Russia. It was not unusual, in eastern Ukraine, for someone to express furious hatred for 'fascists' and then in the same breath rant about the Jews or the gays as the root of all evil in the modern world.

As I soaked up the defiant celebratory mood in Donetsk, news came through that in Mariupol, the grimy port city to the south, violence had flared. I summoned Andrei and we sped down the highway, arriving to a scene of chaos. The police station was on fire and had been hit with heavy weaponry; outside its smouldering skeleton, a dead body lay on the street. Amid the chaos, a man passed walking his dog, and the animal strained at the leash to have a sniff of the corpse. It was a jarring moment, an interregnum between peaceful life and the full onset of war.

The streets were packed with furious locals baying for revenge. People shared frantic snippets of news and gossip with each other. The police had gone over to the side of the rebels, they said, which had prompted the Ukrainian Army to come in and launch an assault on the police station. When I spoke to policemen the next day, it seemed what had actually happened was that protesters had attempted to storm the police station. Barricaded inside on the top floor, the commander had radioed for the help of the army to free his men from the clutches of the baying mob.

Mariupol was a divided city, and the full truth was difficult to get at. The police force, like the rest of the population, was split between those who wanted to remain part of Ukraine and those who supported the Donetsk People's Republic. Rumours spread quickly among the angry crowds. After storming the police station, the Ukrainian Army retreated from the city in panic. An armoured personnel carrier broke down, and was abandoned. Nervy soldiers tried to fend off the angry, violent crowd. Shots were fired; people died.

It being a public holiday, people had started drinking early, and most sober residents had gone home quickly when the violence started. Wisps of smoke escaped from smouldering buildings, and dazed, drunken people stumbled through the streets. Someone had got the abandoned armoured personnel carrier working, and around a dozen young men were hanging off it as it careered around a corner and drove into view.

'This is the Donetsk People's Republic!' one of them yelled, deliriously. Later, they fired its cannon, hitting the corner of a residential building about twenty metres away, but thankfully causing no injury.

I found a woman coherent enough to answer my questions; she was angry with Kiev, and wanted Russia to intervene. 'Look at what they did to our city, on Victory Day of all days, the most sacred day there is.' Like most people, she had the orange-and-black St George's ribbon pinned to her breast. Despite the fact she was giving the 'right' answers, a group of angry women materialized, and on ascertaining that I was a foreigner began physically attacking the poor interviewee with their handbags in slapstick fashion.

'Why are you talking to this foreign scum? They're liars! He will twist everything against Russia! He's a propagandist!' The interviewee and I quickly went our separate ways.

That day in Sevastopol, Putin arrived in Crimea for the first time since the annexation, and gave a Victory Day speech melding the historic liberation of Crimea from the Nazis in 1944 with the recent events. 'We respect the way you have kept your love of the Fatherland through the years and generations,' he told the Crimean crowds.

Russia had wanted Crimea for the Black Sea Fleet at Sevastopol and the historic significance of the region. Its interests in Donbass were different: as it became clear that the whole of eastern Ukraine was not going to join Donbass in its uprising, Moscow had little use for an economically depressed region. Building a defendable border for hundreds of miles around Donbass would be a whole different challenge to seal-ing off Crimea at its narrow isthmus. Two days earlier, Putin had issued a surprise call to the separatists not to 'hurry' with their own referen-dum on independence.

But the historical rhetoric unleashed by Moscow had already created a heady, dangerous atmosphere. A combination of the war excitement, and the chance for a neglected region to gain what seemed on the basis of the Crimean example to be an easy ticket to higher pensions and prosperity, was a tempting offer for many in eastern Ukraine.

As the sun set in Mariupol, a tracksuited man in his early twenties, who was so intoxicated he could hardly stand, lurched towards me and shoved me in the chest, part aggressive gesture, part self-balancing act.

'Where you from?' he slurred menacingly.

'From Moscow,' I said, enunciating my words as Slavically as I could and banking, successfully, on the hope that he was too drunk to notice my light but obvious foreign accent.

'Well listen here, Muscovite,' he said, pushing me again. 'Tell your Putin to send the army in quick. He's a liar. He promised he'd help us, and now he's gone and slapped us across the forehead with his cock!'

He stumbled away from me and began wandering off, but turned while still in earshot to shout some last words.

'Onwards to Berlin! Death to fascists! Happy Victory Day!'

III

The violence in Odessa and Mariupol was a turning point, as the mem-ories and rhetoric of one war helped spark another. There were skir-mishes with newly formed Ukrainian volunteer battalions in the middle of May, and then at the end of the month came another point of no return, when the localized clashes morphed into a full-on war. Donetsk in May had remained a city with a dual power system; the airport con-tinued to function and was controlled by Ukrainian authorities. I flew out on a Turkish Airlines flight to Istanbul for a few days of rest after several weeks in Donetsk, and flew back into the city on 22 May, get-ting a Ukraine stamp in my passport. Four days later, Khodakovsky gave the order for a group of his men to seize the airport. The idea was to prevent the Ukrainians from landing planes of supplies or troops.

But for Kiev, the airport was a red line, and 120 of Khodakovsky's men were pinned down, subjected to intensive bombing raids for several hours. The airport, built brand new for Euro 2012, was destroyed, and a battle began for control of it that would last nearly a year.

As spring turned to summer, the situation at Donetsk Airport became the new norm. The rebels held major cities like Donetsk and Luhansk, while the Ukrainian Army dug into positions on the outskirts. The rebels shelled them from the city centre, then quickly wheeled away the artillery. The Ukrainians fired back, often wildly inaccurately, and caused inevitable civilian casualties. The anti-Ukraine mood among those who had remained in Donetsk hardened quickly.

Putin had backed himself into a corner. The initial help and support given to the rebel movement had prompted many locals to join the fight, but unlike in Crimea, the Ukrainian Army was willing to fight back. Now, there was a real war. Allowing Russia's proxies to be defeated militarily would be humiliating, but Putin was equally unwilling to order a full-on invasion of Ukraine. Incurring the wrath of the West over the Crimea annexation had been worth it, in order to prove Russia had its red lines, but he did not want either the irrevocable break with the West or the huge financial burden that a full-blown invasion of Ukraine proper would entail.

Instead, Russia funnelled weapons and men across the border. When the Ukrainians started using air power, the Russians also sent anti-aircraft missiles. But because of the need for plausible deniability, the men on whom they relied on the ground were proxies who were not fully controlled by the Kremlin. In July, a BUK surface-to-air missile was launched from a field not far from the city of Torez, at what those firing it almost certainly assumed was one of the Ukrainian jets patrolling the skies. The plane turned out to be a Malaysian Airlines Boeing 777, flying from Amsterdam to Kuala Lumpur, flight number MH17. The remains and possessions of the 298 people on board were strewn across the Donbass sunflower fields: here a severed arm, there a wash kit and a stack of holiday reading. Round the corner, the perfectly intact body of a young Malaysian boy landed outside a babushka's cottage. Over the next days, the sun-scorched human remains were sorted into colour-coded bags: black for whole bodies, green for parts. I watched as they were loaded onto a train at Torez station. The rescuers tied bandannas around their faces to stop themselves puking from the overwhelming stench. A few days later, in towns close to where the missile had been launched from, a few people quietly whispered to me that they had seen the BUK system drive past on that day. It was pretty obvious what had happened, and later there would be harder evidence.

The phone lines in the Kremlin rang with furious world leaders demanding to know what had happened, and Putin made a strange middle-of-the-night video address saying it was too early to apportion blame. But one of his court reporters ran a story, which he must have been ordered to write, that suggested the Russian president had launched an enquiry to find out who was responsible, and would disown the rebels if it turned out they had fired the missile.[3] In the end, the Kremlin took the cowardly way out, presumably when Putin was informed that the missile system had in fact come from Russia and thus he was ultimately responsible for the deaths. The Kremlin's media operations launched 'version' after implausible 'version' of how the Ukrainians *might* have shot down the plane, changing the story each time their latest disinformation drive was disproved. The downing of MH17 and the subsequent brazen lying was probably the Kremlin's lowest point in all my years covering Russia.

IV

For the most part, the visible leaders of the separatist movement were all either locals like Khodakovsky or irregular Russians, operating within a murky chain of command. There were Chechens, Cossacks, anarchists, nationalists, Communists, and radical Orthodox Christians, and they all had guns. It was a mess.

Igor Bezler, a wild-eyed and moustachioed former Russian officer, was perhaps the scariest commander of all. Even the other rebel leaders spoke about him in alarmed tones. He went by the nickname *Bes*—the Demon—and he had taken over the town of Gorlovka. In June 2014, he released a video shot in a basement. Two men were stood against a wall, hands tied behind their backs and eyes covered with blindfolds. Complaining that the Ukrainian side had not released a man of his from captivity, the Demon said he was executing two of the eight Ukrainian hostages he had in his possession. 'If my man is not released within the hour, another two will be shot, and so on, until all eight are dead. If the Ukrainians don't need their men, then I certainly don't. Ready; aim; fire!' Two men in balaclavas fired at the men standing by the wall, and their bodies crumpled to the ground.

The Demon did not, as a policy, give interviews, but one of the men fighting alongside him was an admirer of the writing of my long-time friend Marina Akhmedova, a Russian magazine journalist and novelist with a broad fan base, and invited her to come and interview his commander. She agreed to take me with her, and we made the drive from Donetsk to Gorlovka, where we were met at the checkpoint on the outskirts of town by Marina's admirer and driven to a local police base, which the Demon had made his makeshift headquarters.

A small fort had been constructed of sandbags and ammunition crates by the entrance, and we were led up some stairs to an antechamber where we were told to wait for the Demon to emerge. On the wall, there was a portrait of Vladimir Lenin and one of Soviet-era bard Vladimir Vysotsky, with the caption: 'A thief should sit in prison.' One of the fighters made us instant coffee while we waited; the walls shook gently with the sounds of explosions in the not-too-far distance. I went to the bathroom and found a copy of the Ukrainian constitution perched on top of the toilet roll holder; people had ripped out pages to wipe with. Periodically, fighters came dashing up the stairs with news for the boss. Before they entered his office, they had to leave their telephones and weapons on a table. One man wearing a Cossack fur hat deposited two pistols, a Kalashnikov, a foot-long dagger, and an iPhone 5 on the table before he was allowed into the Demon's inner sanctum. It was surreal to think that just a few months ago, this had been a sleepy post-industrial town where nothing much happened.

The door to the Demon's office opened and the man himself emerged, cigarette in hand and wearing a *telnyashka*, the striped Russian naval vest, underneath military fatigues. In an instant the fighters were on their feet, standing rigid and saluting. One meekly informed him that the two journalists had arrived.

'I'm busy. We will talk later. For now, show them the prisoners,' he snapped, striding down the stairs surrounded by heavily armed men.

We were led to a basement room that held six people. Mindful of the ethics of interviewing prisoners, and aware of the presence of one of the

Demon's men by the door, I told the hostages they did not have to say anything to me unless they wanted to, but I would be interested to hear their stories if they wanted to speak.

One of the men began to talk. His name was Vasil Budik and he was a local journalist, he said. He was of Georgian origin, from the Black Sea region of Abkhazia. When war broke out in 1992 between the Georgians and the Abkhaz, one of many bloody conflicts that accompanied the Soviet collapse, he fought for the Georgians. When they lost, he had to flee his homeland, and had been living in Gorlovka for two decades. He had been arrested because the Demon's men had found photographs of him with Right Sector paraphernalia on his telephone. I didn't know if there was any truth to the accusation that he was a Ukrainian radical, and it was hardly the right time or place to ask. He had been in the cellar for a number of months, he said, and had been one of those featured in the execution video. It had all been a setup; the bullets were blanks, and the stunt was an attempt to pressure Kiev into releasing separatist prisoners.

As we were talking, a fighter appeared. 'The bodies have arrived,' he said, and beckoned for us to come upstairs to the main courtyard. He motioned not only to me and Marina, but to the prisoner Budik as well, who obligingly trotted up the stairs, surrounded by guards. A blue transit van, serving as an impromptu hearse, reversed into the premises. In the back was the body of a rebel fighter who had died in combat. The Demon and the other fighters crowded round the open doors of the van to glance at the body and pay their respects. Budik was also emotional.

'I knew him well, since he was eight years old. My wife and I would bring in homeless kids or orphans and try to give them a decent upbringing. I taught him boxing, tried to give him a grounding in life. I helped him out a lot. He was a good lad.'

I remarked that it was an extraordinary testament to the mindless, fratricidal nature of the conflict that he was mourning the death of one of his captors. Budik chuckled. 'You think that's weird. They've got a high-ranking SBU official as a prisoner here, and one of his in-laws is guarding him,' he said.

The Demon turned on his heel and walked inside. A few minutes later, we were back in the room with the hostages and he materialized, announcing he was ready to talk. Marina's first question was to ask the Demon why he did not pity the men he was holding captive. His countenance changed immediately, and the tension among his men was palpable. Marina is a remarkably skilled interviewer, adept at pushing people right to the edge of their comfort zones and then walking them back. I had seen her work this magic trick on numerous interviewees before: bringing people to the very verge of walking out of the interview, before she somehow pulled the situation back from the brink and had the disoriented subject spew forth all kinds of fascinating detail they would never normally have revealed. It was an extraordinary journalistic talent, and in a decade of joint reporting trips, the Demon was the one time I ever saw her get it wrong.

'The only reason they are still here is because they are Ukrainian Army soldiers,' he said, gesturing at the room containing the hostages. 'Those who are fighting with the Ukrainian Army we keep as prisoners. Those who are fighting with volunteer battalions, we question them and then shoot them on the spot. Why should we show them any pity?'

'Because they are human beings too; they have families,' said Marina. His voice grew louder as he became more angry. 'You should see what they have done to my people. They chop off their heads and shit in the helmets! They are fascists! So why should we stand on ceremony with them? Questioning, execution, that's it. I will hang those fuckers from lampposts!'

He was shouting furiously, but stopped in his tracks when he noticed that Marina had her dictaphone switched on, and I was scribbling down his words in my notebook. He grabbed the recorder from her hands and ordered one of the fighters to destroy it. The man took the dictaphone and hurled it at the wall. It bounced off, unharmed, and was chased down the hall by the minion, who stamped on the offending piece of equipment. It proved surprisingly durable, forcing him to jump up and down on it repeatedly, like some strange cartoon sequence. The Demon himself plucked my notebook from my hands, and began to rip out the pages frantically, scattering the torn sheets of paper on the floor.

Protesting only made things worse. He barked commands at his subordinates: 'Burn their notebooks! Seize their electronics! Search everything for compromising material and destroy it! If you find anything suspicious, execute them as spies! Immediately!'

The Demon departed the room and left us in a stunned silence. Western journalists were not the most popular category of people in eastern Ukraine, and I had been threatened on numerous occasions throughout the summer, but it usually felt like a display of bravado rather than genuine danger. This was different. That it was no joke was clear from the fact the Demon's men all looked absolutely terrified at the turn of events. Fumbling in my pocket while a man rifled through my bag, I tried surreptitiously to wipe all the photographs on my phone, which dated back to Maidan and could have been incriminating. But ten minutes later the Demon came back, having had second thoughts.

'Get out! Get out of here now and never come back!'

Relieved at the surprise reprieve, we scurried out of the building and drove back to Donetsk.

Almost exactly a year later, I arranged to meet Budik, the prisoner from the basement, again. He had eventually been released in an exchange, and was now working for the Ukrainian defence ministry, helping facilitate further prisoner exchanges between the two sides. We met in Slavyansk, the first town to have been taken over by the separatists, but which the Ukrainian Army had won back reasonably quickly. Outwardly, the town was now resolutely Ukrainian: yellow-and-blue flags were everywhere, and Vladimir Lenin had been toppled from his perch. Many of those who had openly supported the separatists had been arrested; others had melted away into the background, cursing Kiev in their kitchens but staying quiet in public. A busker strummed his guitar in the late summer sunshine. Budik strutted over to the cafe where we had agreed to meet, in khaki trousers and a grey vest, a pistol swinging from his hip. He cut a very different figure to the man I had met in the basement a year before.

I asked if he remembered my visit, and he chuckled, as he lit a cigarette with a lighter in Ukrainian flag colours. 'You were unbelievably lucky to get out of there alive,' he said. 'I was sure you were finished. When he had that mood, those eyes, there was no stopping him normally. A few days before you came he'd executed a rebel fighter for rape, and he was very angry that day. What a miracle.'

Budik described life as a ward of the Demon in chilling terms, talking of extreme mood swings, extrajudicial executions, and reckless decision-making, but despite all of that, and despite even the fake execution to which he had been subjected, he had a measured assessment of his captor.

'He has all the qualities of a good officer. You know, he applied to join the Ukrainian Army in the 1990s, but they turned him down. The Ukrainian generals didn't need officers who wanted to fight for honour; they were too busy stealing money. This is a man who can recite whole verses of Taras Shevchenko's poetry in Ukrainian, but he ended up fighting for the Russian Army instead.'

I was a little dubious of Budik's characterization of the Demon as a model officer. Was there not a case of Stockholm syndrome here, I asked? Wasn't the Demon simply a psychopath? Budik smiled. Some of the things he knew the Demon had done, he said, were so awful he would only talk about them to a war crimes tribunal. But he also, extraordinarily, said he was still in touch with the Demon, and the pair had spoken by Skype the previous week. You shouldn't break people down into such simplistic categories, he told me.

'The Demon is a product of war. Any time you kill, it demeans you as a human; it breaks you. He lived through Afghanistan, he lived through both Chechnyas. It took me ten years to become normal again after the Abkhaz war. If you'd seen me in 1993, you'd have been surprised at what you saw.

'And don't forget that the Demon gave an oath to the Soviet Union. An oath is something a man should give only once in his life. For all that he fought for Russia, I think he remained loyal to the Soviet Union. You fight for your motherland, and then your motherland disappears. Not everyone can handle that.'

V

Igor Strelkov was the man who 'pulled the trigger'[4] on the Donbass war when he seized the first building in Slavyansk in April. The tall, skinny officer with a pencil moustache, who was chauffeured around Slavyansk in a black Mercedes, quickly became the most notorious man in Ukraine. One summer afternoon in 2014, I spent hours waiting on the twelfth floor of the seized Donetsk administration building, where the rebels met to discuss military strategy, trying to sweet-talk his bodyguards into passing him a message asking to grant me an interview, but to no avail. Eventually the doors swung open, and Strelkov himself came strutting out, vintage wooden pistol holster at his hip and a sextet of armed-to-the-teeth bodyguards cocooning him, radiating an aura of menace. I was too overwhelmed by the scene to call anything out to him, and by the time I had regained my composure he was already two flights further down the steps; when I caught up with them at ground level, he had hopped into one of a convoy of cars that sped off at break-neck speed. It was two years before I finally got to speak with him.

Strelkov had also been deeply affected by the Soviet collapse, but his epiphany came earlier. He was studying at a military history institute during the late *perestroika* years, and chose the Russian Civil War as his specialist subject. He was granted a pass to access top-secret archives, where he was able to read the memoirs of the White émigrés who had fought against the Bolsheviks in the Civil War. The Whites were the last real taboo of Soviet history: if the excesses of Stalinism could be explained as a deviation of the Bolshevik revolution, the Whites stood against its very essence. Strelkov read the memoirs of the former tsa-rist officers who commanded the White armies—reactionary, nation-alist, and with gentlemanly codes of honour. Everything he thought he understood about the Soviet state was turned on its head, as he began to sympathize with the White voices he read. He withdrew him-self from the Komsomol, the Communist youth league, of which he had previously been an enthusiastic member. 'I found things out that almost nobody knew at the time, and almost overnight I changed from a Stalinist to a monarchist,' he told me much later, when we met in 2016. It was somewhat ironic that the man who had sparked a rebellion that drew much on nostalgia for the Soviet Union was actually deeply anti-Soviet.

When the 1991 coup took place, Strelkov was in his final year at uni-versity. Many of his friends went to defend the White House from the reactionary coup forces, but he stayed away. He didn't support either side. While he disliked the Communists, he had no time for the new liberals either; he thought they would sell Russia out to the West. 'I had conflicted views; I understood that the Soviet Union was doomed and that Soviet ideology was dead. I hated it and didn't support it. But on the other hand, I already understood that it would lead to the fall of the state and social upheaval.'

After fighting in a Russian battalion alongside the Bosnian Serbs in the war in Bosnia, he later returned to Russia, served in the army, and then joined the FSB, where he was a serving officer for sixteen years. He fought in both Chechen wars and left 'due to personal reasons' the year before the Crimea events. He spent his spare time attending costumed military reenactments, and had a collection of vintage military memorabilia. All the time he remained furious at how Russia remained a weak vassal state of the West.

He began working in security for Konstantin Malofeyev, a young, deeply religious financier, who had become an influential Kremlin power broker and a proponent of a more aggressive Russian policy in Ukraine. Through shady mechanisms that may never come to light, Strelkov found himself in Crimea during the annexation, and later in the heart of events in Donbass. The Ukrainians, and many Western governments, were convinced he was acting on direct orders from the Kremlin; Strelkov described himself as a Russian patriot in Ukraine of his own accord, in pursuit of a great new Russia. The truth was probably somewhere between the two.

During his short reign over Slavyansk, Strelkov held military tribunals, on the basis of which people were shot for looting. It was all absolutely legal, he told me matter-of-factly, as he had based the tribunals on a 1945 military decree signed by Stalin. In early July, as the Ukrainian Army closed in on Slavyansk, Strelkov retreated to Donetsk and was put in charge of military strategy for the whole rebel system. In Donetsk, Strelkov had a number of hare-brained schemes to defend the city, including a suggestion to blow up a number of high-rise residential blocks on the outskirts of town, to provide obstacles against a potential Ukrainian attack.

Khodakovsky had little time for Strelkov, with his fantasies of a resurgent great Russia. The people who gathered around Strelkov were those who had never built anything in their lives, Khodakovsky complained. 'They are interested in destroying the old world but they don't know what to put in its place. For them, human life is as valuable as toilet paper.' For Strelkov, Donbass was just a piece on a chessboard. His ultimate goal was the recreation of the Russian Empire.

The Kremlin also got sick of Strelkov. He was too much of a loose cannon for the shadowy Moscow operatives running the war in eastern

Ukraine, and when they decided on secret but significant direct Russian military intervention in late summer 2014, one of the conditions was that Strelkov be removed. He reluctantly withdrew.

The Kremlin used Russian nationalists when it needed them, but the last thing it wanted was people like Strelkov whipping up nationalist fury and demanding further incursions into Ukraine. Nationalism was a useful political tool only as a distraction, not as a prescriptive philosophy for military action. On his return to Moscow, Strelkov found himself silenced by the authorities; he was banned from appearing on state television.

After two years of oblique criticism of the current order, he had given up trying to find his niche in the system and set up a political movement in direct opposition to the Kremlin. He predicted a civil war in Russia, due to Putin's unwillingness to go all the way in his confrontation with the West. Blacklisted by the Russian media that had once lionized him, he finally agreed to meet with me, and I went to see him at a spartan office in central Moscow in summer 2016. As we spoke, a sandy-coloured cat the size of a lamb padded into the room and clambered nonchalantly onto the table in front of us. 'His name's Grumpy; he's a Maine Coon,' Strelkov said, stroking the cat's tail, fluffy as a feather duster.

It was hard to square the figure before me with the man I had seen two years previously in Donetsk. The comically large cat added an absurd tinge to proceedings that meant I had to work hard to suppress giggles as Strelkov gravely prophesied the rivers of blood that would flow on Russian soil as a result of Putin's indecision. There was indeed a potential future scenario of economic decay in which the nationalist sentiment that Putin had carefully cultivated could spiral out of control and people like Strelkov could become a threat to the regime. But his grand statements about taking control of the country seemed ridiculous when made from his shabby suite of offices, the entrance hall of which smelled strongly of body odour.

In Donetsk, he had appeared the harbinger of a dark, apocalyptic Russian renaissance, oozing malignant charisma and authority. Maybe, one day in the future, he or people like him would regain that aura. But for now, giant cat on his lap, he just looked like another disgruntled middle-aged man, confused and marooned by the collapse of the Soviet Union.

VI

The Ukraine conflict rapidly became one of those issues like the Israel/ Palestine question, in which both sides become blind to the arguments of the other. The single-mindedness and intransigence of locals was depressing but understandable. For patriotic Ukrainians, it was hardly surprising that with Russia conducting a secret war on their territory, they were not predisposed to listening to the Kremlin's talking points; for residents of Donetsk who stayed behind and were woken up on a nightly basis by Ukrainian shelling, it was natural that the Russian propaganda points found a receptive audience.

It was harder to respect the motives of the cheerleaders and propagandists outside the region, who latched their own narratives onto the conflict. For many Western observers, the conflict in eastern Ukraine boiled down to one thing: Russian aggression. Even mentioning the genuine local grievances and socio-economic causes of the conflict was seen as doing Putin's work. The Russian military intervention, both using arms-length mercenaries and regular troops, was very real and most certainly illegal. But how could it be so easy for Russia to stir up trouble? Why were so many locals so ready to go along with the Russian narrative? Why were many of them ready to pick up weapons, fight, and die for the separatist cause? Beyond labelling them idiots, or brainwashed by propaganda, not many people in Kiev or the West wanted to think more deeply about the problem.

At an embassy garden party in Kiev, I asked a European ambassador what he thought about the language and culture issues in Ukraine, and he looked shocked. 'There is no language issue in Ukraine! No culture issue in Ukraine! There is a criminal, evil, deceitful Russia which is acting like it belongs in another century and that is it! There is no division at all!' He repeated this, pretty much word for word, about ten times, before I was able to sidle off to the drinks table and escape. He had never been to Donetsk, and even though I had just returned from a long trip, he did not think to enquire of me whether I agreed with him.

The lies and simplifications on the other side of the barricades were even more troubling. The most shared item about Ukraine on *The Guardian*'s website during the whole of 2014 was a column by the veteran journalist John Pilger about the awful events in Odessa, which he described as one of many 'US-orchestrated attacks on ethnic Russians in Ukraine'.[5] Pilger's view of the conflict was that it had all been instigated by the Americans, who had turned Ukraine into a 'CIA theme park' and were trying to goad Russia into war.

Pilger was part of a small but influential body of thinkers in the West, who bought the Kremlin's talking points on Ukraine uncritically, convinced that what they were seeing was a replay of the Cold War and the nefarious hand of Washington abroad.

To bolster his repeated references to the Ukrainian authorities as fascists, Pilger recounted a horrific scene from outside the burning building in Odessa. He quoted appalling details from Igor Rozovskiy, a Jewish doctor who was scrambling to rescue people from the building where Russians were being burned to death by the fascist mob: 'I was stopped by pro-Ukrainian Nazi radicals. One of them pushed me away rudely, promising that soon me and other Jews of Odessa are going to meet the same fate. What occurred yesterday didn't even take place during the fascist occupation in my town in World War Two. I wonder, why the whole world is keeping silent.'

Rozovskiy's quote was factually incorrect in the most grotesque manner: in the space of three days in October 1941, tens of thousands of Jews were massacred in Odessa. Some were shot dead, while others were burned alive.[6] The lazy urge to compare everything to the Second World War, and compare everyone to the Nazis, had the double effect of devaluing the very real tragedy which occurred in the trade union building in Odessa, and cheapening the memory of the many thousands more who died in the Holocaust.

Still, the doctor could be excused his hyperbole, so soon after bearing witness to such terrible events. But there was a much more fundamental problem with the story. Nobody in Odessa had ever heard of a doctor called Igor Rozovskiy. When his account of the events went viral, local journalists did some digging, and found that his Facebook profile had only recently been created. His profile picture was actually a photograph of a dentist from a town over a thousand miles away in Russia. Shortly afterwards, Rozovskiy's Facebook page was deleted. The fraudulent nature of the page had been debunked several days before Pilger's piece came out, and had been written about in both English and Russian; just a few minutes online checking out the details would have uncovered the fraud.[7]

In subsequent years, the concept of 'fake news' and invented stories would receive more attention globally, but fake accounts were a frequent and frustrating part of reporting the Ukraine war. In an era of declining newsroom budgets, a reliance on citizen journalism with little quality filter, and social networks as the main source of news, sifting the real from the fake became ever more challenging. But Pilger himself had spent much of his career complaining, often with justification, about the gullibility or collusion of Western journalists with their governments' official narratives. It was an extraordinary dereliction of duty to fall for a crude scam such as this. Later, Pilger frequently ranted about Western coverage of Ukraine. He was disgusted at journalists like me for whitewashing a 'fascist-contaminated junta' in Kiev, and outraged that this was happening 'in the borderland through which the original Nazis invaded Russia'.[8] It was not only Russians and Ukrainians who struggled to transcend the tropes and outlooks of the Cold War and refracted events through the prism of the Second World War.

We later made a correction to Pilger's column to note that Rozovskiy's testimony was probably false, but it was too late. More than sixty thousand people shared the piece on social media,[9] where it found a receptive audience among those who believed the 'mainstream media' was lying to them about US meddling in fascist Ukraine. They happily accepted Pilger's fake doctor as the 'truth' that crooked mainstream journalists were trying to hide from them.

The absurdity of some of the claims coming from the Kremlin and its Western parrots had the additional side effect of blinding supporters of Ukraine to problems that actually did exist. There really was an unpleasant minority of neo-Nazis who fought for Ukraine, centred on the Azov battalion, which used a version of the Nazi-linked *Wolfsangel* as its symbol. The battalion was instrumental in defending Mariupol from an attack of separatist forces backed up by regular Russian army units in late summer 2014, but many of the men from the battalion expressed far-right views. I spent an evening on night patrol around Mariupol with a heavily armed Azov fighter who waxed lyrical about Hitler and his policies and told me he was fighting Russia because he believed Putin was a Jew. The Azov's neo-Nazis were a bizarre mix: mainly Russian speakers from eastern Ukraine, not western Ukrainian Bandera fans, and I even met a Russian nationalist among their ranks, who believed Putin's multi-ethnic Russia was to the detriment of the Russian people and so had decided to fight for Ukraine. Kiev, underprepared to take on Russia, was grateful for anyone who was willing to fight. But even if their exact ideology, and how they fit into the tangled mix of different forces, was complicated, it was deeply problematic that these men with far-right views and symbols were running around the front line. Yet when I wrote about Azov, Ukrainian authorities and even friends became angry, and accused me of doing the Kremlin's work. It was much easier for them to brush off justified criticism as Kremlin propaganda when Russian news agencies and people like Pilger really were spreading lies.

In the months after the deaths in Odessa, I heard again and again from rebel fighters that the 'Odessa massacre' was their tipping point: the event that made them decide it was time to sign up and join the fight. I even met a deeply confused Texan in Donetsk, who had been so moved by what he read online about Odessa that he flew to Russia, crossed the border, and signed up to the rebel cause. He was convinced that World War Three could be averted only if the American-Ukrainian fascist axis was halted in Donetsk.

There were certainly serious questions for the Ukrainian authorities to answer about what happened in Odessa, and the official investigation into the deaths was extremely unsatisfactory. But reinventing it as a Nazi-style massacre, turning an already appalling event into something even worse, could and would have terrible consequences.

Lies and propaganda had an unnerving tendency to become self-fulfilling prophecies. In Donbass, people took up arms against a phantom threat of fascist attack, but faced with losing yet more of the country, Ukraine's weak army and inexperienced volunteer battalions fought back, and before long there really were innocent civilians dying from Kiev's artillery shells. My Donetsk driver Andrei, who had been so dismissive of the low-class fools at the checkpoints when the uprising began, before long became angry with both sides. He still had no time for the rebels but was losing his mind from the sound of shelling in his neighbourhood, and was at his wits' end with the Ukrainian government. He was trying to escape from it all by watching films every evening. After another six months, when I again returned, he was seriously considering joining the rebels, and complaining about the 'fascist Ukies' who had destroyed life in his home city. Thus the self-ful-filling prophecies of war worked their logic. 'When one lot claim that the other lot have massacred women and children, so both sides believe it and do it,' wrote the inter-war satirist and journalist Karl Kraus. 'The act is stronger than the word, but stronger than acts is the echo.'

VII

On a warm afternoon late in the summer of 2014, I travelled to a ram-shackle village deep in the hinterlands of eastern Ukraine's Luhansk region. Like many of the countryside settlements in the area, its rows of topsy-turvy gingerbread cottages simultaneously gave off an air of decaying, oppressive poverty and the feeling of a certain rural idyll. In the pleasant courtyard of one relatively affluent household, a middle-aged woman in tracksuit bottoms wailed inconsolably, tears streaming from her bloodshot eyes. Barking dogs and cawing doves completed a harrowing polyphony. To one side, a glum-faced man was methodically sliding hefty chunks of meat onto two-foot skewers, to make *shashlyk* for the wake.

The low-key ceremony later that evening would mark forty days since Igor's death, though the choice of date was arbitrary. Nobody knew for certain exactly when he had died. His body had only been discovered a few days before. Until the war started, Igor had worked as a shoveller and loader for a nearby coal mine. Like many jobs in eastern Ukraine, it was backbreaking work for a low wage. Igor rarely complained, though. He was lucky to have a job at all. His salary was not much but it kept the family going, and there was even some left over for him to indulge his passion. Igor had been obsessed with doves; there were dozens of them, squawking away from inside a shed-sized cage at the back of the garden. He had travelled across the country to buy different rare breeds, having sought them out on Internet forums. The doves were his pride and joy, said Yekaterina, sniffling.

'He said he looked at them flying and it made him feel free inside, like he could fly away too. Now he's never coming back, and I don't know what to do with them. I'll keep them, of course, but every time I look at them I'm reminded of him.'

She daubed at her blotchy face with one of her wrists and turned to go back into the cottage. Yekaterina had always worried about Igor. After all, given the frequency of industrial accidents in Ukraine's decrepit mines, every shift could be his last. But she could never have imagined he would meet his death at war.

As Donbass descended into conflict, Igor kept working his shifts at the mine, even as more and more of his friends and co-workers joined the rebel armies. He had travelled all over Ukraine to buy his doves, and while he felt far more at home in Donbass than he did in the Ukrainian-speaking west of the country, he had never felt threatened by other Ukrainians. One day, though, he decided he could not remain indifferent any longer. The thought of the fascists in Kiev coming to seize Donbass disgusted him. His boss was sympathetic to the cause and gave him leave. He was killed just a few weeks later.

Due to the ongoing military action in the area, his corpse had been discovered only in recent days, by a rebel patrol that came across it in a wooded area. Time and the summer sun had both taken their toll. Yekaterina was able to identify Igor only by the religious icon he kept in his trouser pocket at all times, and his shoes. The body was so disfigured it could have been anyone, and in these troubled times there was no energy or money for DNA analysis. She wondered if it might all be a hideous coincidence. Perhaps her Igor would return, and it would be the wife of another man, a man with similar taste in icons and footwear, who had become a widow. The ferocity of her tears betrayed how forlorn a hope it was. Yekaterina had not yet found a way to tell her ten-year-old daughter, who was spending the summer with relatives in Russia, that her father was dead. She shook her head vigorously in denial. 'What am I supposed to say to her? How can I tell her?'

There had been tension in the house when Igor said he was leaving. 'Of course I tried to talk him out of it, of course I did. We had a huge argument, there was a terrible scandal. But it was no use. His mind was made up. And do I blame him? No, I can't blame him. He died defending us, defending our children. He's a hero.'

I asked Yekaterina what the decisive factor had been in Igor's leaving his job and joining the armed uprising.

'We were sitting right over there,' she said, gesturing towards the sofa, 'when they said they were going to kill everyone in the east.'

'Who said that?'

'Kiev! They said it openly, that they wanted to kill everyone in the east, or remove them, or something like that. They wanted to clear the region so they could drill for, what's it called, shale gas. It was on the television.'

Most people in Donbass watched Russian television; the entertainment programmes were of higher quality than their Ukrainian equivalents, and it was broadcast in a language they could understand. Yekaterina could not remember which particular programme it was they had been watching that had given them news of this fascist plan of ethnic cleansing; there were many such talk shows and angry rants in the spring and summer of 2014. But she clearly remembered the effect it had. A few minutes after the programme was over, Igor stood up from the sofa. He looked at her, and said firmly and decisively: 'That's it. I'm going to fight.'

VIII

Not long afterwards, in Donetsk, I ran into a prominent Russian state television commentator. I had seen him on air in previous weeks railing about the US State Department's investment of billions to stage a coup in Ukraine, and he was frequently to be found on talk shows ruminating about 'fascist' Ukraine and its threat to Russia, using the tropes of the Second World War in the service of this new war. When we got talking over a drink, though, he struck a very different tone. His real take on Ukraine, he said, was that it was all a cynical battle between different oligarchs. Ukraine's president Petro Poroshenko, far from being some kind of fascist demagogue installed by Washington, was in fact defending the interests of various Russian criminal gangs against those of certain Ukrainian criminal gangs.

Even by the cynical standards of Ukrainian politics, it was an implausibly simplistic analysis, but it was also very different to what I'd heard him shriek about on air. I pointed this out to him, and he laughed.

'America? Don't be silly, that's all just for the television. Nobody really believes in that, it's just a good rallying point for the masses. We need to invoke patriotic spirit somehow.'

I asked him what would happen about the investigation into MH17. He shrugged. 'Look, Russia is fine here. If they nail us with evidence, then we'll be able to pass it off as drunken rebels. If it was really our missile, then I'm sure we've already destroyed the BUK system that was used, and you can be sure the people who fired it will never be heard from again.' While foreign disciples such as Pilger genuinely believed that talk of Russian involvement was a Western media invention, Russian propagandists themselves were less inclined to deny the blindingly obvious in private.

The only hope for peace, he believed, was for Russia to return control over Donbass to Kiev, which in return would accept Russian control over Crimea and give a guarantee to Moscow that Ukraine would never join NATO. I said I thought it unlikely that the Ukrainian people would ever accept Crimea as part of Russia, and it would thus be impossible for any government in Kiev to do such a deal. He raised an eyebrow as if he could not quite believe I could be capable of saying something so stupid.

'They won't *accept* it? Ha! They'll accept whatever the television tells them to accept!' He chuckled, and gulped down the rest of his whisky.

In some ways, it was a breath of fresh air to hear someone speak so honestly about how they felt the world worked. But the problem with such cynicism was that it led to very real victims. Ingesting a daily diet of war and fascists and heroic last stands, men like Igor eventually decided to pick up a gun and go and fight for real. Meanwhile, men like the television journalist drank their whisky and revelled in the rejuvenated status of the new Russia.

IX

By the end of summer 2014, for many in eastern Ukraine, the lofty notions of history had subsided in the brutal reality of conflict. Many of those on the front lines complained it was a futile, fratricidal conflict, whatever the television stations in Moscow and Kiev said. But the logic of confrontation meant there was no turning back.

The centre of Donetsk was largely spared military action, as the suburbs took the toll, but the whole of Luhansk was subjected to a punishing siege over the summer. Most people who had family elsewhere in Ukraine or Russia had left the city; those who remained were those who were too frail to leave or had nowhere to go. A few days after the

Ukrainian siege of Luhansk was broken in early September, I travelled there to assess the damage. It had been a city of 400,000 people, and was the second lode of separatist power. Signs of the hasty Ukrainian retreat littered the road into Luhansk; at one spot there was a burned-out column of eleven tanks and other armoured vehicles, taken out by the sort of precision strikes only the regular Russian Army could manage.

The city itself was coming to life again, but everyone appeared dazed and disoriented. People emerged bleary-eyed from basements; there was little petrol so most were on foot or bicycles, laden with large bags either side of the saddles like mules. At points on the side of the road, crowds of people gathered, waving their mobile phones in the air as if in a strange ritual, trying to get a bar of reception to make a call at the few places where there was still a signal. There were continuous muffled booms coming from the airport outside town, where the rebels were exploding ammunition the retreating Ukrainians had left behind.

Everybody spoke in careful phrases or whispered confidences. For now, the rebels were in charge, but nobody knew who the authorities would be in six months from now, and speaking out of line publicly could be deadly in either scenario. Nerves were frayed and people's emotions squalled unexpectedly. Numerous interviewees burst into tears without warning. This was the aftermath of war; gone was the militarist bravado of the early days.

A concert for talented schoolchildren to mark the first day of the school year went ahead, despite the fact that most of the schools were closed. The local director of education, a stern woman named Valentina with a matter-of-fact manner and a shock of peroxide-blonde hair, was adamant that everything should proceed as planned, because people were reassured if there was a semblance of normality. Before we went in to watch the concert, she served me tea in her office from a china teapot, with the bustling ceremony of a Victorian aristocrat. It was hard to believe she had been sleeping, together with her eighty-six-year-old mother, on the bathroom floor for the past two months, as her district was shelled on a nightly basis. 'I behave as if everything is normal because people know me and they like to see that everything is fine. But of course inside it's hard. Everything feels constantly shaken up,' she confided to me as I sipped my tea.

Although more than half the city's schoolchildren had fled with their families, she was adamant that the annual concert would go ahead, and it was an impressive show: a young girl in pigtails sawed her way valiantly through a violin sonata, and a dance ensemble of eight-year-olds turned out beautifully in matching shiny skirts and cravats did their best to lift the mood. Then, suddenly, the headmistress's adult son took the stage, announcing he would read a poem he had just written. He stood stock still, with no discernible expression, and began to read lines about the horror of war. Gradually, his voice picked up volume, and he worked himself up to an appalling yelling for the finale, about the terror of a Grad rocket attack. Truck-borne Grad launchers sent a salvo of up to forty missiles flying across a wide area. The name literally means 'hail', and the weapons are extremely imprecise. They were a particularly disgusting weapon to use in civilian areas, but both sides in the conflict had employed them relentlessly.

Our hearts ache with despair,
There is no earth, there is no sky.
GRAD! GRAD! GRAAAD!

As he howled the word repeatedly, the children looked on with saucer eyes. Some of the teachers wept silently.

At the morgue, I found dozens of simple pale-wood coffins stacked outside, sometimes with a bloodied bandage or a chunk of yellowed torso visible in the chink between casket and lid. There had been no power for most of August, meaning the bodies could not be refrigerated. Flies swarmed inside and outside the building, and the stench was unbearable. The bodies were arriving too quickly for proper burial; the coffins had been lined up twenty at a time, in a series of hastily dug trenches in a scruffy field around the corner from the morgue.

Inside, I found Anatoly, the sixty-two-year-old morgue director, in a putrid office buzzing with yet more flies. His three colleagues had all fled, leaving him to do all the work. And there was lots of it—he had a list of more than five hundred names and addresses, and now dozens more were arriving each day as the roads finally became safe enough to drive long-dead bodies to the morgue. Sometimes the remains were unidentifiable; he would take DNA samples in the hope that one day someone might appear with the technology to analyse them. Anatoly's family was in western Ukraine, and the natural thing would have been for him to get the hell out as his colleagues had. But then, he said wearily, who would do all the work?

I picked an address at random from Anatoly's grim list and drove there in pouring rain to investigate. It was in a rural suburb of the city, called Bolshaya Verkhunka, which had been right on the front line. The Ukrainian National Guard had taken up a position at one end of the simple main street, and the separatists at the other, less than a mile away. For a month, they had fired shells at each other over the tops of the houses along the street. With the rebel surge in the past week, the Ukrainians had finally been flushed out, abandoning their position. Every single house on the street had some kind of serious damage; many of them were burned to the ground.

I found a gaunt, middle-aged woman named Lyubov wandering aimlessly along the street in the rain like the sole survivor of an apocalypse. Her house was relatively unscathed; it had merely been riddled with bullets. All the windows were shot out, though, and she had no idea where she would get either the money or materials to replace them before the onset of winter. She had spent the past month alone in her cellar, and was clearly in a state of severe shock. Still, she was one of the luckier ones. Next door was a house belonging to Vitaly and Marina, a newlywed couple in their early thirties. They too had hidden in the basement, but their house had taken a direct hit. Rubble had fallen inside, blocking the entrance to the cellar, and the house caught fire. Trapped below ground, Vitaly and Marina burned to death; their charred bodies had been buried in a shallow grave in the back garden. Lyubov walked me down the street, pointing at each house in turn: 'Dead, escaped to Kiev, dead, dead, escaped to Russia, dead.'

The only other house where people were alive and present was the remains of what had once been a handsomely decorated cottage at the end of the street. Nikolai, a sixty-five-year-old who had built the house with his own hands between 1975 and 1981, ushered me into the pathetic remains of his home. For the past month, he and his wife had cowered in their dank cellar as the house he had painstakingly built was pulverized by bullets and mortars above them. No soldiers from either side had been in to ask if anyone was there; there had been no offers of evacuation.

Most of the roof was destroyed, half the walls were gone, and those that remained were like Swiss cheese. His wife was hysterical. 'We were waiting for you, we were waiting for anyone. Why didn't you come before?' Nikolai simply stared into the middle distance, unable to process events. In the space of a month, a whole lifetime of labour had been destroyed. His pride and joy had been a sky-blue Volga 21 sedan, purchased in the 1970s and kept in mint condition, with not a scratch to be seen, flecks of mud carefully polished off at daily intervals. Over the past weeks, it had been reduced to a gnarled tangle of metal, small fragments of the beautiful azure still visible in a few places. Even his bicycle had been mangled, a final indignity. His ninety-year-old mother-in-law, frail and alone, was stranded in a neighbouring village, and with no electricity, no phones, and no transport, the couple were unable to find out if she was still alive.

It was pouring with rain and night was falling, so after some time I turned to leave, promising to do what I could to get the word out about the level of devastation. The three hunched figures waved forlornly at me from the doorstep of the ruined house, as I trudged back to the car in the rain. Of all the horrors of the year—the dead on Maidan, the charred bodies of Odessa, and the butcher-shop carnage of the MH17 wreckage—this affected me the most. The dead are dead, after all, but to see these amiable, decent people come to terms with losing absolutely everything was as devastating as it was pointless.

Everyone was too wrapped up in their favoured narratives to care much about those caught in the middle: the fate of the residents of Bolshaya Verkhunka was the fault of the fascists in Kiev, or the fault of the lunatics in the Kremlin, or indeed it was their own fault for not caring enough about their predicament to fight off one side or the other.

But all I saw was some elderly villagers who had a conflict they little understood thrust upon them in the twilight of their lives. The country they were born in and grew up in had collapsed, and they felt no real sense of belonging either to Putin's resurgent Russia, or to a Ukraine that had done nothing to improve their lives in the years since independence. They spoke a mishmash of Ukrainian and Russian, which my Muscovite ear had to struggle to comprehend, and they had never particularly cared about politics or ethnic labels.

They had toiled all their lives to afford the luxury of seeing out a basic but comfortable retirement in this middle-of-nowhere rural quietude. Now, the fruits of their decades of labour had been pulverized by two groups of men, one of them fighting under the red-black flag of the wartime Ukrainian nationalist army, and the other fighting under the orange-black St George's ribbon symbolizing the Soviet war victory. For a month, the two sides had stood at opposite ends of these people's street and lobbed explosives at each other, over their heads.

PART FOUR

———

The Past in the Future

12

After the war

As the war in the east of the country rumbled on, in Kiev the Ukrainian government passed laws aimed at forcing a final and decisive break with the lexicon and iconography of the Soviet past. The symbolic hauling down of Kiev's central Vladimir Lenin monument during the Maidan revolution was solidified in a set of laws on 'decommunization'. There were more than a thousand other Lenins in towns and cities across Ukraine. The monuments had been removed from the west of the country when the Soviet Union collapsed, but elsewhere they remained standing, as regions were allowed to freelance their own historical memory narratives.

This was no longer an option. The law decreed that all statues glorifying Communist leaders had to go, and all Soviet street names and town names, of which there were thousands, also had to change. It was meant to be a final and decisive break with the past. Of course, in the parts of Ukraine under separatist control, the Lenins remained standing. In Crimea's capital Simferopol, the new Russian authorities gave their biggest Lenin a restoration, reopening him in the main square newly shiny and defiant.

Petro Poroshenko, the post-Maidan president, was himself a billionaire, and while the rhetoric changed dramatically, and many young and dynamic activists entered politics, on the big questions Ukraine continued to function in much the same way it always had, with a few oligarchs controlling all the key financial flows. For Poroshenko to get away with this extraordinary reversion to the status quo after so many had stood on Maidan demanding radical change, he had to make at least some rhetorical concessions, and thus he 'outsourced' memory politics to the radical nationalists, in order to keep them happy while businessmen continued dividing up the financial pie much as before.

In the Russophone regions of the east under Kiev's control, the decommunization initiative received a mixed reception. In Artemovsk, named after the Bolshevik revolutionary Artem, the town's name, the main square's name, and statues of both Lenin and Artem all had to go. Dzerzhinsk, just a few miles from the front line and named after the founder of the Soviet secret police, became Toretsk. I found the oversized concrete torsos of two Dzerzhinskys and a Lenin tossed away in a scrap yard on the edge of town. In Odessa, with deft humour in the spirit of the city's long heritage of satire and swindlers, one of the Lenin monuments remained standing, but was given a cloak and helmet, and transformed into Darth Vader. 'To Darth Vader, the father of the nation, from your grateful children,' read the new inscription. This middle ground, subversion instead of either reverence or annihilation, was perhaps the least harmful way to deal with the Soviet past. Separately, an Odessa artist made a video satirizing the whole decommunization process. In the film, a man arrives with new street signs, pulling down the markers for Lenin Street and replacing them with street names based on Maidan heroes. He walks away, job done, oblivious to the fact the buildings themselves are collapsing and crumbling to rubble behind him. The obvious point was that perhaps, given the state of Ukraine in 2016, there should have been more important priorities than changing the street names.

The Kremlin's domination of the Second World War narrative for propaganda purposes meant Victory Day was now extra-controversial in Ukraine. The government decreed 9 May would no longer be a celebration. Instead of brash, neo-Soviet festivities on 9 May, there would be a solemn commemoration on 8 May, to be known as the Day of Remembrance and Reconciliation. A poppy was adopted as the new symbol in place of the orange-black ribbons, which had been tainted by their use in the separatist cause. (Later, in May 2017, the government actually made wearing the orange-black ribbons an offence punishable by a fine or up to fifteen days in jail.) The change of focus sounded like a welcome move away from bombast and towards reflection in a country that was deeply split over memories of the war. But the poppy was a controversial choice of symbol. In other countries it was linked with the First World War, not the Second World War, and cynics pointed out that its red-black colours were the same as the flag of the Ukrainian nationalist armies. So the replacing of orange and black with red and black did not look like a conciliatory move at all, but instead the replacing of one war narrative with another.

Any sense that the symbolism of the poppy colours could have been mere coincidence was dispelled by the other section of the new decommunization laws. As well as banning relics of the Soviet past, the laws decreed that the wartime Ukrainian nationalist movements should be recognized as 'veterans of the struggle for independence'. A number of streets were renamed after OUN leader Stepan Bandera and UPA military commander Roman Shukhevych.

I went to meet the man who had drafted the history laws, the ageing MP Yury Shukhevych, Roman's son. Born in 1933 and now in his eighties, Shukhevych was almost blind and walked with a stoop, one arm resting on an ornamental western Ukrainian axe turned walking stick, the other supported by a parliamentary aide who helped lower him into an armchair in the foyer of the hotel where he had set the meeting, across the street from the Rada, the Ukrainian parliament building in Kiev.

The Soviets arrested Yury's mother at the end of the war, and put him into an orphanage. He escaped, but was caught, and sentenced to ten years of labour in 1949. His father, who continued an underground battle against the Soviets, was killed in a firefight during his arrest by Soviet agents near Lviv in 1950. Yury spent thirty-one years in prison and further years in exile in some of the remotest parts of the Soviet camp system. It was only in 1989 that he was released and was able to return to Lviv. The decades in Soviet camps and prisons had not dimmed his sense of Ukrainianness, and he was known as an extreme nationalist politician, on the fringes of the political debate. Maidan had given him a late chance to enter mainstream politics, however, and he won election to the Rada on the Radical Party's ticket in 2014, at the age of eighty-one.

His grey hair was swept back and his eyes were squinted almost completely shut. He wore a traditional *vyshivanka* shirt, embroidered in the yellow and blue of the Ukrainian flag. Although he was physically frail, he remained razor-sharp mentally, and spoke to me in accented Russian, peppering his speech with the staccato imperative '*Slushayte!*' ('Listen!'). It was unclear whether it was a turn of phrase or a mark of irritation at my questioning. Shukhevych told me that there was no difference between Hitler's race ideology and Soviet class ideology, and that symbols of both deserved the same treatment. '*Slushayte!* These laws should have been enacted twenty-three years ago, but our society had not matured enough. For seventy years the Soviets filled our heads with lies. You can't imagine how it worked: from kindergarten, to school and university, through literature, television, the press. Of course people in the east are zombified. They purged the whole intelligentsia there.'

I moved on to the question of the lionization of the nationalist movement, and of his father. Surely, Shukhevych had to admit that the nationalists had done terrible things during the war, I said. '*Slushayte!* War is always a crime, there were crimes on all sides. Coventry, Dresden, Hiroshima, these were all crimes against peaceful civilians. Of course it was a cruel battle and there were a lot of bad things that happened.'

I had recently been to Rava-Ruska, a town on the Ukrainian-Polish border, where more than two-thirds of the pre-war population had been Jewish. The current Jewish population was zero. Previously there had been nothing to mark the total extermination of the community, although there had been a monument to the UPA. Now, finally, a monument had been erected to the Jewish victims, funded by a German charitable foundation. It was located in a clearing just outside the town, where some of the mass killings had taken place. The monument had the following inscription: 'Between 1941 and 1944, 3,000 Jews were killed here by the German occupiers and their subservient local structures.'

I asked Shukhevych what he thought. '*Slushayte!* Maybe the ghettos were indeed guarded by local police. But what about the Judenrat, which selected and sorted the Jews? The Jewish police handed over the Jews to the Germans, but they don't like to talk about that, do they? And I saw it with my own eyes.'

The Judenrat, the Jewish councils that worked with the Nazis, were called 'the darkest chapter of the whole dark story' by Hannah Arendt. As part of a long and nuanced debate about the history of the Holocaust, it was perfectly acceptable to explore what role the Judenrat might have played in the killing. As a reflex response to a question about whether Ukrainian nationalists should really be lionized, it was, to put it mildly, distasteful.

It was easy to understand Shukhevych's anger with the Soviet Union and everything that it stood for. It was a system that had locked him up for decades purely because of his surname. It was unsurprising that in this unexpected twilight of his life, as a member of parliament in an independent Ukraine, he felt vindicated and vengeful. But in a country with such delicate historical trauma, he did not seem like the right person to be drafting the laws on history.

Volodymyr Viatrovych, the historian who ran Ukraine's National Memory Institute, was in charge of implementing Shukhevych's laws. His office was in an elegant building on Lypska Street, which had once housed the Soviet secret police in the early days after the Bolsheviks took over Kiev. Was now the right time to be doing this, I asked him, given that the country was torn apart by conflict, and many people in the east were uneasy at the western Ukrainian version of nationalism, and felt nostalgia for the Soviet past? How would this go down in the parts of Donbass that the Ukrainians had won back from the separatists, where Kiev was fighting a battle for the affection and loyalty of the populace?

Viatrovych had a long answer ready. 'I think these laws are more relevant than ever. Russian aggression has based itself on Soviet traditions and Soviet thinking. It works on *homo soveticus*, on those who think of themselves as Soviet people. If we want to remove the threat of this aggression, then we have to do everything we can to de-Sovietize, so that these islands of Sovietness become fewer and fewer.'

Donbass had previously been a paradise for workers, with tough physical labour but good salaries, Viatrovych said. During the Soviet period it was possible to subsidize this, but when the union collapsed it was no longer possible, and so it was that many people in Donbass associated the appearance of Ukraine with a downturn in their own fortunes, and remembered the Soviet period as a golden age. That was why these people missed the Soviet Union, and it was important to explain to them that they were wrong.

I thought Viatrovych had diagnosed the problem splendidly, but I was less sure about his solution. Surely if the reason people missed the Soviet period was largely socio-economic, the solution was to give them economic opportunities, and some hope for the future, not simply ban them from expressing regret that the Soviet era had passed.

Viatrovych disagreed. Lots of people thought you could just let economic progress naturally take its course and the Soviet past would simply dissolve, but the example of Russia showed this is not the case, he said. 'If you don't do anything with the Soviet past, if you don't try to disassociate and remove yourself from it, then it will be reborn. We see many people of my generation, even of the younger generation who were born after the Soviet Union collapsed, who are absolutely Soviet, they look at the world in an absolutely Soviet way.'

It seemed to me that the best way to prevent people from retaining a Soviet identity was to offer a new kind of identity they could be proud of. Those Ukrainians who had made a success of their lives were unlikely to miss the Soviet Union and more likely to be Ukrainian 'patriots' of some stripe or other. Those who hadn't, if they came from western Ukraine, were at least able to take solace in Ukrainian independence and a sense of statehood that had been denied them in the Soviet period. But those Russian-speaking eastern Ukrainians for whom life had got worse since the Soviet collapse had few directions in which to turn, except to seek comfort in a rose-tinted version of the past, happily provided by Russian propaganda.

Kiev's memory policies seemed as though they would only make things worse. It was clearly a good idea to pull down statues that honoured killers like Dzerzhinsky, and to make a clear-eyed evaluation of the Soviet past. But the fight against the Bolsheviks was being carried out using distinctly Bolshevik methods. There seemed little point in renaming the streets if you had no mechanism to change what was going on inside people's heads.

II

While Ukraine was busy erasing all traces of its Communist past, in the Donetsk People's Republic, the Russia-backed quasi-state that had now become entrenched in Ukraine's east, Soviet nostalgia remained strong.

I kept in touch with Khodakovsky, and saw him every time I went to Donetsk, and on his visits to Moscow. We chatted for hours about what he wanted for the region, what he could and couldn't say in public, and how memories of the Soviet past played into current events. I often disagreed with him, but I enjoyed our conversations. He remained surprisingly frank in a way that others were not, including about the failures of the separatists to fulfil their promises to the locals who had backed them.

Although he was articulate and well-read, when I later went through the transcripts of our long conversations, I found that on different days he claimed to adhere to different philosophies, drawing on a hodge-podge of ideas and sources of ideological inspiration. One day, he told me he agreed with the philosopher Lev Gumilev that Russia is more of an Asian power than a European one, and that totalitarian tendencies were perfectly natural. A few months later, he assured me that his ideal was to build a free and democratic society on the European model, in which plurality of opinion could flourish. Sometimes he spoke of the Soviet Union as an ideal; other times he declared he had 'no illusions' about what kind of country it had really been, and had no desire to see it return. Often, I felt that he was having a discussion with himself, and that I was merely a convenient medium through which to do so.

During one of our meetings, Khodakovsky told me a remarkable story about his paternal great-grandfather, whom family legend main-tained had died during the Second World War. But one of his father's cousins did some digging into the family history, by questioning eld-erly relatives, and shared the results with Khodakovsky. It turned out that his great-grandfather had not died in the war after all; he had been arrested in 1937, dragged from his home in the middle of the night, and never heard from again.

Years later, Khodakovsky's father was complaining to his son that everything in modern Ukraine was useless, and that if only Stalin were around today, he would bring order. 'It turned into an argument, and I got angry. I said to him, "Your own grandfather was repressed by Stalin. In 1937, somewhere in the villages of Kharkov region, the NKVD came to his house, and dragged him away with nothing but the clothes on his back, and your grandmother never saw him again." And he just looked at me, and I realized he doesn't know this. He'd forgotten it, or he never knew. Imagine that. It's just an illustration of how short our historical memories are in this part of the world.'

It was a telling and moving tale, and similar to stories I had heard before. But the strangest thing about it was its source. Khodakovsky was one of the leaders of a movement that exploited exactly the kind of nostalgia for the Soviet period and the 'strong leadership' of Stalin that had irritated him in his father. In fact, a portrait of Stalin had recently appeared on Donetsk's central street, outside the opera theatre. Moreover, on the desk in Khodakovsky's Donetsk office, alongside the Orthodox icons, he had a bust of Dzerzhinsky, the founder of the Cheka. Dzerzhinsky had laid the foundations for the later repressions, and had said quite unequivocally, 'We stand for organized terror'. How did that fit with his desire for an open and pluralistic society, or with his anger about his father's loss of memory?

Dzerzhinsky was an abstract moral ideal, Khodakovsky told me. 'He said a security service agent should have a cold mind, clean hands, and a hot heart. He should be a believer and he should serve his country. I spent twenty years serving in Ukraine's state security organs, and I know how mercantile, how corrupt those men were, and how little they were an example of the heights of the human spirit. I'm not going to take them as my examples, am I? You have to take an ideal from somewhere.'

The same logic applied, he said, to the reason why people in Donbass missed the Soviet Union so much, and longed for a Stalin figure. It was less that they were genuinely passionate Soviets, and more that among the miserable selection of options on offer, it seemed like the best one. There were no great political thinkers or insightful philosophers to guide the people, so the current rulers had to use whatever ideals they could find.

'We have a risk that society becomes seriously ill, and that's why we have to grasp onto what we can. We probably can't create our own ideas, we have no intellectual basis for that, we don't understand the world well enough. So we do what we can. And that's why Soviet ideology has served as a kind of magic wand, because we don't have anything else.'

He was vocalizing something I had sensed constantly during my travels in the post-Soviet world: affection for the Soviet heritage was mainly about fighting a dissatisfaction with the present, not about a real longing for the past. 'You need a foundation, so that in your own conscious-ness you don't have an internal crisis. So people use what their historical memory has given them. Of course, they idealize that society, they ideal-ize Soviet ideology, but you can understand and forgive that. It's more psychotherapy than ideology. They have adopted it, and they feel better.'

But this kind of thinking could take on a life of its own. What Russia wanted from Donetsk was not an *actual* reconstruction of the Soviet system; Moscow merely wanted to exploit nostalgia for the Soviet period to harness support in the region. Real appeals to resurrect the Soviet past, rather than just providing people with the therapy of nos-talgic memories of the war victory and of late-Soviet equality, could be as dangerous as the *real* Russian nationalism that Strelkov peddled. After all, Putin's legitimacy was based on an opposition to the wild capitalist excesses of the 1990s, and yet many in his closest circle had become billionaires.

If a political force appeared that espoused genuine socialist ideas, said Khodakovsky, then 80 per cent of the Donbass population would support it, because of how unfair the past two decades had been. 'Why would Russia want a place next door where this kind of ideology was dominant, when in Russia itself there are so many people who are socially disenfranchised, and who would demand the same kind of thing there? We can't let this ideology develop too much because there is a threat associated with it.'

That, he said, was why the separatist authorities had to be so ruth-less at stamping out dissent, and why they were kept on a short leash by their 'curators' in Moscow, who did not want the rhetorical talking points to become inconvenient political rallying cries. It was why the Donetsk People's Republic was such a crude place, where critical jour-nalists were banned, and locals who spoke out against the regime ended up in basements.

'Here's an allegory,' Khodakovsky said. 'You come into an artist's stu-dio full of subtle, delicate equipment, but you only know how to use a hammer and a saw. You're not going to use the things you don't know how to. We don't know how to work delicately with public opinion, nobody taught us. So we have to use more simplistic methods. We can't allow any ideology or any political diversions we don't control to appear in society. We are reasonable people, of course we want to be able to speak normally, to speak openly, and to look our interlocutors in the eye and argue our point of view. But we still feel shakiness in our legs, and we are not yet strong enough.'

I sensed a permanent melancholic undertone to his words, behind the eloquent but flimsy attempts to justify the brutal Donetsk reality. I couldn't help but wonder, given all the bloodshed and the destruction, and his frank appraisal of the current reality, whether he didn't regret his actions. Wouldn't it have been better to have remained part of an imperfect Ukraine than to become mired in the swamp of drawn-out, bloody conflict?

There was no scenario, he insisted, in which the war not occurring would have been better. 'Of course, from the point of view of the social situation, maybe things here would have been calmer, and economic life would have stayed as normal. But there would have been a different kind of pressure, perhaps even scarier. There was a gradual hammering away at our foundations, at our sense of identity and at the way we wanted to develop. Intrusions into the spiritual realm of a person are as scary, if not more so, than intrusions into the physical realm. These aren't things you can prove, of course. You can only feel it, suggest it in a speculative way. Some people might say you've dreamed it all up yourselves.'

Each time I saw him, I asked the same question, and each time he insisted he regretted nothing. I never quite believed him. On one of his trips to Moscow towards the end of 2016, we sat in the lobby cafe of his hotel, chatting until two in the morning. He looked harried, and slightly diminished.

Russia by then was using the Donbass territories as a bargaining chip with the West, leaving the local leaders to do hopeless U-turns as Moscow changed its instructions on what policies they should follow. Unruly separatist leaders who did not toe Moscow's line had a habit of meeting sticky deaths: a motorcade was shelled, a car sprayed with machine-gun fire, a warlord blown up in the lift of his Donetsk apartment block, and another exploded in his office. 'Ukrainian diversionaries' were blamed each time, but nobody believed that. Khodakovsky had so far escaped such a fate, but had been removed as head of the security council and told to keep quiet.

His whole bearing suggested he was beginning to crack under the weight of the Kremlin's cynicism, but Donetsk was his home, and he did not want to flee to Russia, as some of the other rebel leaders had done.

'We're tired of being an experiment. Our people were used and ignored for years on end, and then they had a small taste of what it's like to be part of something real. But now they've lost it again.'

III

The outburst of patriotism prompted by the 2014 interventions was a powerful mobilizing force for Putin, and even though it was followed by Western sanctions and a falling rouble, his ratings remained high. A public opinion survey[1] released in March 2017 asked Russians to list the things that made them proud of their country. Victory in the Great Patriotic War came first, of course, and in second place was the 'return' of Crimea, above the Soviet space programme. Lower down the list came Russian literary and scientific achievements.

In the new, jingoistic atmosphere, the victory legend remained central to the narrative, but efforts were made to augment it with newer celebratory material. As the centenary of 1917 approached, the focus was not on the two revolutions and their confusing, shades-of-grey meaning for Russia, but on slotting other historical events into place to weave a grand narrative of Russian history. Second-tier heroes and victories, including from the tsarist past, could take their place below the Great Victory and the return of Crimea in an unbroken narrative of Russian success.

In November 2016, a monument to Vladimir the Great, the tenth-century ruler of Kiev who had been baptized in Crimea, was unveiled outside the Kremlin, rising seventeen metres high and dominating the central Borovitskaya Square. During the opening ceremony, the awkward fact that Vladimir had in fact been prince of Kiev was not mentioned once. Kirill, the patriarch of the Orthodox Church, said that without Vladimir, 'there would have been no Rus', no Russia, no Russian Orthodox power, no great Russian Empire, and no modern Russia.'

Putin called Vladimir 'a far-sighted politician who created the foundations of a strong, unified, centralized state,' and said it was the baptism of Rus' under Vladimir that had led to the strong morals and values that still defined Russian life.

'It is this solid moral foundation, unity and solidarity that helped our ancestors overcome difficulties, live and achieve victories to the glory of the Fatherland, strengthening its power and greatness from one generation to the next,' said Putin as the monument, cross-in-hand, towered behind him. The Vladimir outside the Kremlin was a thinly veiled tribute to the Vladimir residing within its walls: two bookends of a millennium of Russianness.

The monument was opened on 4 November, the so-called Day of National Unity. State television carried live pictures of the unveiling, and the commentators mused on the theme of the day: 'When you think of our national unity, of course you think firstly about the victory in the Great Patriotic War, as this is the event that binds us all together. But you also think of the times in which we lacked national unity, in 1917, and 1991, and this is equally important.' Thus, the twentieth century's dual collapses were disastrous moments of cataclysm, while a strong united Russia—be it tsarist, Soviet, or Putinist—was to be welcomed.

The Soviet state had always faced a tricky conundrum: its ideology glorified revolution and revolutionaries, but its actions had to stifle any actual protest impulse in its citizens. Putin's narrative faced no such paradox. It fetishised *stabil'nost'*, which meant revolution and state collapse was inherently bad, whether in 1917, 1991, on Maidan in Kiev, or in some future hypothetical Russia.

EPILOGUE

By 2017, it was hard to open a newspaper in London or New York without seeing a news story about Russia interfering in the affairs of Western nations. Intelligence services fretted about what Moscow's next move would be, and CNN ran a documentary about Putin entitled *The Most Powerful Man in the World*. The goal he had set back in 1999, on the eve of his entry into the Kremlin, had been achieved. Russia had indeed become a first-tier nation, in narrow geopolitical terms, and the majority of Russians felt proud of their country again.

But the gradual economic improvement of the oil boom years had tailed off after 2014, as Western sanctions and plummeting oil prices combined to hammer the Russian economy. As the cash flows dried up, it became clear how little had been done to diversify the resource-rich economy during the years of plenty. More than twenty million Russians—around 15 per cent of the population—had incomes below the poverty line, while 38 per cent had problems affording food and clothing.[1] I was reminded of a phrase Stalin's daughter had used in a letter to her children, explaining her defection to the United States in 1967, about the perverse nature of the Soviet system: 'With one hand we try to catch the moon itself, but with the other we are obliged to dig potatoes, the same way it was done a hundred years ago.'[2]

In February 2017, as the Western world pondered allegations that Putin's intelligence services had intervened to help get Donald Trump elected, I travelled to Irkutsk, six hours from Moscow by plane. The town, of pretty wooden cottages and grimy Soviet-era high-rises, was in the midst of a harsh Siberian winter. A few weeks previously, more than eighty people had died in one of Irkutsk's suburbs from drinking a poisoned consignment of *boyaryshnik*, a hawthorn-infused bath tincture that was widely quaffed by poor Russians as it was cheaper than vodka and contained a good percentage of chemical ethanol. An underground laboratory in Irkutsk had made a counterfeit batch that contained methanol instead of ethanol. Those who ingested it were rushed to hospital, but most of them died the same day, following a massive failure of their internal organs. Some health experts estimated that more than ten million Russians still drank this kind of booze substitute on a regular basis.

I met up with Anton, a twenty-two-year-old nationalist and member of Irkutsk's youth parliament. In the aftermath of the *boyaryshnik* tragedy, he and a group of friends had got together to try to rid the city's shops of fake alcohol. He took me on a mission with his friend Ivan to a shop on the outskirts of town. They had received an anonymous tip-off through their social media group that the shop was selling counterfeit vodka under the table. They smoked cigarettes, tousled their hair, and carried pockets of loose change to imitate drunks scraping together their last roubles for a bottle of the hard stuff. They hid a tiny camera in a packet of Winston cigarettes; if the shop sold them vodka, they could turn the footage in to police to make arrests. I waited outside in the cold while they went into the shop; they emerged shortly afterwards, pleased that they had found no illegal alcohol this time. The situation was improving, thanks in part to their sleuthing over previous weeks.

Anton was born in 1995 in a small town not far from Irkutsk called Cheremkhovo. He grew up in a poor family but managed to win a place at Irkutsk University, where he was now living in a dormitory. In 2014, he did his military service in Novosibirsk, a day's journey along the Trans-Siberian towards Moscow. It was the height of the Ukraine crisis, and the unit was on high alert, with frequent drills in which they would deploy to the depths of the tundra and rehearse launching missile strikes. Novosibirsk was the furthest from home he had ever been, but he wanted to see Moscow, Europe, America.

He had gone into politics because he wanted to help people, he said. 'To be a politician is to defend your country and help your people.'

He dreamed of one day becoming president. He was not in it for the money, or at least not yet; when I asked if there was a cafe or bar we could go to for a chat, he had no idea. He didn't normally go to places like that, he said, because he couldn't afford it.

We eventually found a bar and he excitedly ordered a whisky and coke when I offered. Putin had been in charge of Russia since Anton was a five-year-old, and although he conceded that for most people in Irkutsk life was difficult, and that most local politicians were corrupt, he was a fan of the president, especially since 2014. Putin had defended Russia's interests against a rapacious West, Anton said, and by intervening in Syria had saved us all from World War Three, though he was hazy on the details of quite how this had happened. If he became president one day, he would focus on internal problems more, he said, because life was such a hard grind. However, right now, he could not imagine ever speaking out directly against the president. With Russia under attack from the West, the country had to remain united. Political unrest would merely give Russia's enemies an opportunity to act. After we had chatted for a while, Anton said he had a few questions of his own to ask me. The first was about the Second World War.

'What do people in Britain know about the Soviet war effort? Do they realize that the Soviet Union saved the world from fascism?'

'Well, I'm not sure people know all the details,' I said. 'But certainly they know that the Soviets made enormous sacrifices. Everyone has heard of the Battle of Stalingrad.'

'And what about Victory Day? Do you celebrate it?'

'Well, a little. There were some celebrations on the round anniversaries, but in general it's more of a commemoration than a big party.'

'Ah, well that's understandable. No other country lasted more than six months against the Nazis, except the Soviets! So why would you celebrate?' There was nothing confrontational about his tone, he spoke as though he was merely stating the obvious.

Anton was a good kid, and was putting in long hours in an attempt to help his city overcome an awful problem, but he could not stop talking about the war. It infused all his thoughts. When I asked him about his home town, Cheremkhovo, the first thing he told me was that it had produced a lot of coal during the war.

Now that I was actively keeping an eye out for war paraphernalia, I started to see it everywhere, nibbling away at the subconscious from a thousand sources at once. At the hospital where many of the *boyarysh-nik* patients were treated, the head doctor had a 9 May Victory flag on his desk. An ambulance parked outside the entrance to the emergency ward had '1941–1945' emblazoned on its side. After I left the hospital I found my driver tuned to a radio station playing a documentary about the fall of Berlin. I picked up a copy of that week's local newspaper and found three articles about the war: one was a news report from the local veterans' committee, another was about a competition for patriotic school projects to mark the 114th anniversary of the birth of a local war hero, and there was also a full-page spread chronicling the life of a veteran who had died a decade earlier. A few days after I returned from Irkutsk to Moscow, Russia's defence minister Sergei Shoigu announced that in a 'patriotic park' outside Moscow, a mock-up of the Reichstag would be erected. Shortly afterwards, a vast, costumed reenactment of the storming took place.

The war film of the moment was *Panfilov's 28*, a tale of twenty-eight Red Army soldiers who fought so heroically in the Battle of Moscow that they were able to hold off the advance of dozens of Nazi tanks. The men all died, and became true Soviet heroes, immortalized in monuments and history books. But the story had been made up, or at least dramatically embellished. When Sergei Mironenko, director of the Russian State Archive, pointed this out, he was shot down by culture minister Vladimir Medinsky, who said that 'only total scumbags' would question sacred Soviet war legends. Medinsky said he believed the Russian people should treat the Second World War heroes in the same way that the church revered saints. They were untouchables.[3] Mironenko was fired.

Victory, by this point, really was Russia's religion: it had a narrative of martyrdom and glory, and its own symbols and iconography. It demanded a religious level of faith in the truth of its canons, and it had its own saints, sacred texts, and sermons.

Before leaving Irkutsk, I paid a visit to School Number 45, in a run-down suburb that had a reputation as exactly the sort of place where people drank *boyaryshnik*. Inside the school, the corridors were decorated with homework projects about the army, and the children were preparing for 23 February, Defenders of the Fatherland Day.

The headteacher, Lyudmila Baikalova, was a whirlwind of energy, as she raced from classroom to classroom in a shiny white jacket and sparkly matching shoes, rounding up the children for a rehearsal. There were still two weeks to go, but Lyudmila wanted the parade to be perfect, and had the children marching up and down in lines, singing war songs, and saluting each other. 'It makes me want to burst with pride, just looking at them,' she said. 'Patriotism is the most important thing for us. It's beautiful that we remember the previous generations and we are proud of our great country.' Three years earlier, the school had reintroduced the old Soviet uniform, smart black blazers and ties for the boys, and a white apron for the girls, with their hair tied in white ribbons. There had been a discussion among parents and teachers, Lyudmila told me, and it was decided that morale at the school would be improved immeasurably if the old uniform was returned.

In a side room, an extracurricular class for the most patriotic thirteen-year-olds was under way, about the Russian Army and its weapons. The teacher read in a monotone from pre-prepared PowerPoint slides about the characteristics and functions of S-400 missile systems, Soviet and modern Russian tanks, and other weaponry. The students dutifully took notes. I asked them a few questions; they all told me life had become much harder since 2014, and some of their families had been forced to cut back on food. But they expressed approval of Putin, who they said was doing his best to fight corruption among his underlings.

After the lesson was over, Lyudmila ushered me into her office, where she had laid out a lunch spread: fish with mashed potatoes, pickles, and a mayonnaise-drenched salad. 'You're a man, and a man should eat properly,' she said warmly, pushing plate after plate towards me. Since her husband died five years ago, she said, she had more or less lived her whole life through the school, arriving at the crack of dawn and often leaving late at night. She devoted her sizeable reserves of energy towards trying to give the pupils prospects for the future, and wanted to fill them with patriotic thoughts to make them feel part of something big and important.

Her phone rang, and I heard one side of a conversation that was presumably fraught on the other end. Lyudmila's tone was soothingly routine. 'He's kidnapped the kid? . . . And where's the mother? . . . And there's a one-year-old sister? . . . Do we know where the grandparents are? . . . Are there any sober family members? . . . OK, I will raise the alarm and do everything I can.'

She turned to me, with a just a hint of weariness infusing her usual enthusiasm. 'This is a very difficult part of town.'

She enquired as to the subject of my book; I told her it was about the elevation of the war victory to a national idea in Russia, and she beamed a smile of genuine warmth. She was delighted I would be writing about such an important topic. If only more Westerners understood the importance of the Soviet war effort, she said. I thought about her long hours of work in the school, trying to use patriotism and war memory to imbue a sense of meaning into the difficult lives of these kids, and felt a pang of guilt at the fact that the book's contents would be sharply at odds with what she doubtless had in mind.

But even though much of the Soviet war story really was inspiring, and millions like Lyudmila took to its promotion in good faith, I still found the broader cynicism hard to swallow. Putin had faced a truly difficult task, when he took office in 2000, to pull together this creaking, wounded nation. But it was now seventeen years into his rule over Russia. During that time, his old childhood judo partners, his former KGB pals, and the trusted associates he had parachuted into various governmental jobs had amassed fortunes and moved into vast palaces outside Moscow, hidden from the public behind high forest-green fences. Many of them badmouthed the West in public but purchased real estate in London, Miami, or the South of France. They spent their weekends at lavish parties and their holidays on yachts; the wife of one deputy prime minister flew her pet corgis around Europe on a private jet. Meanwhile, here in the Russian heartland, people were drinking themselves to death on poisoned bath fluid because they couldn't afford vodka, while being bombarded with never-ending tales about the glory of a victory that had occurred seventy-two years previously. On state television, shrill news bulletins, shouty talk shows, and bombastic documentaries drilled into viewers that the 'return' of Crimea and the newly assertive Russian foreign policy should be a new source of pride. The international outcry and sanctions were passed off as sour grapes from foreign powers jealous of Russia's resurgence. The presidential election was shifted to 18 March 2018, the fourth anniversary of the official annexation of Crimea, to give a patriotic undertone to the electoral 'contest'.

Putin had largely succeeded in his mission to create a sense of nation and rally Russia around a patriotic idea. But instead of transcending the trauma of the Soviet collapse, his government exploited it, using fear of political unrest to quash opposition, equating 'patriotism' with support for Putin, and using a simplified narrative of the Second World War to imply Russia must unite once again against a foreign threat. Even if protests against the current obscene levels of corruption become a serious threat for Putin, or one day even lead to a change of government, the patriotic rhetoric of his years in charge is likely to endure. These ideas have formed the basis for the upbringing of a whole new generation of Russians, and they will continue to influence the collective Russian psyche long after Putin finally departs from the Kremlin.

Russia's glorious past has become a national obsession, but a prosperous future still seems a long way off.

AFTERWORD TO THE
PAPERBACK EDITION

LATE IN THE SUMMER of 2018, some months after this book first came out, I packed up my apartment in Moscow for good. After fourteen years, it was time for me to leave Russia, although I wasn't going all that far: to Budapest to take up a new job roaming central and eastern Europe, where I now cover seventeen countries that, like Russia and Ukraine, shed Communist regimes three decades ago. My new region was also made up of nations that have spent the intervening years creating or rediscovering national identities, just like Russia and Ukraine. Most of these new countries had managed the journey with fewer convulsions than had been felt in the former heartlands of the Soviet Union, and many of them were already in the European Union. But the same issues borne of decades living with an enforced, prescriptive historical worldview, followed by the requirements of building new nations in the wake of the collapse of Communism, were present to some degree in all of them. The moulding of history to fit contemporary narratives was ever-present.

The way this worked varied from country to country, depending on the differing historical legacies in each of them left by Europe's bloodiest century. In Hungary, the gnawing sense of victimhood over the post–First World War settlement that had left many ethnic Hungarians living outside the country's borders was still a matter of daily public discourse, while the Nazi-allied Hungarian regime's deportation of the nation's Jews to Auschwitz was quietly sidelined. In Poland, the tragic fate of the Poles led to an unsavoury kind of competitive victimhood when it came to discussions about the Holocaust, that consistently poisoned historical debates. While in some places, twentieth-century history was everywhere you looked, in other places, people preferred to keep it buried. In Romania, when I visited the National History Museum, its halls filled with ancient treasures and portraits of medieval princes, the narrative stopped in 1918. I asked one of the staff where I could find the twentieth-century section. "There isn't one," she said curtly, with an irritated shake of the head.

Across the region, the Second World War was still the most complicated historical issue, and the one most put to use by governments involved in nation-building projects. Memories of heroism, betrayal, shame, and genocide jostled to find their place in the narratives. As in Russia, it was unsurprising that such a devastating conflict was the primary source of national myths for the whole continent, but also as with Russia and Ukraine, politicians seeking to boost national pride took a selective approach to historical memory.

It was not just "new Europe" that suffered from a problematic relationship with the war. Back home in Britain, the national discussion (which sometimes felt more like a national shouting match) unleashed by the recriminations of the Brexit vote led to an increased focus on British history and the Second World War victory. As I arrived in Oxford in early 2018 to give a lecture about this book, one of the first things that struck me as I went into the newsagents at the train station was a large, colourful magazine embossed with a Union Jack and the all-caps title BRITAIN'S GREATEST VICTORIES. Politicians, and many ordinary people, evoked the war years as a sign of Britain standing up to foreign aggressors, and drawing implausible parallels with the modern-day European Union. The Conservative MP Marc Francois went so far as to use a television interview to rip up a letter from the German CEO of Airbus warning against the economic impact of Brexit. Accusing him of "Teutonic arrogance," Francois said his war veteran father "never submitted to bullying by any German, and neither will his son." The combination of bluster, arrogance, and trivialization of the war sacrifice made me feel like I was back in Russia. In the US, there has always been a long-standing strain of public discourse that paints American soldiers as the decisive force in the war, reinforced over the years by Hollywood. Donald Trump went further, seeming to echo Putin in his reverence for the war victory in his 2019 State of the Union address. He referred to the D-Day landings as "the most momentous battle in the history of war," something that no doubt came as a surprise to anyone who had studied Stalingrad or numerous other key battles on the Eastern front.

As the eightieth anniversary of the outbreak of the Second World War came around in September 2019, there were fewer and fewer people left alive anywhere in the world who had a direct link to the conflict. Only a tiny handful of veterans remained alive and lucid. In a few years from now, there will be none. And yet the Second World War remains the conflict that the world cannot stop reliving. In many ways, eighty years is the perfect amount of time for those events to be used for all kinds of political grandstanding and national narrative building. Twenty years ago, there were still many people alive who remembered all too well the horrors of war; in twenty years from now, a whole century will have passed, and the outbreak of war will be as distant as was the American Civil War to those alive in the 1960s. Right now, however, we are in a sweet spot. Most people alive in Europe have a grandparent or great-grandparent who was involved in the conflict in some way, yet there are few people left with real, lived memories. This combination, of visceral personal links combined with an absence of actual knowledge, creates ripe ground for the war as a perfect nation-building device.

The complex, all-embracing nature of the Second World War makes it a helpfully flexible friend to politicians, too. Depending on the needs of the day, it can be used to herald the benefits of global alliances with unsavoury partners, or can be used to show that such regimes should be firmly dealt with before they become a major threat. It can be used to warn of the devastating effects of war or used as a rallying call to fight new wars. As far-right parties win a stronger foothold in European politics, it can even be used in a way unthinkable a decade ago. In my new job, I met politicians in a number of countries who praised aspects of Nazi Germany, something that would have resulted in ostracism from the public debate not so long ago. Now, some of these people had parliamentary seats and all the legitimacy that conferred (and, ironically, some of them were backed by Russia, ostensibly the lodestar of anti-fascism).

In Russia itself, the cult of victory continued to march on as forcefully and unstoppably as ever. In the city of Nizhny Tagil, the 2019 celebrations saw people dressed up as Nazi prisoners of war paraded through the city streets inside cages. As on every 9 May, my Facebook timeline was filled with anguished Russians, bemused at the West's refusal to acknowledge the enormous price the Soviet Union paid to defeat Nazism and angered at criticism of the pomp and parade, sprinkled with a few affronted liberals despairing at the "privatization" of victory by Putin and the militarism and aggression of the day. A poll in 2019 showed that victory remained the overwhelming winner in surveys of what made Russians proud, soaring ahead of the achievements in space or any intellectual achievements. Another 2019 survey showed record approval ratings for the historical role of Stalin, with 70% of Russians saying he had played a positive role in Russia's development. Among 18- to 24-year-olds, only 13% said they had a negative view of Stalin's historical role.

And yet there were some signs in both Russia and Ukraine that other narratives are possible and other stories could be told. I returned to Kiev in April 2019 to see Petro Poroshenko, who had risen to power on the hopes and aspirations of Maidan, be soundly defeated by Volodymyr Zelenskiy, a television actor and comedian who had no political experience except playing the president in a sitcom. Poroshenko had ramped up his nationalist rhetoric in the run-up to the vote, trumpeting a new, Ukrainian church and running on a "language, faith, army" platform. Zelenskiy also said he was a Ukrainian patriot who detested Russian aggression, but he spoke of a softer, more inclusive vision of Ukrainianness, one that could allow for but not necessitate the worship of Bandera, for example. On 9 May 2019, shortly before his inauguration, he made a point of laying flowers at the grave of his grandfather, who had fought for the Red Army. There were many questions about how effective a president he could be, but his election certainly showed an appetite for a new kind of national identity in large parts of Ukraine.

My final assignment for *The Guardian* in Russia was to cover the football World Cup in June and July 2018, spending a month criss-crossing the country to games in various cities, culminating in the final at Moscow's Luzhniki stadium, where France lifted the trophy in driving summer rain. For a month prior to that, Moscow had turned into a 24-hour party city, as the streets were filled with boisterous football fans from across Europe and South America. Argentinians drank and danced the night away in Nizhny Novgorod, Portuguese and Iranian fans mingled with locals in the dusty outpost of Saransk. The vast majority of fans who travelled to the tournament had a fantastic time and marvelled at the incredible sights of Russia, while most Russians took delight in showing off their country to the visiting hordes. The tedious Russian visa process was relaxed for anyone who held a match ticket, and many people felt vindicated that the visitors were able to see how much Russia had to offer visiting tourists, and to show a different side of the country to the one that is so often in the headlines.

One night, several hours after the games that day had finished, I walked down Nikolskaya, the pedestrianized street that runs from Red Square to the Lubyanka, and which had become the unofficial hub for fans of all countries. The dawn was about to break, but thousands were still out in the street, singing, dancing, and mingling in good humour, with Russians in the majority but fans of all the competing nations joining in the fun. A few cops looked on smiling, having been ordered to ignore the law banning public alcohol consumption for the month. As I pushed my way through the crowds and finally came out onto Lubyanka Square, around 100 people were dancing to the tune of a techno beat, blasting from speakers mounted on top of a parked SUV. Such a scene, in the shadow of the feared FSB headquarters, where normally just loitering would invite the swift approach of a policeman, felt dizzyingly transgressive and liberating.

There was, for sure, a Potemkin-village feel to much of the official bonhomie. Russia did not become a different place overnight, and it always had fascinating historical sights and a raucous nightlife open to those who were intrepid enough to look, existing alongside all the more sinister repressive state apparatus. But there was something different in the air for that month. It was everything Putin had wanted the Sochi Olympics to be, and more, four years later and amid much lower expectations. There was a warmth, a joy, and most importantly a pride located not in historical grievances but in the present. It was a tantalizing taste of another Russia, one which might one day materialize.

Budapest, summer 2019

AUTHOR'S NOTE

I have used Kiev and Odessa instead of Kyiv and Odesa, as they are accepted English spellings. For towns in Russophone areas of eastern Ukraine I have used Russian names, so Konstantinovka and not Kostiantynivka, etc., as these were the names most often used by the locals.

I have occasionally changed people's names and, on a very small number of occasions, amended minor details, in cases where people asked me not to use their real names, or where I took my own decision to protect a person's identity.

ACKNOWLEDGEMENTS

My thanks to Masha Kortunova for the long hours of transcription and other help; and to Veronika Dorman, Roland Oliphant, Tom Parfitt, Masha Turchenkova, Elena Volochine, and Emma Wells for being good company and thoughtful colleagues on reporting trips.

I'm thankful to Ksenia Bolchakova for generosity with contacts and ideas for Magadan, and Sergei Raizman for showing me around the city. Pavel Polian was helpful on the deportations, Bryan Glynn Williams on the Chechens and Crimean Tatars, and Tom de Waal on Chechnya. Lana Estemirova helped me on some Chechen-language issues. Many people at Moscow Memorial were helpful on various aspects of the Soviet period. Simon Shuster dug out useful audio from Belbek.

In Kiev, Kristina Berdynskykh has always been wonderfully generous and collegiate; Anastasia Magazova was also very helpful with contacts in Crimea and elsewhere in Ukraine. In Donbass, there are many people who helped at various times with logistics, transport, and safety on both sides of the lines to whom I owe thanks.

I am extremely grateful to Essie Chambers, Amie Ferris-Rotman, Sally Foreman, Suzy Hansen, Michael Idov, Polly Jones, James Lanman, Maria Lipman, David Marples, Sophie Pinkham, David Priestland, Elena Racheva, Douglas Smith, Nargis Walker, and Joshua Yaffa for the time they spent reading parts or all of the text and giving extremely valuable comments and suggestions. Particular thanks to Sarah Topol, who valiantly ploughed through an early draft.

It has been an honour to work for *The Guardian*, the newspaper I grew up reading and always wanted to write for. Jamie Wilson has been a perfect foreign editor, giving me the latitude to pursue the stories I found interesting, and providing guidance without interference. Everyone else on *The Guardian*'s foreign desk has been nothing but a delight to work with. I also owe much gratitude to Andrei Zolotov Jr for giving me a chance to start out in journalism in Moscow back in 2005.

Daniel Kunin and Kirsty Giles gave me places to write in, respectively, Tusheti and Crystal Palace. Spending three weeks at the MacDowell Colony in New Hampshire was an amazing opportunity and helped me get the draft finished, and Simon Morrison was kind enough to put me up for ten days at Princeton to do the final edits. Tracy Bohan and Kristina Moore at Wylie, and David McBride and Claire Sibley at Oxford University Press have helped me through the process of putting the book together.

Finally, I must mention my enormous debt to Marina Akhmedova, one of my oldest friends and my long-standing reporting partner. Her generosity with time and contacts has been absolutely invaluable. We often disagreed about the things we saw, but without her, many of the characters featured in this book would never even have spoken to me.

NOTES

Chapter 1

1. Gevorkyan, Timakova, Kolesnikov, *First Person*, 78–79.
2. Gevorkyan, Timakova, Kolesnikov, *First Person*, 80.
3. Talbott, *The Russia Hand*, 197.
4. There is compelling circumstantial evidence that these explosions may have been a 'false flag' operation carried out by elements of the state. See, for example, Satter, *Darkness at Dawn*.
5. http://www.levada.ru/2016/04/19/bolshe-poloviny-rossiyan-sozhaleyut-o-raspade-sssr/.
6. Available at http://www.ng.ru/politics/1999-12-30/4_millenium.html.
7. Interview with David Frost, 5 March 2000, http://news.bbc.co.uk/hi/english/static/audio_video/programmes/breakfast_with_frost/transcripts/putin5.mar.txt.
8. For more detail on the idea of the post-Soviet cityscape as palimpsest see Oushakine, *The Patriotism of Despair*.

Chapter 2

1. http://kremlin.ru/events/president/transcripts/21421.
2. Quoted in Ivo Mijnssen, "The Victory Myth and Russia's Identity," *Russian Analytical Digest* 72, no 10 (9 February 2010): 7.
3. http://kremlin.ru/events/president/transcripts/24938/videos.
4. See, for example, Rolf, *Soviet Mass Festivals*, 182–183.
5. Quoted in Service, *Russia*, 287–288.
6. Artizov and Naumov, *Vlast' i Khudozhestvennaya Intelligentsiya*, 494.
7. See, for example, Korney Chukovsky's words in Artizov and Naumov, *Vlast' i Khudozhestvennaya Intelligentsiya*, 494, 524.

8. For example, the aunt of the dissident Andrei Sakharov, whose husband had been murdered by the Bolsheviks, found the war a sort of relief noting that 'for the first time in years I feel that I am Russian'. See Braithwaite, *Moscow 1941*, 356.

9. Andrew and Mitrokhin, *The Mitrokhin Archive*, 122.

10. Merridale, *Night of Stone*, 215.

11. See, for example, Hellbeck, *Stalingrad*, 15–19.

12. Naimark, *Stalin's Genocides*, 88.

13. Quoted in Remnick, *Lenin's Tomb*, 403.

14. Statistics on the deportation of the Kalmyks are from author interview with Vladimir Ubushayev in 2007, and his book *Kalmyki: Vyselenie i vozvrashchenie 1943–57*, available online at http://www.memorial.krsk.ru/Articles/Ubushaev.htm.

15. Figures from Supplement 1 of Polian, *Against Their will*. There were also the mass deportations of Balts and Ukrainians just after the war began.

16. Williams, *Inferno in Chechnya*, 75.

17. Williams, *Inferno in Chechnya*, 81.

18. Ubushayev, interview with the author, 2007.

19. Polian, *Istoriomor*, 174–175.

20. Nataliya Narochnitskaya, *Rossiya dolzhna aktivnee protivodeistvovat' popytkam nizvesti na net ee glavenstvuyushchuyu rol' v pobede nad natsizmom*, http://narotchnitskaya.com/interviews/nataliya-narochnitskaya-rossiya-dolzhna-aktivnee-protivodeystvovat-popyitkam-nizvesti-na-net-eyo-glavenstvuyushhuyu-rol-v-pobede-nad-natsizmom.html?view=full.

21. It is probable that the controversy was used by those who wanted to shut the channel down for other reasons, but it was at the very least indicative of the climate in Russia that 'inappropriate' references to the war were pounced upon as something that could be used against the channel.

22. Beevor, *Berlin*, 412.

23. Antony Beevor, interview with the author, August 2015.

24. While the average American might be better acquainted with saccharine Hollywood renditions of camaraderie among US troops than with the internment camps or with the ethical dilemmas around dropping the atom bombs on Japan, when I typed 'Japanese internment camps' into amazon.com I found dozens of books on the topic. On Ozon, the Russian equivalent of Amazon, searches for books about the wartime deportations gave a mere two results. One promised to unmask the slanders of 'Russophobes' and their supposed lies about the deportations, while another had a print run of 1,500. By comparison, the same site had 48 different titles about the Battle of Kursk, and 138 on Stalingrad. Recently there has been impressive work on the deportations by a few Russian historians ploughing this lonely furrow, most notably Pavel Polian.

Chapter 3

1. http://news.bbc.co.uk/2/hi/europe/586691.stm.
2. Bullough, *Let our fame be great*, 326.
3. Naimark, *Stalin's Genocides*, 96.
4. http://news.bbc.co.uk/hi/english/static/audio_video/programmes/
   breakfast_with_frost/transcripts/putin5.mar.txt.
5. Smith, *Allah's Mountains*, xviii.
6. It should be noted that Laurel Fay, among others, has cast significant
   doubt on whether these words were actually Shostakovich's.
7. Swank, at least, fired her manager and apologized after her turn at the
   concert was reported by me in *The Independent* and picked up elsewhere,
   claiming she had not been properly informed about the situation in
   Chechnya. The others did not.
8. This quote, and one small quote later on, is taken from an earlier interview
   with Apti Bolotkhanov carried out by my friend and reporting partner
   Marina Akhmedova of *Russky Reporter* magazine.
9. Polian, *Istoriomor*, 82.
10. Elena Milashina, "Kak lomali Ruslana Kutayeva, i
    pochemu on ne slomalsya," *Novaya Gazeta*, 12 July
    2014, https://www.novayagazeta.ru/articles/2014/07/12/
    60323-kak-lomali-ruslana-kutaeva-i-pochemu-on-ne-slomalsya.
11. https://www.youtube.com/watch?v=qmJYN8LQegM.

Chapter 4

1. Applebaum, *Gulag*, 88.
2. The town had different names depending on who was in charge.
   Stanisławow was the Polish name, Stanislau the Austro-Hungarian,
   Stanislav the post-war Soviet name. In 1962, Soviet authorities changed
   the name to Ivano-Frankivsk, after the Ukrainian poet Ivan Franko. It still
   bears this name today.
3. Applebaum, *Gulag*, 440.
4. Quoted in Remnick, *Lenin's Tomb*, 50.
5. Merridale, *Night of Stone*, 306.
6. Stalin himself had used the phrase, 'When wood is cut, chips fly'.
7. Schlögel, *Moscow 1937*, 472.
8. Getty and Naumov, *The Road to Terror*, 243.
9. Quoted in Merridale, *Night of Stone*, 203.
10. Grossman, *Everything Flows*, 62.
11. Shaun Walker, "Stalin's Secret Police Finally Named but
    Killings Still Not Seen as Crimes', *The Guardian*, 6 February
    2017, https://www.theguardian.com/world/2017/feb/06/
    stalin-secret-police-killings-crimes-russia-terror-nkvd
12. One of the many problems with this line was that it presupposed that the
    Soviet Union was not an empire, doing little justice to the hundreds of

thousands of Poles, Ukrainians, Chechens, and Crimean Tatars, among others, who died in ethnically based repressions. The insistence that it was all an internal matter contributed to the poisoning of contemporary relations between ethnicities, whether it be Chechens, Poles, or Ukrainians, who felt Moscow refused to accept responsibility for the crimes of the past.

13. This site was also not without controversy, as it was reopened in 2015 with the focus more on memory of incarceration rather than of repression.

14. For a discussion of this see Buruma, *The Wages of Guilt*, 21.

15. Quoted in Encarnación, *Democracy without Justice in Spain*, 81–82.

Chapter 5

1. See Zygar, *All the Kremlin's Men*, 254.

2. Saakashvili suggested to Putin that if he was so upset, he should open a Museum of Georgian occupation in Moscow. (Georgian government source, interview with the author, 2006.)

3. There has been much debate on these points, but this chimes with what I saw on the ground, and learned from interviews, and is also the conclusion of the thousand-page, exhaustive report authored by a Swiss diplomat that found that 'operations started with a massive Georgian artillery attack' but also stated that 'much of the Russian military action went far beyond the reasonable limits of defence'. See Shaun Walker, "Georgia Began War with Russia but It Was Provoked, Inquiry Finds," *The Independent*, 30 September 2009, http://www.independent.co.uk/news/world/europe/georgia-began-war-with-russia-but-it-was-provoked-inquiry-finds-1795744.html.

4. This is the account given by Putin in a Russian television documentary made a year after the annexation.

Chapter 6

1. Snyder, *The Reconstruction of Nations*, 121.

2. This policy of 'taking root' was promoted across the Soviet ethnic republic in the 1920s before being rolled back during the 1930s.

3. Recounted in Snyder, *Bloodlands*, 50.

4. Dolot, *Execution by Hunger*, 211.

5. Dolot, *Execution by Hunger*, 197–202.

6. Snyder, *Bloodlands*, 47.

7. Snyder, *Bloodlands*, 56.

8. Grossman, *Everything Flows*, 137–138.

9. Rossolinski-Liebe, *Stepan Bandera*, 177.

10. Rossolinski-Liebe, *Stepan Bandera*, 181.

11. They took the city from the Soviets, who had annexed western Ukraine in 1939.

12. Rossolinski-Liebe, *Stepan Bandera*, 207.

13. Many Ukrainians went to great lengths to help Jews, and Israel has to date recognized 2,272 citizens of Ukraine as 'Righteous among the Nations' for sheltering Jews during the Holocaust (see Plokhy, *The Gates of Europe*, 271). Nevertheless, elements of the Ukrainian nationalist movement willingly embraced Nazi anti-Semitism. Close to a million Jews from Ukraine were killed in the Holocaust—around one in six of all the victims—and in at least some of the massacres, locals played a part.

14. Reid, *Borderland*, 214.

15. Reid, *Borderland*, 222.

16. Maria Danilova, "Ukraine Marks Anniversary of Great Famine," Associated Press, 22 November 2008.

17. Rudling, "The Cult of Roman Shukhevych in Ukraine," 34.

18. There is circumstantial but troubling evidence that mass killings of Jews took place under the guise of 'fighting partisans' during this time; see Rudling, "The Cult of Roman Shukhevych in Ukraine," 39–41.

19. Interview with Mikhail Tyaglyy of the Ukrainian Centre for Holocaust Studies.

20. One such town was Rava-Ruska, where a memorial appeared only in 2015.

21. Talbott, *The Russia Hand*, 80.

22. Plokhy, *Yalta*, 121.

23. Plokhy, *Yalta*, 75.

24. A scene witnessed, and recounted to me, by the Dutch reporter Olaf Koens.

25. https://www.kyivpost.com/article/content/ukraine-politics/poll-half-of-ukrainians-dont-support-kyiv-euromaidan-rb-334469.html.

Chapter 7

1. Pleshakov, *The Crimean Nexus*, 90.

2. http://www.rferl.org/a/ukraine-crimea-bases-targetted/25306141.html.

3. The report is available online at http://old.president-sovet.ru/structure/gruppa_po_migratsionnoy_politike/materialy/problemy_zhiteley_kryma.php. While the official results are extremely dubious, the figures in this report also seem incorrectly skewed in the other direction when compared with informal conversations during the month I spent in Crimea.

4. From remarks made in a meeting with businessmen quoted by *Kommersant*, among others, *Uvolen za nesootvetsvie zanimaemoi territorii*, 22 August 2005, http://kommersant.ru/doc/602759.

5. "Voennaya doktrina Rossiiskoi Federatsii," http://rg.ru/2014/12/30/doktrina-dok.html.

Chapter 8

1. Sebag-Montefiore, *Potemkin*, 275–276.

2. Sebag-Montefiore, *Potemkin*, 272.

3. Quoted in Glyn Williams, *The Crimean Tatars*, 8.

4. Figes, *Crimea*, 422.
5. Quoted in Glyn Williams, *The Crimean Tatars*, 63.
6. It was never overtly specified that the Crimean Autonomous Soviet Socialist Republic was meant to be specifically *Crimean Tatar*, and thus bring with it the attributes and privileges that being a titular ethnicity brought with it, but the evidence suggests this probably was the intention. The distinction, while seemingly irrelevant, was important in terms of ethnic claims to the territory, and is still argued about in Crimea today.
7. Glyn Williams, *The Crimean Tatars*, 77.
8. Pleshakov, *The Crimean Nexus*, 88.
9. Elvedin Chubarov, interview with the author, 2015.
10. Uehling, *Beyond Memory*, 4.
11. Thousands of Crimean Tatars tried to make the journey back to their homeland unofficially, but the Soviet system required the place of residence to be stamped in the passport. Police quickly deported those who did not have it, with up to six thousand Crimean Tatars who had returned unofficially re-deported in 1968 alone. See Glyn Williams, *The Crimean Tatars*, 128.
12. Ablayev, *Rossiiskaya Federatsia protiv Mustafy Dzhemileva*.
13. Uehling, *Beyond Memory*, 90.
14. Uehling, *Beyond Memory*, 44.
15. Quoted in Wilson, *Ukraine Crisis*, 107.
16. Many Crimean Tatars felt he had been a dictatorial head of the *mejlis* and some even alleged he had misappropriated funds meant for repatriation. However, nobody doubted his record of dissidence during the Soviet period, and his political activities were widely respected in the community.
17. After the Russian annexation, realizing that Dzhemilev and other pro-Ukraine Crimean Tatars were a useful tool to portray the Ukrainianness of Crimea to an international audience, there was a sudden interest in Crimean Tatar history and culture in Ukraine. This had not been particularly in evidence during the years that Crimea was controlled by Ukraine, however. While it was welcome, it also smacked a little of opportunism.

Chapter 9

1. Video available at https://www.youtube.com/watch?v=wozJ5Px4s6c; the exact wording used by Mackevicius, which is difficult to translate precisely, was *my rabotaem v silovoi sfere* and *my siloviki*.

Chapter 10

1. There was a persistent rumour in Donetsk that Khodakovsky had closer relations with Akhmetov than he let on with me, with the most notable piece of evidence being that members of Vostok guarded Akhmetov's

lavish residence outside town at one moment when it seemed locals might be readying to storm it. Khodakovsky denied any contact other than the initial, fruitless negotiations to me.

Chapter 11

1. The fullest account of the Odessa violence came from Howard Amos, the only Western journalist to be in the city when it happened, who returned a year later to piece together the build-up: Amos: "'There Was Heroism and Cruelty on Both Sides': The Truth behind One of Ukraine's Deadliest Days," *The Guardian*, 30 April 2015, https://www.theguardian.com/world/2015/apr/30/there-was-heroism-and-cruelty-on-both-sides-the-truth-behind-one-of-ukraines-deadliest-days.

2. On the two-year anniversary of the tragedy in 2016, Ukrainian authorities actually banned relatives of the dead and well-wishers from laying flowers at the site, in a deeply unsavoury episode. (See Shaun Walker, "Tensions Run High in Odessa on Anniversary of Deadly Clashes," *The Guardian*, 2 May 2016, https://www.theguardian.com/world/2016/may/02/odessa-ukraine-second-anniversary-clashes.)

3. Andrei Kolesnikov, "Vladimir Putin khochet pereproverit' informatsiyu, kotoruyu on poluchayet ot podchinennykh," *Kommersant*, 29 July 2014, http://www.kommersant.ru/doc/2534737.

4. A description of his own role during an interview Strelkov gave in 2015.

5. https://www.theguardian.com/commentisfree/2014/may/13/ukraine-us-war-russia-john-pilger.

6. Gilbert, *The Holocaust*, 218.

7. See, for example, http://blogs.pravda.com.ua/authors/savanevsky/5365f834c31e7/ in Ukrainian or http://www.rferl.org/a/ukraine-unspun-odesa-doctor-dentist-false-claim/25372684.html in English, published more than a week prior to Pilger's piece.

8. Pilger's Edward Said Memorial Lecture given in September 2014, reproduced at http://johnpilger.com/articles/breaking-the-last-taboo-gaza-and-the-threat-of-world-war.

9. As of early 2017. Available at https://www.theguardian.com/commentisfree/2014/may/13/ukraine-us-war-russia-john-pilger.

Chapter 12

1. http://www.levada.ru/2017/03/01/gordost-i-styd/.

Epilogue

1. *The Russian Economy Inches Forward: Will That Suffice to Turn the Tide?*, Russia Economic Report, no 36, 9 November 2016, online at http://www.worldbank.org/en/country/russia/publication/rer, and *Naselenie Rossii v 2016 godu: Dokhody, raskhody, i sotsialnoe samochuvstvie. Monitoring NIU VShE*, online at https://isp.hse.ru/monitoring.

2. Nicholas Thompson, "My Friend, Stalin's Daughter: The Complicated Life of Svetlana Alliluyeva," *The New Yorker*, 31 March 2014, http://www.newyorker.com/magazine/2014/03/31/my-friend-stalins-daughter (I have slightly amended the quote for grammar).

3. Vladimir Medinsky, interview with *Rossiisskaya Gazeta*, 27 August 2015 http://www.pravmir.ru/vladimir-medinskiy-iz-vseh-iskusstv-dlya-nas-vazhneyshim-yavlyaetsya-istoriya/.

BIBLIOGRAPHY

Ablayev, Remzi. Foreword to *Rossiiskaya Federatsiya protiv Mustafy Dzhemileva: Omskii Protsess Aprel' 1976 goda*. Simferopol: Odzhak, 2003.

Adamovich, Adam. *Khatyn*. English translation. London: "Glagoslav" publications, 2012.

Aksyonov, Vassily. *The Island of Crimea*. London: Abacus, 1986.

Alexievich, Svetlana. *Second-Hand Time*. London: Fitzcarraldo, 2016.

Andrew, Christopher, and Vasily Mitrokhin. *The Mitrokhin Archive: The KGB in Europe and the West*. London: Allen Lane, 1999.

Artizov, Andrei, and Oleg Naumov. *Vlast' i khudozhestvennaya intelligentsiya: Dokumenty TsK RKP(b)—VKP(b)—VChK—OGPU—NKVD o kul'turnoi politike 1917–1953gg*. Moscow: Demokratiya, 1999.

Boym, Svetlana. *The Future of Nostalgia*. New York: Basic Books, 2001.

Braithwaite, Roderick. *Moscow 1941: A City and Its People at War*. Croydon: Profile Books, 2006.

Bullough, Oliver. *Let Our Fame Be Great: Journeys among the Defiant People of the Caucasus*. London: Allen Lane, 2010.

Buruma, Ian. *The Wages of Guilt: Memories of War in Germany and Japan*. London: Atlantic, 2009.

Carleton, Gregory. *Russia: The Story of War*. Cambridge and London: Harvard University Press, 2017.

Clover, Charles. *Black Wind, White Snow: The Rise of Russia's New Nationalism*. New Haven: Yale University Press, 2016.

De Custine, Marquis de. *Journey for Our Time: The Journals of the Marquis de Custine: Russia 1839*. London: Phoenix Press, 2001.

Desbois, Patrick. *The Holocaust by Bullets: A Priest's Journey to Uncover the Truth behind the Murder of 1.5 Million Jews*. New York: St Martin's Press, 2008.

Dolot, Miron. *Execution by Hunger: The Hidden Holocaust*. New York: Norton, 1987.

Encarnación, Omar G. *Democracy without Justice in Spain: The Politics of Forgetting*. Philadelphia: University of Pennsylvania Press, 2014.

Esch, Christian. *"Banderites" vs. "New Russia": The Battle Field of History in the Ukraine Conflict*. Reuters Institute for the Study of Journalism Fellowship Paper. Available online at http://reutersinstitute.politics.ox.ac.uk/.

Etkind, Alexander. "Post-Soviet Hauntology: Cultural Memory of the Soviet Terror." *Constellations* 16, no 1 (2009): 182–200.

Figes, Orlando. *Crimea: The Last Crusade*. London: Allen Lane, 2010.

Gaddis, John Lewis. *George F. Kennan: An American Life*. New York: Penguin, 2011.

Gall, Carlotta, and Thomas de Waal. *Chechnya: A Small Victorious War*. London: Pan, 1997.

Gayev, S., M. Khadisov, and T. Chagayeva. *Khaibakh: Sledstvie prodolzhaetsya*. Grozny: Kniga, 1994.

Getty, J. Arch, and Oleg V. Naumov. *The Road to Terror: Stalin and the Self-Destruction of the Bolsheviks, 1932–39*. New Haven: Yale University Press, 2002.

Gilbert, Martin. *The Holocaust: A History of the Jews of Europe during the Second World War*. New York: Henry Holt, 1985.

Ginzburg, Evgeniya. *Into the Whirlwind*. London: Collins Harvill, 1989.

Grach, Leonid. *Eshche ne vecher*. Kiev: Oriyani, 2007.

Grossman, Vasily. *Everything Flows*. London: Harvill, 2009.

Gudkov, L. D., B. V. Dubin, and N. A. Zorkaya. *Postsovietskii chelovek i grazhdanskoe obshchestvo*. Moscow: Moskovskaya Shkola Politicheskikh Isledovanii, 2008.

Hellbeck, Jochen. *Stalingrad: The City That Defeated the Third Reich*. New York: Public Affairs, 2015.

Hill, Fiona, and Clifford Gaddy. *Mr Putin: Operative in the Kremlin*. Washington, DC: Brookings Institution Press, 2015.

Hobsbawm, Eric J. *Nations and Nationalism since 1780*. Cambridge: Cambridge University Press, 1990.

Jones, Polly. *Myth, Memory, Trauma: Rethinking the Stalinist Past in the Soviet Union 1953–70*. New Haven and London: Yale University Press, 2013.

Kalinin, Ilya. "Nostalgicheskaya Modernizatsiya: Sovetskoye proshloye kak istoricheskii gorizont." *Neprikosnovenny Zapas* 74, no 6 (2010): 6–16.

Kalinin, Ilya. "Boi za istoriyu: proshloye kak ogranichenny resurs." *Neprikosnovenny Zapas* 78, no 4 (2011): 330–339.

Kuromiya, Hiroaki. *Freedom and Terror in the Donbas: A Ukrainian-Russian Borderland, 1870s–1990s*. Cambridge: Cambridge University Press, 1998.

Levine, Peter A. *Trauma and Memory: Brain and Body in a Search for the Living Past. A Practical for Understanding and Living with Traumatic Memory*. Berkeley, CA: North Atlantic Books, 2015.

Lieven, Dominic. *Empire: The Russian Empire and Its Rivals from the Sixteenth Century to the Present.* London: Pimlico, 2003.

Luciuk, Lubomyr. *Searching for Place: Ukrainian Displaced Persons, Canada, and the Migration of Memory.* Toronto: University of Toronto Press, 2001.

MacDonald, Ian. *The New Shostakovich.* London: Pimlico, 2006.

Marples, David. "Introduction: Historical Memory and the Great Patriotic War." *Canadian Slavonic Papers* 54, no 3–4 (2012): 284–294.

Medinsky, Vladimir. *Mify o Rossii: O russkoi gryazi i vekovoi tekhnicheskoi otstalosti.* Moscow: OLMA Media Grupp, 2015.

Merridale, Catherine. *Night of Stone: Death and Memory in Twentieth-Century Russia.* New York: Penguin, 2000.

Mijnssen, Ivo. "The Victory Myth and Russia's Identity." *Russian Analytical Digest* 72, no 10 (2010): 6–9.

Mishra, Pankaj. *Age of Anger: A History of the Present.* London: Allen Lane, 2017.

Naimark, Norman M. *Stalin's Genocides.* Princeton: Princeton University Press, 2010.

Nelson, Todd H. "History as ideology: The Portrayal of Stalinism and the Great Patriotic War in Contemporary Russian High School Textbooks." *Post-Soviet Affairs* 31, no 1 (2015): 37–65.

Ostrovsky, Arkady. *The Invention of Russia: The Journey from Gorbachev's Freedom to Putin's War.* London: Atlantic, 2015.

Oushakine, Serguei Alex. *The Patriotism of Despair: Nation, War and Loss in Russia.* Ithaca, NY: Cornell University Press, 2009.

Pavlovsky, Gleb. *The Russian System: A View from the Inside.* Moscow: "Europe" publishing house, 2015.

Petrov, Vladimir. *June 22, 1941: Soviet Historians and the German Invasion.* Columbia: University of South Carolina Press, 1968.

Pilunsky, Leonid. *Bilet v Teatr Gryoz: Publitsisticheskie stat'i, rasskazy, stikhi.* Simferopol: Dolya, 2002.

Platt, Kevin M. F., and David Brandenberger, eds. *Epic Revisionism: Russian History and Literature as Stalinist Propaganda.* Madison: University of Wisconsin Press, 2006.

Pleshakov, Constantine. *The Crimean Nexus: Putin's War and the Clash of Civilizations.* New Haven and London: Yale University Press, 2017.

Pobol, N. L., and P. M. Polian. *Stalinskie deportatsii 1928–1953 (Rossiya XX vek: dokumenty).* Moscow: Materik, 2005.

Polian, Pavel. *Against Their Will: The History and Geography of Forced Migrations in the USSR.* Budapest: CEU Press, 2004.

Polian, Pavel. *Istoriomor, ili Trepanatsia pamyati: Bitvy za pravdu o Gulage, deportatsiyakh, voine, i KHolokoste.* Moscow: AST, 2016.

Politkovskaya, Anna. *A Russian Diary: A Journalist's Final Account of Life, Corruption, and Death in Putin's Russia.* London: Random House, 2009.

Pomerantsev, Peter. *Nothing is True and Everything Is Possible: The Surreal Heart of the New Russia.* New York: PublicAffairs, 2014.

Plokhy, Serhii. *The Gates of Europe: A History of Ukraine.* London: Penguin, 2016.

Plokhy, Serhii, *The Last Empire: The Final Days of the Soviet Union.* New York: Basic Books, 2014.

Plokhy, Serhii. *Yalta: The Price of Peace.* New York: Viking, 2010.

Politkovskaya, Anna. *A Dirty War: A Russian Reporter in Chechnya.* London: Harvill Press, 2001.

Reid, Anna. *Borderland: A Journey through the History of Ukraine.* Boulder, CO: Westview Press, 2000.

Remnick, David. *Lenin's Tomb.* London: Penguin, 1993.

Ricoeur, Paul. *Memory, History, Forgetting.* Chicago: University of Chicago Press, 2009.

Rolf, Malte. *Soviet Mass Festivals, 1917–1991.* Pittsburgh: University of Pittsburgh Press, 2003.

Rosenberg, Tina. *The Haunted Land: Facing Europe's Ghosts after Communism.* New York: Random House, 1995.

Rossolinski-Liebe, Grzegorz. *Stepan Bandera, the Life and Afterlife of a Ukrainian Nationalist: Fascism, Genocide, and Cult.* Stuttgart: ibidem Press, 2014.

Rudling, Per Anders. "The Cult of Roman Shukhevych in Ukraine: Myth Making with Complications." *Fascism: Journal of Comparative Fascist Studies* 5 (2016): 26–65.

Sakwa, Richard. *Frontline Ukraine: Crisis in the Borderlands.* London: Tauris, 2015.

Satter, David. *Darkness at Dawn: The Rise of the Russian Criminal State.* New Haven and London: Yale University Press, 2003.

Satter, David. *The Less You Know the Better You Sleep: Russia's Road to Terror and Dictatorship under Yeltsin and Putin.* New Haven: Yale University Press, 2016.

Schlögel, Karl. *Moscow 1937.* Cambridge: Polity Press, 2012.

Sebag-Montefiore, Simon. *The Romanovs 1613–1918.* London: Weidenfeld & Nicolson, 2016.

Service, Robert. *Russia: Experiment with a People.* London: Macmillan, 2002.

Sherlock, Thomas. "Confronting the Stalinist Past: The Politics of Memory in Russia." *The Washington Quarterly* (Spring 2011): 93–109.

Sherlock, Thomas. "Russian Politics and the Soviet Past: Reassessing Stalin and Stalinism under Vladimir Putin." *Communist and Post-Communist Studies* 49 (2016): 45–59.

Shirokorad, A. B. *Velikaya Deportatsiya: Tragicheskie itogi Vtoroi mirovoi.* Moscow: Veche, 2015.

Snyder, Timothy. *Bloodlands: Europe between Hitler and Stalin.* New York: Basic Books, 2010.

Snyder, Timothy. *The Reconstruction of Nations: Poland, Ukraine, Lithuania, Belarus, 1569–1999.* New Haven: Yale University Press, 2003.

Subtelny, Orest. *Ukraine: A History.* 4th ed. Toronto: University of Toronto Press, 2009.

Uehling, Greta Lynn. *Beyond Memory: The Crimean Tatars' Deportation and Return*. New York: Palgrave Macmillan, 2004.

Williams, Brian Glyn. *The Crimean Tatars: From Soviet Genocide to Putin's Conquest*. London, 2015.

Williams, Brian Glyn. "Commemorating 'The Deportation' in Post-Soviet Chechnya: The Role of Memorialization and Collective Memory in the 1994–96 and 1999–2000 Russo-Chechen Wars." *History and Memory: Studies in Representation of the Past* 12, no 1 (Spring/Summer 2000): 101–134.

Wilson, Andrew. *Ukraine Crisis: What It Means for the West*. Totton, Hampshire: Yale University Press, 2014.

Wood, Elizabeth. "Performing Memory: Vladimir Putin and the Celebration of WWII in Russia." *The Soviet and Post-Soviet Review* 38 (2011): 172–200.

Wood, Elizabeth, William Pomerantz, Wayne E. Merry, and Maxim Trudolyubov. *Roots of Russia's War in Ukraine*. Washington, DC: Woodrow Wilson Center Press, 2016.

Zygar, Mikhail. *All the Kremlin's Men: Inside the Court of Vladimir Putin*. New York: Inside Affairs, 2016.

INDEX